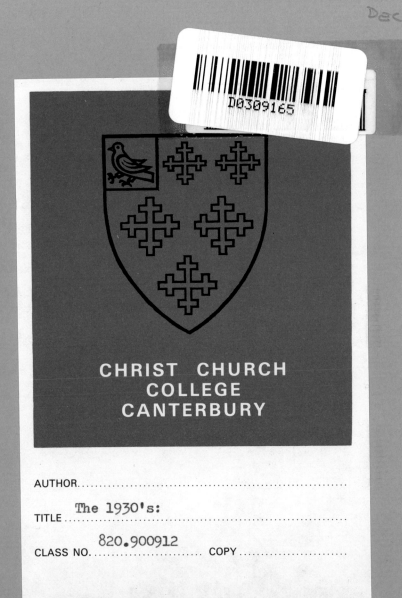

CHRIST CHURCH
COLLEGE
CANTERBURY

The 1930s

The 1930s:

A Challenge to Orthodoxy

Editor JOHN LUCAS
Professor of English, University of Loughborough

THE HARVESTER PRESS · SUSSEX

BARNES & NOBLE · NEW YORK

First published in Great Britain in 1978 by
THE HARVESTER PRESS LIMITED

Publisher: John Spiers
2 Stanford Terrace, Hassocks, Sussex

and in the USA by
HARPER AND ROW PUBLISHERS, INC.
BARNES AND NOBLE IMPORT DIVISION
10 East 53rd Street, New York 10022

© John Lucas and The Harvester Press Limited, 1978
Chapter 8 © Arnold Rattenbury, 1978; Chapter 10 © Enid Slater, 1978; the illustrations © Ruth Boswell, 1978.

British Library Cataloguing in Publication Data

The 1930s.
1. English literature – 20th century – History and criticism
I. Lucas, John, b. 1937   II. Nineteen thirties
820'.9'00912

ISBN 0-85527-533-2

Barnes and Noble
ISBN 0-06-494399-2
LCN 78-67473

Printed in Great Britain by
Bristol Typesetting Co. Ltd,
Barton Manor, St. Philips, Bristol

Contents

Contributors

Edgell Rickword well-known as poet, critic and literary journalist and editor.

John Lucas, Professor and Head of the Department of English and Drama at the University of Loughborough. His most recent books are *Egils Saga* (the poems), 1975, and *The Literature of Change*, published by Harvester Press and Barnes and Noble, 1977.

H. Gustav Klaus spent two years teaching at the University of Warwick before returning to West Germany where he now lives in Bremen. He has edited and translated *Marxistische Literaturkritik in England* (1973) and a collection of Raymond Williams' essays. At present he is completing a full-length study of the literary and theoretical writings of Christopher Caudwell.

Roy Johnson was a mechanical design engineer before taking a first degree in English and American Literature at Manchester University as a mature student. He is now a W.E.A. tutor in Manchester.

Tom Paulin Lecturer in English at Nottingham University, the author of *Thomas Hardy: The Poetry of Perception* (1975) and *A State of Justice* (1977) which was an award-winning volume of poems.

Michael Draper A research student at Nottingham University, where he is writing a thesis on H. G. Wells' fiction. Some of his poems have appeared in *The Honest Ulsterman*.

William Myers Lecturer in English at Leicester University. He is author of *Dryden* (1973) and contributed a number of essays to books and periodicals. He is currently working on George Eliot's didacticism.

P. J. Widdowson Head of the division of English at Thames Polytechnic, an editor of the journal *Literature and History*, and the author of a book and several articles on nineteenth and twentieth century fiction.

Arnold Rattenbury is the author of two volumes of poetry, *Second Causes* (1969) and *Man Thinking* (1972), and a prose and doggerel play, *A Comedy of Good Intentions*, first produced in 1974. He is currently putting together a third volume of poems and completing a long study of the Nonconformist conscience.

Introductory Note

This book is about the 1930s. It may look an unwise choice. With so much attention paid to that near-fabulous decade by way of biography, memoir, exhibitions and critical studies, it seems reasonable to suppose that all that can usefully be said has by now been said. Reasonable, but wrong. For 'world is crazier and more of it than we think', especially the world of the 1930s; and too many of the accounts of it which either wear or are thought to wear a look of officialdom turn out to be partial, partisan, or exercises in special pleading. The present book cannot escape all of those charges. But then it isn't meant to. There are good cases to be made for the writers whose work is discussed (and occasionally presented) in the following pages, although one might not think so judging from what most of the self-appointed historians of the 1930s have had to say, or have left unsaid. I hope (and think) that the cases have been made. If they have it will help to ensure that 'the 1930s' isn't a clearly charted episode of lit. hist. but that the very different kinds of achievements it produced are alive and troubling. Which is surely how it ought to be?

*   *   *

A great many people helped to make this book possible. Thanks are especially due to the following:

Montagu Slater's widow, Enid Slater and his daughters Anna Standen and Bridget Kitley, for reminiscences and access to his papers; Randall Swingler's widow, Geraldine Swingler and his daughter Judy Williams, for ditto; Ruth Boswell for permission to use work by the late James Boswell; John Saville for access to material as yet unpublished in his *Dictionary of Labour Biography*; the late Sylvia Townsend Warner, Amabel Williams-Ellis and Edgell Rickword for recollections about the Thirties;
A*

Marx Memorial Library for the loan of rare and relevant books; the late Benjamin Britten, O.M., C.H.; and above all Arnold Rattenbury, without whose help and guidance the book would not have been possible.

John Lucas

An Interview with Edgell Rickword

John Lucas

Not so long ago the Carcanet Press published a collection of Edgell Rickword's critical writings: *Essays and Opinions, 1912–1931*. The volume was respectfully reviewed but more than one commentator implied or said straight out that Rickword had committed intellectual suicide when he joined the Communist Party in the 1930s, so that 1931 came to look like a terminal date. Such tidying-up of history (Clive James' review in the *New Statesman* had a particularly brisk and no-nonsense air) seemed to me of a piece with Julian Symons' *The thirties: a Dream Revolved*, and one of the things I wanted to find out from Edgell Rickword was whether he thought his work within the party had been a colossal blunder and, more particularly, how he now looked back at his involvement in the periodical, *Left Review*, which he edited for a while, and which Symons and other commentators on that period have tended to treat with a mixture of scorn, condescension or benign tolerance.

Edgell Rickword lives with his wife in a small, neat town house in Islington. The walls of the downstairs room where we talked were lined with books, piles of books and records spilled across the floor, were heaped on chairs, on and under tables. A coal fire poured out heat, pushing back the cold of a December afternoon. Rickword's thick mass of grey-white hair is combed back from a high forehead, and he moves slowly, perhaps because of physical frailty – he is, after all, in his late seventies – or more probably because he is very nearly blind. When he spoke his voice fluttered, died, sprang to sudden life, and it was some time before I could be sure I was understanding him aright. But of two things I was in no doubt. One, that for all the apparent guardedness of his speech he was full of mischievous wit. Two, the energy of his commitment to the cause of letters as well as the cause of Marxism in the thirties and beyond, and the fact that such commitments followed in a clear line from the days when he had edited the *Calendar of Modern Letters*. (And as Arnold Rattenbury testifies elsewhere in this book, Rickword is not only a poet and critic of genius, he was also an editor of genius, and continued to be one long after he was supposed to have killed himself off with that fatal dose of Marxist orthodoxy.)

He tested warily each question I put to him, not because he was suspicious of it (I hope), but because he wanted to give the most accurate, truthful and ample answer that he could. There were therefore liable to be long silences between question and answer, and silences often occurred somewhere along the thread of the answer itself. But no gaps, the thread never broke.

I began by asking him if there was any link between the *Calendar* and the *Review,* or whether he saw them as entirely different enterprises.

'Oh, there were connections, certainly. You see, when I ran the *Calendar* I was always on the lookout for good new writing, I wanted to encourage writers. But at the same time those of us around the magazine were socially conscious and as we moved into the 1930s that consciousness grew. By 1933 we were all appalled at the collapse of the economy, the whole social set up in Britain, and by the things that were happening on the Continent. If one had any awareness at all at that time one was bound to be shocked by the state of affairs in Europe as a whole.'

The *Calendar* had of course finished some years previously. Who thought up the *Review* and how did it actually come to exist?

'Well, the only thing I can remember is meeting in a room over a pub in Fitzrovia. There were about fifteen of us, Hugh MacDiarmid, I think, Bert Lloyd, Ralph Fox, Amabel Williams-Ellis, Tom Wintringham, and others. Someone had the idea of founding the Society for the Defence of Culture, as I now think it was rather childishly called. And we had the notion of setting up a group of Revolutionary Writers. Yes, it was as political as that.'

It therefore seemed proper to ask if the people at the meeting were party members.

'No, certainly not all, two or three. I think the real lead came from Wintringham, he'd been in Russia, you see, and was a terrific driving force. He had been given six months for belonging to the Central Committee, and consequently disbarred from his profession. But we all shared a dissatisfaction with the state of literature as such, not only the safe attitudes of most of the better-known contemporary writers, but also its whole commercial basis, content and packaging. After the first meeting there was one to launch a society of revolutionary literature and obviously such a society needs an organ. So the organ was started and the society rather faded out. And that's how *Left Review* was born.'

Could he remember at all what had been meant by Revolutionary Literature?

'I think it was literature that expressed and reflected the actual struggle of the down-trodden, as it were, or could convey by realistic treatment, reportage, their actual conditions of work and communicate their humanity and the plight of their position in a flourishing society – you know, a society that was bilious with riches at the top.'

Proletkult?

'No, not at all. We didn't know about it, not in '34. I think that came in the following year, but we certainly didn't know about it at the time of founding *Left Review*.'

But the *Review* did encourage proletarian writing, didn't it?

'Certainly that was basically the thing we most wanted to do. We didn't want to fill the pages with our own stuff. And we hoped that through the party and also the W.E.A., the Workers' Music Association and the one or two drama groups – that sort of thing – working people would get to hear of us and send us their work. It seemed reasonable to imagine that there must be a good deal of work painfully written out on old school sheets, old school books, exercise books.'

And did a lot of work find its way to the offices of *Left Review*?

'Well, a good deal, but I'm forced to admit that much of it was very bad. Of course a certain kind of critic will sneer, and say "what do you expect?" But after all, most of the stuff that had been submitted to the *Calendar* was equally bad and much of that was by people with respectable names in the literary world. That was one reason why we had stopped the *Calendar*. And why we stopped the *Review*. We couldn't get work of the quality that would have justified us carrying on.'

I asked him if he thought that *Left Review* had unearthed any talented writers, and after some thought he threw out several names.

'There was Julius Lipton, a garment worker in a sweat

shop in the East End. He wrote poems. I recall a volume
called *Poems of Strife*, with an introduction by the then
poet laureate. I met him during the war but he'd got a bit
embourgeoisified by then. But there were certainly some
quite good radical Jewish writers in London at the time, who
contributed. Simon Blumenfeld, he wrote some pieces for us,
and did a novel. And there was Willie Goldman, he wrote
two or three novels. And a Welsh miner, Lewis Jones.
Douglas Garman took time with him going over the text of
his novel. But when all's said we could contact only a small
fringe, you know, so I don't think we did too badly. Of
course, you could say that we narrowed the range too much
by going mostly for work by party members, but if a good
poem had come along on a non-political subject I should
hope that we would have put it in. Besides, there were other
good working-class writers that *Left Review* didn't discover
but with whom it certainly identified – James Hanley and
Grassic Gibson and Ralph Bates. Harold Heslop, too. He
represented the British proletarian writers at the first International Congress of Revolutionary Writers in the Soviet
Union. He wrote several very interesting novels, of which I
particularly remember *Last Cage Down.*

He was emphatic that *Left Review* hadn't ended with its
successive editors feeling that they had been let down or disillusioned.

'I was disappointed, naturally, not so much because I
was expecting a lot of literary masterpieces, as because I
was hoping for more reportage and controversy, and although there was some it didn't get to a very high level. So
it was the same with *Left Review* as with the *Calendar*. I
was disappointed. We seemed to have worked through the
available material all too quickly. And I honestly don't think
we could have got much stuff at that time in England. You
must also remember that I was living in Winchester, and
politically active there, hardly visiting London by the time
Left Review ceased publication. Looking through its last
issue recently to refresh my memory, I find a distinctly more
optimistic view expressed in Randall Swingler's editorial.
He presents a long and careful analysis of the journal's three
year existence, making the quite reasonable claim that a
number of authors, and to some extent a new kind of

writing, had become established. Taken together with other remarks in that issue – particularly those by Allen Lane, the founder of Penguins, and Donald Kitchin, the *Review's* manager – it seems quite clear that Swingler and Kitchin at least were convinced that there would be a militant successor to the *Review,* cheaply priced and with a large publishing house at its back – very probably what eventually proved to be the rather unmilitant *Penguin New Writing.* This cannot have been what they intended. Nonetheless there is some force to the idea that the early *Penguin New Writing* derived directly from work we had done in the *Review.* I suppose one distinction between the *Calendar* and the *Review* is that anyone who knows anything about literature knows about the *Calendar*; it has had an enormous influence quite out-weighing the number of issues it produced. Whereas *Left Review* hasn't so far been properly assessed. Rather unfair, I think.'

But hadn't he thought of asking some of the already famous to contribute?

'Well, some of them did, but it would have altered the character of the *Review* if they'd taken over. I should think that Spender would have offered. He liked to think of himself as on the left in those days.'

Spender was clearly regarded with suspicion. How about Day Lewis?

'Very genuine. Do you not think so?'

I said that I didn't much admire his poetry.

'Ah, the poems. I don't think he was a good poet, but he was genuine about it.'

And Auden.

'He was a bit left then, wasn't he? He went out to Spain, too, to give him his due. I think he was serious. He was very aware of the decadence of bourgeois society. He didn't really know what the alternative was, and neither did Spender or any of his friends. Of course, Spender was in Spain, too. Running around making a fearful fuss. I think he was looking for his young friend who'd joined the British battalion and was now, Stephen really believed, in danger of death from the firing squad for some dereliction of duty.'

And since, inevitably, we had now drifted into the subject of the Spanish War I asked him about his own part in it.

'Well, naturally, I was an ardent supporter of the communist side. By then I was a party member, you see, and was doing Branch work, propaganda, and the editors of the *Review* had fairly regular meetings with party high-ups. We came in for some mild criticism for not giving the right emphasis here or there, no more than that. And then came Spain. I wasn't any good for fighting, you know, I had lost an eye' (he'd been injured fighting in the First World War) 'and so I wouldn't have been any use. Anyway, there were enough people ready to fight. But I went over there with a delegation. I couldn't do much except by way of propaganda. So I went to Madrid, with Sylvia Townsend Warner, Valentine Ackland and, of course, Spender. We were about the only people the Writers Delegation could rumble up. All the others were either fighting, or clearing out, or were on the other side. Of course, there were quite a few Americans there. Hemingway was rumoured to be about but I didn't meet him. He was a man of action, wasn't he? Loosing off machine guns, that kind of thing.'

And it was not long after this time that Rickword wrote the famous "To the Wife of a Non-Interventionist Statesman".

'Yes, that just had to come out, I thought I couldn't let it go. The problem was to make it come across without overdoing it. I read it through again the other day and I think it's all right.'

But not many good poems had come out of the Spanish war, I suggested.

'No, that's true. The compiler of a recent anthology[1] in which it appeared wrote to me to say that it wasn't just about a war situation but a human situation. Well, I hope that's right, but I do agree that most of the poetry about the Spanish war was about taking sides. John Lehmann was able to collect a short volume of poems for Spain which were all pretty good, John Cornford's standing high above the rest. It included Auden's *Spain* which the author later disowned.'

Talking of taking sides, had he known any of the British writers who'd been on Franco's side? Roy Campbell, for example?

'Oh yes, I was a great friend of his up to the time I joined the party. He was very good fun, by no means a fool. But where he got this crappy, hysterical sort of fascism from, I

don't know. At one time I thought his wife might be responsible. She was a catholic convert.'
Wasn't Campbell one as well?

'Yes, he was. She might have made him turn over to the
faith. Anyway, we rather lost contact, though I did see him
once or twice when he was at the B.B.C. where I heard his
arguments sometimes took an unruly turn. Pity.'
From what he had just said I wondered whether he had found
it necessary to drop former friends when he joined the party?

'Oh no, it wasn't like that, although naturally differences
tended to become sharper. But like all active members I had
a lot of work to do for the party – street corner meetings,
chalking notices of rallies and so on – and a good deal of
reading also. Not that I read much in the way of economics.
But there was the historical part of *Das Kapital* and the
Manifesto. And there were compilations of Marx and Engels
on literature, I remember. I read those. In fact if you look
up what's advertised at the time I probably read it all.
There was beginning to be a native Communist literature,
John Strachey, Fox – he was a good populariser, though I
don't think he was very deep. West, too. And Caudwell,
especially. I thought his general articles on studies in a dying
culture were tremendous, though I wasn't so keen on his
poetry or his theories of poetry and I would be hard put to
it to make a case for them without reading him through
again. And I had a lot of French political books, as well. So
it was a busy time.'
And had that anything to do with his almost ceasing to write
poetry.

'How do you mean?'
Well, hadn't he more or less stopped writing poetry in the
thirties?

'Yes, yes, I did.'
Because of involvement with the party?

'No, not at all.' A long pause. 'It was just because I hadn't
any impulse to write poems. I would have quite liked to but
I was getting into rather a different mood, less subjective I
suppose, and I think poetry must have much of the subjective in it. I had stopped writing poetry well before I
became a party member so all that stuff about how being a
communist killed me off as a poet is nonsense. And very

impertinent too, I think. I don't see why these people should think they know what went on in my mind better than I do.'

Had he, though, perhaps hoped that becoming a party member might act as a spur to him as a writer?

'I don't think so. Anyway, it didn't.'

But had he tried to write poems during the thirties?

'I don't think I tried very hard because for some time I had had the news that it had ceased. I simply wasn't in a mind to write poems. But my acquaintance with Marxism didn't act as a psychological brake on my writing life. Lyric poets tend to finish early, you know. It's less likely to happen to a painter, I think. They go on. Whereas sometimes a poet finds himself writing again after a lapse of many years. Do you know Upward's novels? I think they give a very good picture of the situation at the time. A bit narrow perhaps, not quite intensively unified for the purpose, but still good. And he understands about the way in which some writers felt that they could only come to terms with their work if they were politically committed. It's a sense of revelation almost. That being committed makes you a poet, or even becomes a very worthy subject for poetry. And I believe that I tried to think like that, but then nothing happened. I didn't flog it. You can't force a poem.'

And the poetry hadn't dried up because of his editorial commitments to *Left Review*?

'Not at all. I was only actually editor for two years and it wasn't terribly time consuming. I suppose I put in a day or so each week, more of course towards press day; and then, besides *Left Review*, I had other editorial work elsewhere, on the book publishing side.'

Had he thought of starting another journal when *Left Review* finished?

'No, by then I was living in the country, doing freelance work and I didn't see any chance of getting back to London.'

Was he still a party member then?

'Yes, right through the phoney war period I stayed in the party. It was a very odd time. When we were in favour of the war we got knocked off the platform, which I thought was rather a laugh, and when we were against we were also pushed off. But I stayed with the party for a good long time.'

He hadn't left the party because of anything he might have

found out about Stalin's shifty dealings over the Spanish war?

'No, it wasn't like that. I think some party members had joined because of a sudden intellectual flash, or moment of conviction, or feeling. And they were the ones who just as suddenly lost the feeling. It was all very emotional, sloppy really. Whereas others of us joined not because of some sudden enthusiasm but because the Communist Party seemed to be the only one that was actually *doing* something. I joined in 1934, early on. If there was any one thing that helped me to make up my mind it would have been the February riots in Paris, when the fascist attack was from the députés, remember? And Hitler was obviously beginning to run Germany on fascist lines, and was truly frightening, and the only organisation that seemed to take this at all seriously was the Communist Party. It was doing propaganda, and it got at people in London – I'm not so sure how well it was set up in provincial cities at that time – and it had its paper, the *Daily Worker*, and so it represented something that was diametrically opposed to fascism. And that was why I joined.'

I wonder whether, when he was editing *Left Review*, he accepted the line for literature which Gorki laid down at the First Congress of Soviet Writers in 1934. I had the speech with me and quoted:

'Party members who work in literature must not only be teachers of the ideology that organises workers of all lands for the final battle for freedom. In all its behaviour party leadership must be a morally authoritative force; this force must above all inculcate in writers a consciousness of their collective responsibility for everything taking place in their midst. With all its diversity of talent and the growth in the number of new and gifted writers, Soviet literature must be organised as a united and collective whole, a mighty weapon of socialist culture.'

Did he remember reading those words at the time, and if so did they have any bearing on his editorial work?

'I don't remember them, no. It sounds more like Zhdanov than Gorki, but I suppose he's taking the Zhdanov line. The point is, I think, that in general one would approve and say, yes, all right, but it's likely to make for a very crude notion of base and superstructure – superstructure determined in a rigid way by the base. Well, I've never felt that. I go along with the marxists who argue that it's always extremely problematic relating superstructure to base and that you can never criticise a writer in the way that Lukács, for example, criticised Kafka for eccentricity, because eccentricity might be exactly what you wanted at that moment. Not that I took to Kafka when I read him.'

But would he have published him in *Left Review*?

'I doubt it. He had a very lowering effect on one, you know. But there weren't any great pressures from the party to make us toe a conforming line. And the same applied to the monthly journal *Our Time*. Much of the spirit of *Left Review* was embodied in that journal, with an editorial board which included several of the strongest supporters of *Left Review*.'

And what about the *Review* particularly deserved to be remembered?

'I think on its literary side it demonstrated that there could be a fruitful relationship between literature and politics, which in academic and conventional circles at that time were consciously kept separate. The *Review*, as consciously, regarded them as inseparable – as had always been recognised at times of social stress. Of course we weren't always successful in what we set out to do – though I think our artists were perhaps more successful than our writers. They too were reaching back into English tradition with that truly striking barrage of sardonic cartoons upon the hypocrisies of the politicians laid down by the three Jameses, as we called them – James Boswell, James Fitton, James Holland.'

NOTES
1 *Political Verse and Song from Britain and Ireland*, ed. Mary Ashraf, London (1975).

Socialist Fiction in the 1930s: Some preliminary observations

H. Gustav Klaus

To the memory of Alick West

The interest in the 1930s is steadily growing. The year 1975 saw the publication of the first fairly comprehensive account of *The Poetry of the Thirties* by A. T. Tolley and a new edition of Julian Symons' *The Thirties: a Dream Revolved*. In the same year the greater part of Alick West's *Crisis and Criticism,* which together with Caudwell's *Illusion and Reality* and Ralph Fox's *The Novel and the People* forms the main body of Marxist writing on aesthetics of the time, was made available again. In 1976 the 1930s received even greater public attention through the exhibition *Young Writers of the Thirties* held at the National Portrait Gallery and the publication of Samuel Hynes' widely acclaimed study, *The Auden Generation: Literature and Politics in England in the 1930s.*[1]

What is significant about this new interest in the Thirties is that it seems to come mainly from a generation which has not itself seen and lived through the period. This opens up for the first time the possibility of checking and eventually overcoming the kind of selective historiography which has so far dominated the writing about the cultural side of the period. By this I mean not only the breast-beating accounts of the more prominent figures of the Thirties movement, but also the Auden-orientated view of the time taken for granted by most scholars.[2] More books, articles and theses have probably been written about the so-called Auden/Spender group and their poetry alone than about all the other cultural aspects of the Thirties taken together. With the weight of this partial representation in mind, Edgell Rickword has remarked aptly that the movement some people are talking about in retrospect is not the one he remembers.[3] But correct as this assertion may be, it is not enough to stress that there was another kind of Thirties. What is needed in order to establish a less selective, less personally coloured assessment of the period, is thorough research into all its aspects, until finally it will be possible to synthesise the various accounts. This article takes a look at the Socialist fiction of the Thirties which, despite the fact

that there has never before (or since) been a period in Britain
with such a high output of it, has been unduly neglected.[4] Of
course, quantity is not in itself a sufficient argument, and the
following discussion will disclose a number of weaknesses in some
of these novels. But it would be ludicrous to speak of such weaknesses without first analysing and taking into account some of the
obstacles and difficulties which faced Socialist writers and in the
end prevented the composition of even more and better novels.

What is meant here by Socialist fiction? Basically the term is
used in order to embrace working-class novels as well as works
written by middle-class intellectuals, with a clear Socialist intention and perspective. This is of course only a very rough definition, but to avoid an extended terminological discussion suffice
it to say that 'working-class novel' in English tends to denote the
fiction produced by worker-writers (authors still in the production-
process) or writers with a working-class background, depicting
the life of this class. This does not necessarily make them
Socialist novels, for they may still affirm the *status quo*. To
distinguish such novels from the more politically motivated or
outspoken works the term 'proletarian revolutionary' was introduced in the international debate in the Twenties and early
Thirties to define the latter category. On the other hand, in the
German and Russian discussions of that time the background of
authors and/or the theme of their books were thought more and
more to be insufficient criteria and were later replaced or
supplemented by others, such as writing for a proletarian public
and the reproduction of the proletarian mode of consciousness.
These later definitions certainly enlarged the narrow original
concept which had left little space for the creative work of
Socialist intellectuals, and it was only a matter of time before a
new term was coined, though not without a number of serious
political struggles and controversies. As is well known, the outcome was 'Socialist realism'. My own use of the blanket term
'Socialist' does not have quite the same implications, nor does it
prevent me from recurring to 'working-class' or 'proletarian
revolutionary' wherever this is demanded by the material of a
study whose main emphasis is on the (early) phase when these
were still current terms.

*   *   *

It was not until the end of 1934 that a major debate took place in Britain on the function and objectives of a Socialist literature. The initiative came from *Left Review* which in its first number (October 1934) published the statement of aims adopted at the foundation conference of the British Section of the International Union of Revolutionary Writers (Writers' International) in February of that year. The general analysis of the situation was clear enough. The statement spoke of a crisis of ideas and the decadence of modern literature: in short, of 'the collapse of a culture'.[5] What was not clear at all, however, was in which direction to proceed from this point. On the one hand, the writer was asked to recognise the necessity of constructing a new order, and this was said to be the task of the working-class and taken inevitably to mean revolution. On the other hand, though, as a result of the rise of European Fascism a possible take-over by the proletariat seemed far from being the order of the day. And it seems to have been principally this second aspect of the situation which was taken into consideration when the criteria for membership of the Writers' International were established. Membership was open to writers:

>   *(a)* who see in the development of Fascism the terrorist dictatorship of dying capitalism . . . who are opposed to all attempts to hinder unity in the struggle or any retreat before Fascism or compromise with fascist tendencies;
>   *(b)* who, if members of the working-class, desire to express in their work, more effectively than in the past, the struggle of their class;
>   *(c)* who will use their pens and their influence against imperialist war and in defence of the Soviet Union . . . .[6]

This succession of points is hardly arbitrary. Compared with the five-point programme of the German League of Proletarian Revolutionary Writers of 1928 (one, promoting a proletarian revolutionary literature; two, working out a corresponding literary theory; three, criticising bourgeois literature for its notion of 'pure' art; four, combining all proletarian and middle-class revolutionary writers; five, defending the Soviet Union),[7] it clearly indicates the shift of emphasis due to the victory of Nazism in Germany. But although the statement adequately reflects the general defensive position of the European labour movement at that time, it still remains surprising to see that it refrained from stating any aims similar to those of the League.

Alec Brown's contribution to the ensuing discussion contains an indirect criticism of this one-sided alignment of the new association. According to Brown the Writers' International ought to focus on the development of a revolutionary literature, and this for him means plainly proletarian literature. Brown postulates nothing less than: 'LITERARY ENGLISH FROM CAXTON TO US IS AN ARTIFICIAL JARGON OF THE RULING CLASS.'[8] The source of this brand of cultural anarchism is not too difficult to detect. It is a very crude and simplified version of an argument used by the Left Opposition (Litfront and L.E.F.) in the Russian Association of Revolutionary Proletarian Writers (R.A.P.P.) in its fight against the psychological novel (with its picture of the inner life of the hero) and for the portrayal of factory life and proletarian themes. Also one must not forget that the R.A.P.P. itself, while combating such leftist ideas, officially pursued the establishment of a pro-letarian class literature. Nor should this tendency be seen as developing in a historical void. It was accompanied on the political level by the Comintern's distinct move to the left on the strength of its expectation of coming revolutions in Western Europe. It does not come as a surprise, then, to learn that Brown (who, incidentally, read Russian) relates all Socialist literary activity to this final aim: 'all our writing has one end in view, the revolu-tionary end of establishing a socialist republic.'[9]

If there is still something extraordinary about his remark it is less in what he says than in when he says it. After all the R.A.P.P. (and all the other Soviet writers' groups) had been dissolved in 1932 and replaced by a single unified body. Similarly the first congress of the new association (that is, the First Soviet Writers' Congress held in Moscow from 17 August to 1 September 1934) which had called for the appropriation of the bourgeois cultural heritage, ought to have made it clear that the strictly proletarian episode in Russian literature was over and that this would not be without consequences for the cultural policy of other Communist parties.

There are two possible explanations for this delay. Firstly it can be taken as symptomatic of the general backwardness of cultural discussions in the Communist Party. In the Twenties there had been a few sporadic, if ineffectual, attempts to keep up with developments elsewhere. *Labour Monthly* and *Plebs* had published a series of articles on the Proletkult, and after the General Strike the small but active Workers' Theatre Movement had attracted growing working-class audiences to its amateur performances in clubs and halls. But, on the whole, Harold Heslop's description of the state of working-class literature in Britain given at the Second International Conference of Proletarian Revolutionary Writers in Kharkov (1930), was to the point: 'proletarian art in Great Britain is in a very backward position and is in fact hardly begun'.[10] It has been argued that there were some fruitful British-Soviet literary relations in the Twenties. H. G. Wells had visited the Soviet Union, Lunacharski had ordered D. H. Lawrence's early novels to be published, and the *Calendar of Modern Letters* had for the first time published a number of Soviet authors in Britain.[11] But by comparison with the exchanges going on between the Weimar Republic and Soviet Russia these were really negligible. If the setting-up of an organisation where worker-writers could overcome their isolation, discuss their work and perhaps get it printed is to be considered as an elementary step towards the development of working-class literature, then certainly even in the United States such writers were, after 1929 when the John Reed Clubs were founded, in a more enviable position than those in Britain.

As to Brown's intervention in the debate about the aims of the newly established Writers' International, there is still the other possibility that he was acting as spokesman for a group who felt, not unjustly, that the statement of aims said too little about the question of how a proletarian literature could be built up.[12] If such a group did exist, then it certainly proved incapable of expounding its views intelligibly. Numerically and intellectually inferior to people like Randall Swingler, Montagu Slater, Cecil Day Lewis, and Douglas Garman who supported the statement of aims, theirs was a lost cause from the start.

The First Soviet Writers' Congress, at least in the way it was presented, was another argument in favour of the majority. In its second number *Left Review* printed a report on the Congress by Amabel Williams-Ellis who was an editor of the journal and had been the only British delegate in Moscow. Strangely enough in her report she neither mentioned the concept of Socialist Realism nor gave much space to the other leading theme, the taking-over and critical revaluation of the bourgeois literary tradition, and one cannot help wondering whether she fully understood what was on the agenda. But even so, in rendering only the speeches of Ehrenburg, Gorki, Leonov, and Radek, the latter of whom in particular had been at pains to demonstrate the utter decadence of modern fiction (Joyce, Proust),[13] and passing in silence over the more discriminating voices like Bukharin, Herzfelde and Malraux, her article gave the impression of the Congress's having been unanimous in its denunciation of formal experiments in the arts and in upholding the great bourgeois works of art of the nineteenth century as models from which the contemporary Socialist artist would have to learn before he could proceed to greater things.[14] This was precisely the position of those who had conceived and subsequently defended the statement of aims which had said in this respect: 'Journalism, literature, the theatre, are developing in technique while narrowing in content.'[15]

Wintringham's impatience, when he closed the debate in March 1935, is revealing. He made it clear that, whatever differences there remained, the issue had been settled:

> 'These questions certainly need discussion – but our main work, as revolutionaries, is to get a 'united front' for common action among all those who are not revolutionaries, but feel the need to defend culture and literature against the effects of modern Capitalism, Fascism, war.'[16]

The last part of this sentence anticipates the formula which was to sum up the new line. The famous international conference of writers which met in Paris in June that year was convened under the heading 'For the Defence of Culture.'[17] Even Aldous Huxley could be won for such a noble aim.

What is so far clear, then, is that, successful as the Writers' International was in its mobilisation of writers for an anti-fascist front – and the same is true of the corresponding association of artists (A.I.)[18] – it did not become nearly as active in the field of literature proper, in clarifying such questions of method as how a Socialist novelist's technique was to differ, if at all, from a non-Socialist's, or how to go about systematically building up a working-class literature. This judgment does not imply that it was wrong to mobilise intellectuals of a middle-class background or outlook in the tactically motivated interests of the labour movement (the defence of liberal democracy, the prevention of war) – it took the Comintern a considerable time to understand the lessons of the defeat in Germany, but in the end it did react – nor should it be read as being in agreement with views like those of Brown. But it can be argued that the development of Socialist literature in general and working-class fiction in particular did not derive much benefit from the fact that the first British Socialist writers' association was, right from the start, subordinated to the aims of the united front policy. In fact it is in this that the Writers' International differs from all the other organisations in Soviet Russia, Germany, France, and the U.S.A. As long as the R.A.P.P. or even further leftist ideas influenced the international scene (as they did around the end of the Twenties and the beginning of the Thirties), cultural discussions in the Communist Party were almost non-existent. When a kind of R.A.P.P. organ (*Storm*) was eventually founded, it was, from an intellectual point of view, already anachronistic. When finally all the necessary material conditions were given (a writers' organisation, a publishing company ready to print the respective authors, a chain of bookshops, a potential reading public), the fight against Fascism was spelt with a capital 'F', the worker-writer with a small 'w'.

Three notable exceptions, though none of them wholly satisfactory, deserve to be mentioned. The first and probably most important was a series of competitions, each on a given theme ('Strike', 'A Shift at Work', etc.), run by *Left Review* which encouraged workers to describe their work conditions. The prizewinners had their pieces printed by the journal. Encouraging as the result was, with up to fifty entries being received per competition, the whole enterprise (with Amabel Williams-Ellis telling the workers to avoid the use of jargon) had something patronising about it and was, as Alick West later pointed out, based on a critical standard 'which is indistinguishable from the aesthetics current at the end of the nineteenth century'.[19]

Another work that might have sparked off not only aesthetic discussions, but also the odd literary product, was Ralph Fox's analysis of the state of the novel. Although the main thrust of his argument was really a transposition of the popular front from the political sphere to the novel, which explains why he went to such lengths in reminding the contemporary middle-class writer of the progressive tradition of bourgeois literature, Fox in the last third of his book pinpoints a number of crucial problems for the Socialist novelist. Given the limited scope of this article, I can pick out only one, his treatment of the hero. Fox's discussion of this theme stems from his central belief that 'the Marxist writer should present man, as being at one and the same time a type and an individual, a representative of the mass and a single personality',[20] and he criticises both the modern bourgeois novelist for his 'abandoning the creation of personality, of a hero, for the minor task of rendering ordinary people in ordinary circumstances'[21], and

> the mistake made by many Socialist novelists who have used all their talent and energy to depict a strike, a social movement, the construction of Socialism, a revolution or a civil war, without considering that what is supremely important is not the social background, but man himself in his full development against that background.[22]

Fox's own solution was to plead for the return of the hero, whose death in literature he had analysed before in detail. When in this context he quotes Fielding's view that the novelist ought to ' "be universal with all ranks and degrees of men" ',[23] it becomes finally clear that he is recommending the traditional nineteenth-century technique of empathy (Einfühlung), the technique, that is, whereby the author 'feels himself' into his hero. Serious objections had, however, been raised against this technique by the Russian writer Tretyakov and by Brecht in their controversy with Lukács and others in the Thirties. For Tretyakov a novel written in this way could not fulfil its aim of showing the social process at work from a Marxist perspective, since it was bound to present reality through a subjective filter, the eyes of the hero. He wrote:

> The interrelations between the persons in the classical novel, which is based on the biography of an individual hero, remind one of Egyptian frescoes. In the centre, there is a colossal pharaoh, beside him, a little smaller, his wife, still smaller the ministers and generals, and then as copper points the anonymous mass of the population, servants, warriors, slaves.
> In the centre of this edifice stands the hero. The whole world is embodied through him. What is more, the whole world is basically only a collection of his accessories . . . .
> In the novel the leading hero absorbs and subjectivises the whole reality.[24]

Brecht therefore had no hesitations in calling this technique hopelessly outdated,

> although many people are shouting that without it there will be no more art or aesthetic experience. Of course, we still consider it our task to present complicated social processes; but the process of feeling oneself into a central individual ('Mittelpunktsindividuum') has entered into a crisis precisely because it paralysed

this presentation. It is not only a question of not getting the real motives for the inner movements of man in a novel, but also that the world itself is insufficiently reproduced, if it appears only in the mirror of the feelings and contemplations of the hero.[25]

It is a sad fact that no one in Britain at the time was capable of seeing the limitations of Fox's approach to the composition of a Socialist novel and of developing a counter-strategy.

The last attempt worth mentioning to help working-class prose writers get on their feet came from *New Writing*. Founded by John Lehmann in 1936, *New Writing* differed from *Left Review* in that it was 'first and foremost interested in literature' and from *New Verse* in that 'prose will form the main bulk of the contributions'.[26] Lehmann evidently made a great effort to get in touch with and encourage prospective working-class writers, though he cannot claim to have discovered any single author, since B. L. Coombes, George Garrett, Willy Goldman, and Leslie Halward whose work he printed had already published stories elsewhere. *New Writing* with its much bigger format than other literary journals not only introduced a number of important European writers but also provided British Socialist prose writers with an organ ready to print their work at a time when *Left Review*, for example, had already ceased publication. But, in public at least, Lehmann never explained his premisses for choosing this or that prose piece, so that the pages of *New Writing* radiate a certain eclecticism on the part of the editor.

*   *   *

The difficulties hampering the full development of a Socialist fiction, as they have been described so far, can be categorised as resulting either from the political constellation of the time or the organisational and intellectual weakness of the still very small Communist Party. A further factor was the rare combination of ignorance and negligence displayed by the Marxist literary criticism of the day with regard to the *proletarian* heritage. For example, it is a striking fact that at no time in the Thirties was an attempt made to make available some of the poetry and prose of the Chartist movement which, after all, quite apart from its political impetus, had also been the first to attempt to challenge the ruling class in the domain of literature.[27] This is not to suggest that the aspiring proletarian novelist could have made direct use

of works such as Thomas Martin Wheeler's *Sunshine and Shadow*
or Ernest Jones' *De Brassier*: the character drawing in Wheeler's
novel, for example – 'sunshine' denoting the moral superiority of
the Chartist Arthur Morton, 'shadow' testifying to the pitch-black
character of the Capitalist Walter North – is much too simplistic
for the purposes of the Thirties novelist, although the mere fact
of creating a positive proletarian hero at that time should not be
underestimated in its revolutionary implications. But an awareness of this Chartist literature would at least have enabled the
working-class writers of the Thirties to feel that they were not
starting from scratch, that a tradition of working-class literature
did in fact exist and had only to be unearthed, and that they
could learn just as much from the achievements and mistakes of
this tradition as they were supposed to acquire from the appropriation of bourgeois works. It is perhaps a truism, though one
easily overlooked, that it is as important to study the cultural past
of the labour movement, including its literary manifestations, as
it is to investigate its political or economic history; for what the
labour movement stands and fights for is not a new economic or
political structure as such, but the heightening of human life, that
is the creation of an entire Socialist culture.[28]

Just as the place of Chartist literature within the cultural
heritage was never defined, the reasons for the great success of
Robert Tressell's *The Ragged Trousered Philanthropists* were
never laid bare. This is even more surprising in view of the fact
that this novel, which was reprinted twice in the Thirties,[29] had,
in its adaptation for the stage, already been a major success of the
Workers' Theatre Movement,[30] was *read by workers* and sold
during the first forty years of its 'censored' publication more than
100,000 copies[31] – an almost unbelievable figure, if one considers
that the average edition of a working-class novel in the Thirties
was 1,500 copies, of which often less than two-thirds were sold.[32]
What was the secret of this unprecedented success? The nature
of its subject-matter apart, was it perhaps due, as has been maintained recently,[33] to its use of certain formal strategies, such as
the gradual building up of a panorama of life in Hastings (in
contrast to a traditional novel plot with its exposition, climax and
solution of conflict), the corresponding change from one literary
style to another, or the abandonment of a central positive hero
(which would have invited readers to identify, but not necessarily
to think)? Could such technical devices be made fecund for the

work of the contemporary worker-writer? Such questions were never asked.

Of course, with hindsight it is easy to recognise these deficiencies. It is no good pretending that Marxist literary criticism could have solved all of these problems. When it began, it had even less ground to tread on than Socialist fiction. As indicated earlier, in the Twenties there had been a lack of everything. The Communist Party, which anyway never numbered more than a few thousand members, had hardly any creative writers or literary intellectuals on whom it could count. Charles Ashleigh, Ralph Fox, T. A. Jackson, Tom Wintringham are the names that spring to mind, but this is already a fairly comprehensive list, and they could hardly have been expected to run a cultural journal between them. Nor did it seem to be a matter of urgency. In turning the pages of the Twenties periodicals I came across a letter in *Plebs* which referred to an article by one H. W. L. Dana who had spoken of the 'Place of Literature in Workers' Education'.[34] The letter-writer comments: yes, art should be a weapon in the class struggle; yes, the Marxist theory should be applied to works of art; but for heaven's sake, spare us Marxist aesthetics – there's no time for that, anyway. This appears to have been an opinion shared by many militant Socialists of the time.

The same letter-writer cites three names which in the middle of the Twenties apparently stood for attempts at such aesthetics: Trotsky, Bogdanov, Calverton. A less unified trio, or one more divergent in the views of its members, is difficult to imagine. Certainly there is much to be learnt even today from Trotsky's *Literature and Revolution*, published in England in 1925. Trotsky, however, denied that there could ever be a genuinely proletarian culture: firstly, because under Capitalism the basis on which one might be built could not exist; secondly, because during the transitional period of the dictatorship of the proletariat – which he saw as a regime fighting a revolutionary struggle – there would only be a general revolutionary culture; finally, because in the eventual classless society culture would not, by definition, bear the stamp of any class whatsoever. Such a position was clearly a dead-end for the development of a proletarian literature. From A. Bogdanov, the theoretician of Proletkult, on the other hand, some impulses towards the creation of a proletarian literature did no doubt derive.[35] But his almost mystical adoration of the work-process and machines, combined as it was with his demand for a

separate autonomous cultural mass-organisation, did not arouse
the suspicions of both Lenin and Trotsky for nothing. V. F.
Calverton, finally, founder of the American *Modern Quarterly* in
1923 and an occasional contributor to the *Sunday Worker,* was
certainly one, if not the first, American critic to use Marxist
concepts and a Marxist terminology in literary criticism, but his
'analyses' reduced literary works more than anything to the
class-outlook of their authors.

Not surprisingly, no British Marxist critic was mentioned by
the letter-writer in *Plebs.* Some kind of Marxist literary criticism
was first cautiously attempted in the *Sunday Worker.* And
fortunately so, because it helps to track down the few (today
forgotten) working-class novels written in the Twenties. One such
novel, H. H. Barbor's *Against the Red Sky* (1926), was reviewed
by Charles Ashleigh. I have been unable to get hold of a copy of
this now very rare book and shall therefore uncritically reproduce
the reviewer's opinion. The novel depicts the take-over by the
proletariat of Britain. Ashleigh is offended first of all by the fact
'that there is no mention of Russia'. He criticises the illusionary
perspective of the author (weapons are abolished after the revolution) and regrets that the hero is not a worker, but a middle-class
intellectual 'who goes over to the Workers' cause and renders
loyal service'.[36] But finally, in the absence of anything comparable, he cannot but recommend the novel to his readers. It is
naturally impossible to say whether the reviewer does justice to
the book, but what makes it conspicuous is its theme. I cannot
think of any other twentieth-century novel which depicts a
victorious Socialist revolution in Britain.

Against the Red Sky, then, seems to be one of the few English
novels of the Twenties that can be labelled proletarian revolutionary literature. Harold Heslop's miner's novel *The Gate of a
Strange Field* (1929) is an even better example. (Thanks to this
work, incidentally, and an earlier one published to this day only
in a Russian translation,[37] the author was invited to the Kharkov
Conference.) Heslop is very successful when he deals with matters
with which he is evidently closely in touch. The description of the
work underground is penetrating and full of interest. There is a
scene one is not likely to forget where the hero and another miner
are trapped in a flooded pit and only rescued after having been
buried alive for seventeen days. Yet when the author tries to
convey the atmosphere of the General Strike, this realism tends

to get lost in vagueness. Rather than springing from the actions and wills of the workers involved, the strike comes almost like a cosmic intervention. Alick West has touched on a symptomatic sentence in this respect: 'And so the world and its people plunged into the days that were to bring them nearer the gate of a strange field.'[38] Had all the miners looked upon the strike in this indifferent, quasi-fatalistic way, it would never have been brought about in the first place.

Though it would be premature at this stage to pronounce a final judgment on the proletarian revolutionary fiction of the Twenties, it can be said without great risk that it has no O'Casey or MacDiarmid to offer.

*   *   *

While working-class writers saw themselves confronted with a variety of immediate material problems, a number of Socialist intellectuals were tormented by difficulties of a quite different order. Owing to their bourgeois upbringing, taste and habits they were plagued by bad conscience about the class with whom they wanted to associate themselves, a syndrome which in certain cases went so far as to paralyse their creative energy. This sometimes deeply felt sense of guilt can be found in writers as various as Edward Upward, George Orwell, and Christopher Caudwell. Upward is most explicit about it:

> How could he, a bourgeois misfit, a favoured weakling who in spite of his expensive education and many undeserved advantages had become a wretched failure, presume to ask to associate with people who, though born into sordid and hard conditions, had not succumbed but had fought back, on behalf of the whole class they belonged to, against their exploiters?[39]

The autobiographical hero, Alan Sebrill, asks himself this question in *In the Thirties* (1962), when he is about to make up his mind whether to join the Communist Party. This novel was written or at least published more than twenty years after the period in which it is set. Yet its strength lies in the authenticity with which the atmosphere of the period, experienced by a sensitive middle-class intellectual, is preserved. His doubts, fears, and uneasiness come out again, as he finally takes heart to knock at the door of the committee rooms:

B

Why had he been so stupid to put on such a bourgeois-looking
coat this evening? He had done it for the very bourgeois reason
that he had been afraid that if he had worn his fairly disreputable-
looking mackintosh he might have caught a cold in this end-of-
October weather. And now he would be regarded, when he went
into the rooms, as a middle-class interloper; or worse, he might
be suspected of being a police spy or even a runaway mental
patient.[40]

George Orwell, in a mood not too dissimilar from Sebrill's,
sought to inflict punishment upon himself by descending into the
ranks of the down-and-out, sharing their poverty and contempt
for the established order. Even Christopher Caudwell who, it
must be remembered, saw himself primarily as a creative writer,
'a rank and file member of the profession of novelist', as he once
called himself, was harrowed by doubts in this respect. In one of
his unpublished stories the central figure exclaims:

> We both need a religion, but what religions are there nowadays?
> Communism remains, I suppose, but before I can embrace that
> I must go down to the depths, and be one of what a Communist
> must believe alone has the right to exist today, the anonymous
> proletariat.[41]

And in his decision to settle in a typical working-class district,
join the Party there and remain anonymous, Caudwell acted
accordingly.

That this psychological barrier was very powerful, then, cannot
be disputed. What is in question, however, is its 'rationalisation',
the assumption that often went hand in hand with it, namely that
the intellectual as a member of the middle-class had his share in
the exploitation of the working population. In his book *After the
Thirties* Jack Lindsay has demonstrated how abstract such a view
was, how it ignored the basic fact that, on a world scale, the main
burden of exploitation had long shifted from inside the Capitalist
countries to the Colonies, from which the proletariat of the
Western industrial societies profited willy-nilly in about the same
way as, according to this notion, the middle-class intellectuals
profited from, and were held partly responsible for, the exploitation of the workers of their own countries.[42] Lindsay also rightly
rejects the corresponding assumption that the worker, who did
not suffer from this sense of guilt, therefore had easier access to
literary creativity. Our foregoing discussion leaves little ground

for this supposition, anyway, but Lindsay makes a further point:

> Of all the working-class writers thrown up by the turmoils of the 1930s, not a single survivor has remained politically militant. The few writers who have kept on striving to take a revolutionary viewpoint through the difficult years since 1939 have all been middle-class in origin.[43]

Now though there is some truth in this statement, it needs to be modified in several respects. Firstly, and most evidently, it overlooks the fact that two of the most gifted Socialist novelists who were not of middle-class origin died before the decade was over (Lewis Grassic Gibbon and Lewis Jones), others (James Barke, Walter Greenwood) remained firm Socialists until their deaths or at least (Harold Heslop) have never renounced their Socialist commitment to this day, even if their later work does not match the earlier in immediacy and raw power. And, secondly, I would contend that in so far as there has been a retreat, a depoliticisation, or an abandonment of novel writing by worker-writers after the Thirties, this is also due to the relative neglect with which they were treated at the time.

In his own massive contribution to Socialist fiction Lindsay has striven to give shape to the idea contained in *After the Thirties* that the Socialist novelist must be rooted in the people. He is unique in the Thirties in attempting this in the field of the historical novel. But whereas the type of historical novel evolved by Walter Scott, 'this profound dialectical relationship, this deep interwoveness of the historical representative of a popular movement with the popular movement itself',[44] was characterised by a deep veneration for the great historical personalities, Lindsay can claim to have 'democratised' the *genre*. It was his avowed aim to make the reader aware of the revolutionary tradition of the English people. To carry out this plan, he developed an ingenious device: a number of historical personalities do make their appearance in his novels, but their actual role in the plot depends on how much in real history they helped to further historical progress. Thus the great historical figures obstructing social progress recede into the background before the leading men of the popular movements, while these in their turn diminish behind the fictive heroes, taken from the anonymous mass of the people.

In *1649* the role accorded to Cromwell and the other Grandees is negligible compared with the prominent parts given to the

Levellers Lilburne and Overton or the leader of the Diggers, Winstanley. But the real heroes are two fictive figures, Ralph Lydcot, a Leveller whose gradual transformation from a courageous fighter for freedom and democracy into a merchant solely interested in his trade, abjuring politics, is intended to reflect the Capitalist outcome of the Revolution; and Roger Cotton, a bookseller's apprentice, in whose person are fused the religious radicalism of the era and the vision of an egalitarian communism as perceived by Winstanley. 'However, before Lindsay dissolves the picture of English society in the year 1649 into individual actions, the first chapter, which describes the execution of Charles I, shows the full strength of the people.'[45] The moment of the strength of the people is the weakness of tyranny. Ralph, through whose eyes we follow the incidents on the scaffold and the reaction of the masses, is conscious of the historical meaning of this moment:

> He was not in the least concerned in the personal reactions of the actors on the scaffold, bishop or executioner or king. It was a drama that rose above all personal considerations or feelings.[46]

The executioner's axe which separates the head from its trunk symbolically divides one era from another:

> . . . the axe upflashed. Suddenly it was all over . . . from the watching masses came a strange cry, something of fear, something of exultation, both half strangled, and more than fear or exultation, a thankfulness that it was over, a mere statement that what had happened had happened irrevocably.[47]

This initial chapter is the best in a book which otherwise is not free from contradictions. As Alick West has acutely observed, the opposition which the author constructs between revolution and commerce comes near to a mis-reading of the actual character of the events of 1648-49. The English Revolution was headed not by the people, but by the bourgeoisie. Therefore its outcome does not collide with, but is in complete harmony with, Ralph's development. Yet West has to admit that this contradiction in the novel finds a parallel in the dual character of the Revolution itself, which on the one hand was carried out by a class whose interests were confined to the expansion of the market and the retention of private ownership of the means of production, but which on the other hand, however, cannot be interpreted exclusively in terms of 'the victory of a particular class in society over the *old political order*'. Rather it was 'the *proclamation of the political order for the new European society*', and as such 'expressed the needs of the particular world at that time even more than the needs of the particular parts of that world',[48] in which it took place.

In removing the class-struggles from present-day England to the past (Ancient Rome or English history from the sixteenth to the nineteenth centuries)[49] Lindsay's work bears resemblances to the fiction of other Socialist intellectuals. The subject-matter of Ralph Bates's two interesting novels (*Lean Men*, 1934; *The Olive Field*, 1936) is taken from pre-Civil war, revolutionary Spain, most of Mulk Raj Anand's novels are situated in India, and Ralph Fox chose the East (Siberia) for his work *Storming Heaven* (1928). From a preliminary survey it would appear that not one novel has been written in the Thirties about social revolutionary struggles in Britain. To this it might be objected that there was no revolutionary situation either. True, but this supposes in the novelists a clear-headed analysis which is alien to the *Zeitgeist*. On the contrary, as we saw earlier on, the general feeling among Socialist writers was one of a final crisis: revolution seemed to be just round the corner. Nor does it account for the fact that worker-writers in the Thirties continued to locate the class struggles where Tressell, Barbor, and Heslop had located them, in the production process, the only place with which they were thoroughly familiar.

Goldmann in his *Sociology of the Novel* has argued that Malraux set his revolutionary novels in China (*La Condition Humaine*) and Spain (*L'Espoir*), because these were the places where the revolutionary movements were at their strongest, and to situate them elsewhere would have put their realistic quality in danger.[50] Yet, for all its apparent persuasiveness, this is a rather unsatisfactory, almost formalistic explanation. It presumes that the novelist first decides that he wants to write a revolutionary novel and then looks round for his material, whereas in the actual praxis of the writer these can hardly be conceived of as separable, consecutive steps. Since I have no ready solution myself, all I can do here is call attention to this problem which needs to be studied not only in terms of the Thirties (in England), but in the wider context of the revolutionary writing of other periods and countries.[51]

Another empty space one is bound to notice at some stage

when assessing the Socialist fiction of the Thirties is the remarkable absence of novels of factory life, which could have claimed to deal with a situation familiar to and typical of millions of people. Of course, aspects of factory life were treated in individual chapters or scenes (for example, in Walter Greenwood's *Love on the Dole*, part III of Lewis Grassic Gibbon's *A Scots Quair*, and Mulk Raj Anand's *Coolie*), but it appears that there were no such books as Willi Bredel's *Maschinenfabrik N. & K.* in Germany or James Steele's *The Conveyor* in the United States, set in a huge Hamburg machine factory and the Detroit car plants respectively. Often in British stories or novels the industrial unit is rather the small workshop as in the case of Simon Blumenfeld or Jack Hilton. Leaving miners' novels aside, the one major exception to this rule is *Living* (1929) by Henry Green who, ironically, not only stood outside the labour movement and the left-wing intelligentsia of the Thirties, but moreover rose to the position of general manager in the company in whose workshop the 'plot' unfolds. That is to say, there is scarcely any plot to speak of. Not much happens. The only action, if it may be called so, Lily Gates's elopement with her friend Bert Jones, is a miserable failure. So at the end of the novel she returns, disillusioned, alone, and everything goes on as before. Walter Allen, writing in the Sixties, has credited *Living* with being the 'best English novel of factory life' in the last thirty years,[52] a judgment which in the sheer absence of any serious rival may have some justification. Allen supports this view by pointing to the author's ability to capture the 'poetry of working class life':

> . . . one morning in iron foundry, Arthur Jones began singing. He did not often sing. When he began the men looked up from work and at each other and stayed quiet. In machine shop, which was next iron foundry, they said it was Arthur singing and stayed quiet also. He sang all morning.
>
> He was Welsh and sang in Welsh. His voice had a great soft yell in it. It rose and rose and fell then rose again and, when the crane was quiet for a moment, then his voice came out from behind noise of the crane in passionate singing. Soon each one in this factory had heard that Arthur had begun and, if he had 2 moments, came by iron foundry shop to listen. So all through that morning, as he went on, was a little group of men standing by door in the machine shop, always different men. His singing made them all sad. Everything in iron foundries is black with the

burnt sand, and here was his silver voice yelling like bells. The
black grimed men bent over their black boxes.

When he came to the end of a song or something in his work
kept him from singing, men would call out to him with names of
English songs, but he would not sing these . . . .

Still Arthur sang and it might be months before he sang again.
And no one else sang that day, but all listened to his singing.
That night son had been born to him.[53]

This might indeed be called poetry. If one nevertheless hesitates to join in Allen's high praise, this is because he has
forgotten to say that the passage quoted is a rare one in the book,
unequalled in its power to grasp the imagination of the reader
and heighten his sense of awareness of beauty under the harshest
work conditions. True, in some such moments the novel springs
to life, but the overall impression one gets of the life of the
workers is still one of hopelessness, monotony and lethargy, and
it is telling that the more vivid scenes are those which deal with
eternal, 'timeless' events in the life of this class like conception,
pregnancy and birth, whereas there is nothing to suggest that the
workers ever take matters into their own hands to improve the
harsh conditions under which they live and work. They endure,
but they never act.

Let there be no misunderstanding. *Living* has a number of
qualities not always to be found in Socialist novels: brevity of
style, vernacular dialogue, power of observation. But what we are
concerned with is whether it presents a truthful picture of factory
life. The answer is no, for although the author, as far as I know,
never professed to be a Socialist, a novel about the situation of
the working-class published within three years of the General
Strike (which even finds an occasional mention in the book), yet
omitting altogether the essential quality of factory life, the
solidarity of the workers and the action which they take, exposes
itself to the kind of reproach Engels had made with regard to Mrs
Harkness' *City Girl*: '. . . the working-class figures as a passive
mass, unable to help itself and not even showing [making] any
attempt at striving to help itself'.[54]

Arthur Jones, the singer in *Living*, is a Welshman. This is no
accident. In Wales and Scotland, generally speaking at the peri-
phery of industrial civilisation, the oral tradition of peasants and
workers was then still alive. It does not come as a surprise
therefore that some of the best Socialist novels were written by

men who had access to this culture and drew heavily on it.[55]
There is no space here to discuss the achievements of all the
novelists in question: Lewis Jones, Gwyn Jones, James Barke. I
have to content myself with a very brief treatment of what is
generally held to be the outstanding Socialist prose work of the
inter-war period, Grassic Gibbon's *Scots Quair* trilogy (1932-34).

A Scots Quair is set in such a 'border country', first in a peasant
community *(Sunset Song)*, then in a small rural town, already
slightly affected by industrial change, where there is a textile mill
(Cloud Howe), and finally in a typically Scottish industrial city
(Grey Granite). This slowly rising movement towards industrial
life reflects the gradually changing environment as experienced
and reacted against by the people. The peasant community in the
first volume, then, is not a self-contained world, but serves to
demonstrate how under developed Capitalism the lives of the
people in the most distant parts of the country are affected by
social and political decisions taken elsewhere. The capitalisation
of agriculture, the disappearance of the last small tenants, the
migration to the towns, the First World War, the industrial
proletariat, the General Strike, the Great Depression, the hunger
marches are all there – not as abstract events from history books,
but in their impact first on the crofters and then on the towns-
folk, and in the responses they evoke in them.

Gibbon, who was of peasant origin, saw very clearly the losses
inflicted by this historic change. And no one who has read the
trilogy can deny that the perishing of the oral tradition meant a
real loss. So impressively does the author succeed in recording
the dialogues, songs, gossips, quarrels, dreams and lusts in their
original popular idiom.

Sometimes one has the feeling that one is listening to the
voices of a collective rather than reading the narrative account of
an individual. Yet, for all the vividness of his earthy sketches of
the crofter way of life, Gibbon never falls into the trap of
idealising a village life of whose drab aspects he is well aware. His
is a panorama of change, conflict, struggle and progress:

> Change who ruled the earth and the sky and the waters under-
> neath the earth . . . whose right hand was Death and whose left
> hand Life, might be stayed by none of the dreams of men, love,
> hate, compassion, anger or pity, gods or devils or wild crying to
> the sky. He passed and repassed in the ways of the wind,
> Deliverer, Destroyer and Friend in one.[56]

It is this element of recognition of the inevitability and necessity of historical change which prevents him from aspiring to turn
back the wheel of history, from succumbing to a nostalgic,
idealising view of the past, an attitude which mars the work of
many a European writer in the early twentieth century, among
them some of the great names such as Hamsun, D. H. Lawrence
and Unamuno.

But in the context of this study we are less interested in an
evaluation of Gibbon's place in world literature than in his
specific contribution to the Socialist fiction of the Thirties, and
his undoubted greatness as a portrayer of the circumstances and
consequences of the transition from country to town should not
blind us to the fact that precisely in his treatment of the industrial
scene a number of inconsistencies creep in. Authentic as, for
example, the bitterness of the energetic and militant minister
Colquohoun may be in view of the sell-out of the Trades Union
Congress's General Council in the General Strike, his subsequent
withdrawal into a dream-like mysticism is scarcely convincing.[57]
And this points to another disappointing feature of the trilogy.
The plot centres for too long on the intellectual. Only in the final
volume, when Ewan gets himself a job in the steelworks, do the
industrial workers enter the scene. But, probably as a result of
the author's not being closely acquainted with factory workers,
they never abound with the vitality of a Long Rob or Chae
Strachen, the peasants in *Sunset Song*:

> When we meet the 'keelies' alongside Ewan at the steelworks, we
> are mainly conscious of their negative attitudes towards him as
> an intellectual toff . . . Even when the negative aspects of
> working-class life are stressed, the individual personalisation on
> the whole lacks substance and flesh-and-blood vividness.[58]

Worse is to come. At the end of the novel Ewan becomes a
Communist, but loses all humanity. His change is described as a
hardening into a granite block *(Grey Granite)*, a steel machine.
He separates from his girl-friend because, under the threat of
losing her job as a school-teacher, she agreed to sign a paper
which forbids her to attend party meetings. His behaviour at this
point has rightly been called sectarian.[59] When he is finally
ordered into Communist Party Headquarters in London, the
picture of the heartless, insensible Communist is complete. He
knew, it is said,

B*

that if it suited the party purpose Trease [i.e. the local secretary] would betray him to the police tomorrow, use anything and everything that might happen to him as propaganda and publicity, without caring a fig for liking or aught else. So he'd deal with Mrs. Trease, if it came to that . . . . And Ewan nodded to that, to Trease, to himself, commonsense, no other way to hack out the road ahead. Neither friends nor scruples nor honour nor hope for the folk who took the workers' road.[60]

However one may interpret this and similar passages in the third part of the trilogy – whether as a true image of some Scottish Communist Party officials the author might have known personally, whether as a warning against such a dehumanising disposition, a vision, as it were, of Stalinism, or simply as an unreflecting adoption of anti-Communist propaganda – Gibbon left little doubt about where he stood. In a passionate contribution to the discussion over the statement of aims referred to at the beginning of this article, he confessed, 'I am a revolutionary writer' and 'I hate capitalism . . . . But because I'm a revolutionist I see no reason for gainsaying my own critical judgment'. His indictment of the prophecy that bourgeois culture was a dying culture proved far-sighted. 'Capitalist literature, whether we like it or not, is in decay.'[61] That this voice from the wilderness was silenced by an untimely death, at the age of thirty-four, turned out to be the greatest loss for Socialist fiction and as such was another impediment to its fully-fledged constitution in the Thirties.

NOTES

1 Already in 1974 there appeared two important articles on specific aspects of the period: the Workers' Theatre Movement and the foundation of the Writers' International. See Leonard Jones, 'The Workers' Theatre Movement in the Thirties', *Marxism Today*, XVIII, 9 (September, 1974), pp. 271-280. Karl Klaus Walther, 'Zur Entstehung und Geschichte der britischen Sektion der Internationalen Vereinigung Revolutionärer Schrifsteller', *Zeitschrift für Anglistik und Amerikanistik*, XXII (1974), pp. 5-17.—I wish to thank Kiernan Ryan for his careful reading of the manuscript and for greatly improving the text with regard to style.

2 Seen in this perspective the exhibition in the National Portrait Gallery which once more celebrated the Big Five was a marked set-

back. Hynes' book on the other hand is less obsessed with the Auden Group than its title might suggest, though the dismissal of the whole working-class literature of the period with one casual remark ('Virtually no writing of literary importance came out of the working class during the decade.' p. 11) clearly defines the limits of his approach.

3 'A Conversation with Edgell Rickword', *The Review*, no. 11/12 (n.d.), 'The Thirties – a Special Number'.

4 Since the first publication of this article the Spanish scholar Ramón López Ortega has published *Movimiento Obrero y Novela Inglesa* (Salamanca, 1976) which deals mainly, though not exclusively, with the 1930s. Organising his material according to specific themes, such as the apotheosis of work, industrial conflict, unemployment or the portrayal of the trade unionist, Ortega examines about a dozen Thirties novels, among others by George Blake, Walter Brierley, Lewis Grassic Gibbon, Walter Greenwood, Harold Heslop, Gwyn Jones and Lewis Jones.

5 *Left Review*, I, 1 (October, 1934), p. 38.

6 *Ibid.*

7 Cf. Helga Gallas, *Marxistische Literaturtheorie: Kontroversen im Bund proletarisch-revolutionärer Schriftsteller*, (Neuwied, 1971), pp. 31-34.

8 *Left Review*, I, 3 (December, 1934), pp. 77 (Brown's emphasis).

9 *Ibid.* p. 76.

10 Literature of the World Revolution (Moscow, 1931 – no. 1 of *International Literature*), p. 226.

11 Cf. Karl Klaus Walther, 'Literarische Beziehungen zwischen der englischen und der russischen Literatur von der Oktoberrevolution bis zum Ende der zwanziger Jahre', *Wiss. Zeitschrift der Universität Halle*, XXII (1973), pp. 37-44.

12 The lesser-known worker-writers, Simon Blumenfeld and J. MacDougal Hay, in their contributions to the debate, expressed views which resembled those of Brown.

13 See his notorious remark: 'a heap of dung crowded with worms, filmed through the lenses of a microscope—that is the work of Joyce', quoted from *Sozialistische Realismuskonzeptionen: Dokumente zum 1. Allunionskongreß der Sowjetschriftsteller*, ed. by H.-J. Schmitt and G. Schramm (Frankfurt, 1974), p. 205. This book, which contains thirty-seven items, is the only one in print in any language where all the major speeches can be looked up.

14 Admittedly she had a few critical things to say about Radek's over-estimation of the influence of Joyce, Shaw, and Wells on the English intelligentsia and working-class, but this objection in no way changed the main emphasis of her report.

15 *Left Review* I, 1 (October, 1934), p. 38.

16 *Ibid.* I, 6 (March, 1934), p. 225.

17 In the same way it was only logical that once the popular front policy had been officially endorsed by the Comintern at its Seventh World Congress, the International Union of Revolutionary Writers and all its national sections should be disbanded in order to reappear under the name of the International Association for the Defence of Culture.
18 Cf. Donald Drew Egbert, *Social Radicalism and the Arts: Western Europe, A Cultural History from the French Revolution to 1968* (New York, 1970), pp. 497-503.
19 *Left Review*, I, 9 (June, 1935), p. 368.
20 Ralph Fox, *The Novel and the People* (London, 1937), p. 108.
21 *Ibid.* p. 89.
22 *Ibid,* p. 107.
23 *Ibid.* p. 104.
24 'Die Biographie der Dinge', in: Sergej Tretjakov, *Lyrik Dramatik Prosa* (Leipzig, 1972), pp. 201-202 (My translation—HGK).
25 Übergang vom bürgerlichen zum sozialistischen Realismus', in: Bertolt Brecht, *Gesammelte Werke* (Frankfurt, 1975), vol. XIX, p. 377 (My translation—HGK).
26 Both quotations from the 'Manifesto', printed in *New Writing*, No. 1 (Spring, 1936).
27 The nearest thing to a reconstruction of the literary documents of what after Lenin has been called the 'second culture' was the *Handbook of Freedom* (London, 1939), edited by Jack Lindsay and Edgell Rickword (repr. 1977).
28 See in this respect Alick West's rejection of the formula 'culture is a weapon in the fight for Socialism' as a half-truth, in his autobiography *One Man in His Time* (London, 1969), p. 190.
29 In 1935 and 1938; cf. F. C. Ball, *One of the Damned: the Life and Times of Robert Tressell, author of 'The Ragged Trousered Philanthropists'* (London, 1973), p. 257.
30 See Leonard Jones, 'The General Strike and the Workers' Theatre', in: *Essays in Honour of William Gallacher* (Berlin, 1966), pp. 155-156.
31 Cf. Brian Mayne: 'The Ragged Trousered Philanthropists: an Appraisal of an Edwardian Novel of Social Protest', *Twentieth Century Literature*, XIII, 2 (1967), p. 77.
32 I am indebted to Edgell Rickword for this information. Rickword worked first at Wishart & Co. which in 1936 merged with Martin Lawrence Ltd. to form Lawrence & Wishart. Both Wishart & Co. and Lawrence & Wishart, under Rickword's guidance, published a number of interesting working-class novels.
33 Ingrid von Rosenberg, 'Robert Tressells Arbeiterroman "Die Philanthropen in den zerlumpten Hosen",' *alternative*, no. 90 (1973), p. 150.
34 Dana's article appeared in *Plebs*, XVIII, 11 (November, 1925),

pp. 431-438, the letter in the following number, pp. 485-486.
35 The influence of Proletkult in Britain still awaits research.
36 *The Sunday Worker*, 14.3.1926.
37 *Under the Sway of Coal* (Moscow, 1925). For a summary of the contents see E. Elistratova, 'The Work of Harold Heslop', *International Literature* 1 (1932), p. 99.
38 Alick West, *Crisis and Criticism* (London, 1937), p. 137. Unfortunately this chapter has been left out of the new edition, *Crisis and Criticism and Selected Literary Essays* (London, 1975). This is against the intention at least of the original version, which precisely puts the general aesthetics worked out in the theoretical parts of the book to the test of a bourgeois novel (*Ulysses*) as well as a proletarian one.
39 Edward Upward, *In the Thirties* (Harmondsworth, 1969), p. 41.
40 *Ibid.* p. 43 – It should be kept in mind, however, that Sebrill's story is not only one of tormenting inner conflicts, but also of his successful overcoming of them and of his acceptance and integration into the ranks of the Party.
41 I am indebted to Caudwell's brother, T. Stanhope Sprigg, for giving me access to the complete version of 'To Aldous Huxley', an essay of which short extracts were published by *Left Review* III, 11 (December, 1937), pp. 657-661. The second quotation is from Samuel Hynes's introduction to *Romance and Realism* (Princeton, 1970, p. 11.
42 Jack Lindsay, *After the Thirties: the Novel in Britain and Its Future* (London, 1956). In fairness it must be added that of the three writers mentioned at least Orwell, through his first-hand knowledge of colonial reality, very clearly saw this: 'What we always forget is that the overwhelming bulk of the British proletariat does not live in Britain but in Asia and Africa . . . . This is the system which we all live on.' *The Collected Essays, Journalism and Letters of George Orwell*, vol. I (Harmondsworth, 1970), p. 437. But Orwell's insight does not invalidate the point that this guilty state of mind was prevalent among a number of Socialist writers in the Thirties.
43 Lindsay, *After the Thirties*, p. 39.
44 Georg Lukács, 'Der historische Roman', in: *Probleme des Realismus*, vol. III (Neuwied, 1965), p. 48 (My translation—HGK).
45 Manfred Hecker, 'Besonderheiten des sozialistischen Realismus in Jack Lindsay's Romanen zur englischen Geschichte', *Zeitschrift für Anglistik und Amerikanistik*, XXI (1973), p. 148 (My translation—HGK).
46 Jack Lindsay, *1649: a Novel of a Year* (London, 1938), p. 13.
47 *Ibid.* p. 17.
48 Karl Marx, 'Die Bourgeoisie und die Kontrerevolution', in Marx and Engels, *Ausgewählte Schriften in zwei Bänden*, vol. I (Berlin, 1951), p. 60; quoted by Alick West, *The Mountain and the Sunlight* (London, 1958), p. 8 (emphasis only in the German original version).

49 Only after the Second World War did Lindsay switch to 'Contemporary Novels of the British Way', as he calls them.

50 Cf. Lucien Goldmann, *Soziologie des Romans* (Neuwied, 1972), p. 71.

51 This point can only properly be clarified when the wider role of intellectuals is taken into consideration. For example, intellectuals can be mobilised by and for the great and sometimes 'exotic' causes like the Spanish Civil War in the Thirties, Hungary and Egypt in the Fifties, Cuba and Vietnam in the Sixties. The workers, on the other hand, are firmly rooted in the class struggles of their own country.

52 Walter Allen, *Tradition and Dream* (Harmondsworth, 1965), pp. 234-235).

53 Henry Green, *Living* (London, 1964), pp. 89-90.

54 Friedrich Engels, 'Letter to Margaret Harkness', in: (ed.) David Craig, *Marxists on Literature: an Anthology* (Harmondsworth, 1975), p. 270.

55 See Craig's remark 'what typifies the socialist poet is his ready and fertile adaptation of popular styles quite as much as his solidarity with exploited people' and the discussion preceding it in his essay 'The New Poetry of Socialism' in: David Craig, *The Real Foundations: Literature and Social Change* (London, 1973), p. 222.

56 Lewis Grassic Gibbon, *Grey Granite:* Book Three of *A Scots Quair* (London, 1973), p. 220.

57 Though, admittedly, it makes one thoughtful that still a generation later, in Raymond Williams's novel *Border Country* (1960), Morgan, the union secretary, who had devoted himself throughout to a successful outcome of the Strike, 'collapses' after the decision of the TUC Council, abandons his railway job, and rises (or rather sinks) to the position of a cynical small entrepreneur. The extent of what was then destroyed in the minds and hearts of the workers involved is immeasurable.

58 Ian Milner, 'An Estimation of Lewis Grassic Gibbon's "A Scots Quair" ', *Marxist Quarterly* I, 4 (October, 1954), pp. 214-215.

59 Lindsay, *After the Thirties*, p. 51.

60 Gibbon, *Grey Granite*, p. 197.

61 All quotations from *Left Review* I, 5 (February, 1935), pp. 179-180.

A Bibliography of Socialist Novels of the 1930s

The following bibliography would need confirmation and perhaps complementation in a number of cases, but as a preliminary survey it gives an idea of the relative flowering of Socialist fiction in the 1930s. My general guideline was not to apply too restrictive a set of criteria for the selection of works; for knowledge of and background information about this particular aspect of the cultural front in the Thirties is still so scarce that, even at the risk of including doubtful cases, a fairly exhaustive list of authors and titles is what is needed.

That list would, of course, be longer still if one also included other prose works such as stories (e.g. Leslie Halward, *To Tea on Sunday*), sketches (e.g. *Seven Shifts*, ed. Jack Common), autobiographies by working men (e.g. B. L. Coombes, *These Poor Hands*) and reportage (e.g. George Orwell, *The Road to Wigan Pier*). These form an important body of working-class and Socialist literary expressions, but they pose aesthetic problems distinct from those of the novel form.

As one might expect, for some authors only those books are included which reflect their move to the left and the subsequent change in the point of view and subject matter of their novels. Thus, for example, Jack Lindsay's novels on Ancient Rome published before 1937 have been omitted.

As for the grouping of the titles, a chronological order seemed best to serve the purpose of demonstrating the sudden increase in output due to the coming into existence of the Thirties movement. For each individual year the books are listed alphabetically.

1930
J. C. Grant, *The Back-to-Backs* (Chatto & Windus)
Harold Heslop, *Journey Beyond* (Harold Shaylor)
Stacey Hyde, *The Blackleg* (Longman)

1931
George Blake, *Returned Empty* (Faber)
James Hanley, *Boy* (Boriswood)

1932
Frederick C. Boden, *Miner* (Dent)
Lewis Grassic Gibbon, *Sunset Song* (Jarrolds), Part One of
  A Scots Quair

1933
James Barke, *The World His Pillow* (Collins)
F. C. Boden, *Flo* (Dent)
Lewis Grassic Gibbon, *Cloud Howe* (Jarrolds), Part Two of
  A Scots Quair

Walter Greenwood, *Love on the Dole* (Cape)
A. P. Roley, *Revolt* (Arthur Barker)

1934

Dot Allan, *Hunger March* (Hutchinson)
Ralph Bates, *Lean Men* (Peter Davies)
Lewis Grassic Gibbon, *Grey Granite* (Jarrolds), Part Three of
  A Scots Quair
Harold Heslop, *Goaf* (Fortune Press)
Harold Heslop, *The Crime of Peter Ropner* (Fortune Press)
James Lansdale Hodson, *Harvest in the North* (Gollancz)
William Holt, *Backwaters* (Nicholson & Watson)
Jack Jones, *Rhondda Roundabout* (Faber)
Storm Jameson, *Company Parade* (Cassell), Part One of
  The Mirror in Darkness
Montagu Slater, *Haunting Europe* (Wishart)
Geoffrey Trease, *Bows Against the Barons* (Martin Lawrence)
Geoffrey Trease, *Comrades for the Charter* (Martin Lawrence)

1935

Mulk Raj Anand, *The Untouchable* (Wishart)
Anthony Bertram, *Men Adrift* (Chapman & Hall)
Simon Blumenfeld, *Jew Boy* (Cape)
F. C. Boden, *A Derbyshire Tragedy* (Dent)
George Blake, *The Shipbuilders* (Faber)
Walter Brierley, *Means Test Man* (Methuen)
Alec Brown, *Daughters of Albion* (Boriswood)
James Hanley, *The Furys* (Chatto & Windus), Part One of
  The Furys
Harold Heslop, *Last Cage Down* (Wishart)
Storm Jameson, *Love in Winter* (Cassell), Part Two of
  The Mirror in Darkness
Jack Jones, *Black Parade* (Faber)
Naomi Mitchison, *We Have Been Warned* (Constable)
Geoffrey Trease, *The Call to Arms* (Martin Lawrence)

1936

Mulk Raj Anand, *The Coolie* (Lawrence & Wishart)
James Barke, *Major Operation* (Collins)
Phyllis-Eleanor Bentley, *Freedom, Farewell!* (Gollancz)
Ralph Bates, *The Olive Field* (Cape)
George Blake, *David and Joanna* (Faber)

James Hanley, *The Secret Journey* (Chatto & Windus), Part Two of
   The Furys
Storm Jameson, *None Turn Back* (Cassell), Part Three of
   The Mirror in Darkness
Gwyn Jones, *Times Like These* (Gollancz)
Irene Rathbone, *They Call it Peace* (Dent)
John Sommerfield, *May Day* (Lawrence & Wishart)
Gabrielle Vallings, *The Tramp of the Multitude* (Hutchinson)

1937
Mulk Raj Anand, *Two Leaves and a Bud* (Lawrence & Wishart)
Simon Blumenfeld, *Phineas Kahn* (Cape)
Walter Brierley, *Sandwichman* (Methuen)
James Curtis, *There Ain't No Justice* (Cape)
Ralph Fox, *This Was Their Youth* (Lawrence & Wishart)
Gwyn Jones, *The Nine-Days' Wonder* (Gollancz)
Lewis Jones, *Cwmardy* (Lawrence & Wishart)
Arthur Calder Marshall, *Pie in the Sky* (Cape)
Liam O'Flaherty, *Famine* (Gollancz)

1938
Simon Blumenfeld, *Doctor of the Lost* (Cape)
James Curtis, *They Drive by Night* (Cape)
Terence Greenidge, *Tin Pot Country* (Fortune Press)
James Hanley, *Hollow Sea* (Lane)
Jack Hilton, *Champion* (Cape)
Jack Lindsay, *1649* (Methuen)
John Sommerfield, *Trouble in Porter Street* (Lawrence &
   Wishart)
Amabel Williams-Ellis, *The Big Firm* (Collins)

1939
Walter Allen, *Blind Man's Ditch* (Michael Joseph)
Mulk Raj Anand, *The Village* (Cape)
James Barke, *The Land of the Leal* (Collins)
Simon Blumenfeld, *They Won't Let You Live* (Nicholson &
   Watson)
Joe Corrie, *Black Earth* (Routledge)
Frank Griffin, *October Day* (Secker & Warburg)
Leslie Halward, *Gus and Ida* (Michael Joseph)
Lewis Jones, *We Live* (Lawrence & Wishart)
Jack Lindsay, *Lost Birthright* (Methuen)

Lewis Grassic Gibbon and 'A Scots Quair': Politics in the Novel

Roy Johnson

Although it is now becoming more widely acknowledged that
Lewis Grassic Gibbon's trilogy *A Scots Quair* has been unjustly
neglected outside Scotland during the forty years since its publication, those few critics who have written about it have given their
approval to the work's traditional qualities as a novel of manners
and social life – probably because it covers a long time span in
the history of a family, has a detailed social background, and is cast
in the seasoned form of a three-volume novel. It is usually praised,
in other words, for being a well-executed and distinctly Scottish
version of the nineteenth-century triple-decker. But what this
type of commendation ignores is the fact that whilst Gibbon
chose a traditional form it was being put to completely new uses.
He employed it to write Britain's most powerful 'novel of commitment' (long before the term became current) to convey his
own passionately held beliefs about the relationship between
history and politics, and to write a novel which would ultimately
express a militant working-class point of view. In fact this combination of politics, class consciousness, and proletarian viewpoint
made it in many ways the first important 'proletarian novel',
particularly since these characteristics are bound together and
expressed in a language which often recasts orthodox literary usage
to generate a 'speech of the people'. *A Scots Quair* is triumphantly
political in the widest sense – concerned profoundly with the connections between history, economic life, social classes, and the
development of individual political consciousness – but it is in
danger of being trapped by praise which confines it within the
narrow category of being simply a 'social novel'.

Kurt Wittig, as a typical instance, in commending the triology
says that 'the story moves on three distinct levels: personal,
social, and mythical',[1] but this doesn't go far enough. He fails to
mention the sense of historical development which provides the
foundation upon which all the other 'levels' are built. For it is
primarily Gibbon's grasp of history which gives him the base for
his insight into the political relationship between man and society.

And although he is principally concerned with the events of twentieth-century Scottish history and even reflects its socio-economic development in a compressed form by using the country, the town, and the city for the consecutive settings of the three volumes, his consciousness goes much further back – back to the origins of the region with which he is concerned:

> Kinraddie lands had been won by a Norman childe, Cospatric de Gondeshil, in the days of William the Lyon, when gryphons and suchlike beasts still roamed the Scots countryside and folk would waken in their beds to hear the children screaming, with a great wolf-beast, come through the hide window, tearing at their throats.[2]

At the outset of his first volume he gives a potted version of several centuries of Kincardineshire history – from Cospatric, through the English invasions, the Reformation, and the emigrations of the eighteenth and nineteenth centuries, up to a period just before the First World War. The tone is often humorous (Cospatric's slaying of the gryphon), but the intention deadly serious; for the purpose, instigated in *Sunset Song* and running continuously through the subsequent volumes, *Cloud Howe* and *Grey Granite*, is to show a materialist, militantly Marxist view of history as the outcome of perpetual class struggle. The three volumes themselves show that process taking place between land-owners and tenant farmers, factory owners and the working class, but Gibbon also shows the extent to which the process is continuous by integrating its historical past. When young Chris Guthrie visits Dunnottar Castle with Ewan Tavendale she is reminded by a commemoration plaque of her ancestor's struggles in 1685:

> In walls little slits rose up, through these it was that in olden times the garrisons had shot their arrows at besiegers; and down below, in the dungeons, were the mouldering clefts where a prisoner's hands were nailed while they put him to torment. There the Covenanting folk had screamed and died while the gentry dined and danced in their lithe, warm halls . . . . Her folk and his they had been, those whose names stand graved in tragedy.[3]

She has inherited this hatred of class privilege from John Guthrie, her father, and she will pass it on to Ewan, her son. For through his youthful studies of archaeology he too comes to a concept of history charged with an outrage at what has been passed over, ignored, and hidden – as it has been experienced and forged by the uncelebrated majority:

> Why did they never immortalise in stone a scene from the Athenian justice-courts – a slave being ritually, unnecessarily tortured before he could legally act as a witness? Or a baby exposed to die in a jar – hundreds every year in the streets of Athens. . . . . Why not a head of Spartacus? Or a plaque of the dripping line of crosses that manned the Appian Way with slaves – dripping and falling to bits through long months, they took days to die, torn by wild beasts. Or a statuary group of a Roman slave being fed to fishes, alive in a pool.[4]

The sense of indignance, rebellion and resistance associated with this underdog's view of history reverberates throughout the novel in acts of defiance against the aristocracy, the police, and the owners of production as well as isolated acts of stubborn independence: but its principal continuity is shown through the lives of the two main characters, Chris and her son Ewan.

For a girl who grows up in a relatively isolated farming community, Chris has an eventful life during her first twenty or so years. Whilst she is still a child her father is refused the lease to his farm for standing up to the insults of a landowner's wife, the whole family have to move to another farm, her mother murders two of her children and commits suicide to escape the sexual insistence of her father, the rural locality is depopulated through war, her father dies, she gets married then suffers intense disillusion when her husband is brutalised by military life, mourns him passionately when he is shot as a deserter, then gets married again to a new minister in the local church. Right up to the end of the third volume of the trilogy, her life is a continuous series of changes – of which she is very conscious. She knows what the struggles of her ancestors have been, and throughout her own personal life she has known only the hard life of a farmer's daughter then a farmer's and a minister's wife – a life which appears on the surface to be economically static but which for her is experienced as a continuous process of fluctuations to which she must adjust herself. This is one of the principal themes of the novel – history at a personal level seen as a process of *change*. And even as a young girl Chris sees the significance of the fact that 'Nothing endures':

Sea and sky and the folk who wrote and fought and were learned, teaching and saying and praying, they lasted but as a breath, a mist of fog on the hills.[5]

Her adult life continues in a similar manner: she stands by her second husband while he tries to organise the people of the town that they move to, suffers the death of her second child, then the death of her husband in the pulpit as he rages against the political iniquities of the post-war period; she moves to Duncairn, an industrial city on the East coast, and shares the ownership of a boarding house with an older woman, gets married again, then finally separates from her third husband and moves back to the farm where she was born to take up her life on the land again. All this by the time she is forty years old.

Her response to this change is to endure stoically and take what comes along in a tough realistic manner – but all the time she is looking for something unchanging to which she can cling amidst such an exhausting process. In each of the volumes she regularly leaves her social situation to make solitary excursions to high places from which she can look down. She climbs to the Standing Stones above Kinraddie, to the hills behind the Manse at Segget, and makes trips back into the Mearns to escape the claustrophobia of the city. But these symbolic and spiritually refreshing occasions have another purpose besides giving her a chance to 'take stock': she is also making a physical reconnection with the land. For it is that which she sees as a sheet anchor to which she can attach herself. Early in her storm-tossed years as an adolescent she feels that 'nothing endured at all, nothing but the land she passed across'[6] and magnifying this love of the countryside which she has inherited from her mother she erects the land into a form of salvation, with almost a pagan attachment to it:

So, hurt and dazed, she turned to the land, close to it and the smell of it, kind and kind it was, it didn't rise up and torment your heart, you could keep at peace with the land if you gave it your heart and hands, tended it and slaved for it, it was wild and a tyrant, but it was not cruel.[7]

So as she passes into middle age at the end of the trilogy she turns away from human relations to live alone, returning to an elemental relationship with the one thing with which she feels at ease, although she has learned that there is nothing she can do to arrest the process of change even though she might appear to hide away from it.

Her son Ewan starts off with similar attachments, but ultimately his response to the process of change is to transcend this form of neo-primitivism. As a child he is an isolated individual, independent, and quite happy to pursue his enthusiasm for archaeology, which gives him an active sense of history and cultural development. He is an advanced student academically and has all the makings of someone who will gravitate from the working class to become a middle-class intellectual. But when change brings the death of his stepfather Robert Colquohoun he gives up his studies to become an engineering apprentice so that he won't be an economic burden on his mother. He lives in grim city conditions and finds himself in conflict with the rough proletarian youths he works and lives amongst. Subject to the additional conflict with his bosses and the prospects of future unemployment he takes the first major steps towards making a positive response to these changes in his life: he unites with his fellow apprentices and leads them in resistance against the factory management. The position of aloof independence is abandoned: instead of observing history and change from the outside he becomes involved in helping to shape the course of social events:

> A hell of a thing to be History!—not a student, a historian, a tinkling reformer, but LIVING HISTORY ONESELF, being it, making it, eyes for the eyeless, hands for the maimed.[8]

Like his mother has done before him he gives up his studies as so much childish dilettantism and throws himself into the difficulties of political organisation. But his response has even a further stage to go, for when, following the defeat of the Means Test demonstration and Ewan's torture at the hands of the police, he joins the Communist Party and puts himself almost at its full-time disposal, he feels himself to be not only a shaper of History but an *agent* of necessary change through class struggle. He accepts the place which is presented to him as a militant leader whilst at the same time completely abandoning any considerations of personal satisfaction or idealist notions of glorifying the class he will be fighting for. He hasn't

> a single illusion about the workers: they weren't heroes or gods oppressed, or likely to be generous and reasonable when their

great black wave came flooding at last, up and up, swamping the high places with mud and blood. Most likely such leaders of the workers as themselves would be flung aside or trampled under, it didn't matter, nothing to them, THEY THEMSELVES WERE THE WORKERS.[9]

Chris tries to step outside history and the problems of coping with the inevitability of change: her son gives himself *to* history and is prepared to subjugate his own personality in becoming an agent of change. Despite many similarities in their respective characters they have these fundamentally opposing attitudes to the process of historical development with which the novel is so deeply concerned.

The concentration of political interest and events precipitated by this process of development accelerates at the same pace as the narrative of the trilogy. What Gibbon presents is a synthesis of modern Scottish political history in a way that no other modern British writer has done: from a rural agricultural economy to urban industrialisation; from a semi-feudal aristocracy endured by tenant farmers to monopoly capitalists being fought by a class-conscious proletariat. And as a political novelist he shows his greatest strength in having all political considerations arise out of the lives of his characters – not specially imported from outside to illustrate a thesis.

In the first volume, *Sunset Song*, political issues are most of the time kept rumbling a long way below the surface in accordance with the relatively primitive nature of the economy and society before 1914. Chris Guthrie's girlhood and early marriage take place in a community whose form of production has hardly changed since the eighteenth century – small-scale tenant farming under the dominance of virtually absentee landowners. A harsh and difficult way of life which is dominated by the elements (Gibbon skilfully reflects both the personal and the nature themes by dividing the volume into four major 'agricultural' sections – 'Ploughing', 'Drilling', 'Seed Time', and 'Harvest'). Pitting themselves against very unyielding conditions the farmers exhaust themselves in a year-round battle with the soil and survive only through the relatively stable levels of prices and rents. Chris's father, John Guthrie, drives himself and his family with a puritan asceticism and rigid pride which eventually contribute to his early death. But before he dies he becomes faintly conscious of changes taking place beneath the apparently static surface of the community:

> Now also it grew plain to him . . . that the day of the crofter was fell near finished, put by, the day of folk like himself and Chae and Cuddiestound, Pooty and Long Rob of the Mill, the last of the farming folk that wrung their living from the land with their own bare hands.[10]

The event which changes the rural pattern of existence with such shattering force is the First World War, the responses to which illustrate with pointed detail the complex nature of political consciousness in a small farming community. Hitherto, any forms of political awareness have been divided between deep-seated Toryism and conservatism amongst the aristocracy, the landowners, and the petty-bourgeoisie, and rare isolated cases of radical independence in people like Long Rob, who is a sceptic and materialist with his intellectual roots in the tradition of David Hume. But the majority are so far removed from the battle of ideas and world affairs that they are politically unconscious:

> Britain was to war with Germany. But Chris didn't care and Ewan didn't either, he was thinking of his close that the weather might ruin . . . they could fight till they were black and blue for all that he cared.[11]

which might appear as a healthy anti-militarism, but is later shown to be political innocence when Ewan is persuaded to enlist by the war propaganda being made from the press, pulpit, and the petty bourgeoisie. Gibbon exposes these warmongers with blistering irony:

> "Man, some of those editors are right rough creatures, God pity the Germans if they'd their hands on them!"[12]
> "Mr Gibbon's gone, he's a Colonel-chaplain in Edinburgh now, or something like that; and he wears a right brave uniform with a black hanky across the neck of it. His father's come down to take his place, an old bit stock that drinks German blood by the gill with his porridge, by the way he preaches."[13]

And he makes quite clear the economic advantages accruing to those who are so active in calling up atrocity stories of bayoneted children in Belgium whilst staying safely at home. Nor does he shrink from exposing the naivety and cruelty of the working man he is otherwise prepared to celebrate: under the influence of jingoist propaganda, Long Rob is attacked by a gang of locals as pro-German because of his resistance to the war, and there are several sections narrated from the 'average man's' point of view to highlight his gullibility and confusion.

But these social disasters are only the manifestations of a more fundamental economic and political disaster which begins to show itself towards the end of the war. There appears to be economic prosperity in the region, but it is an artificial boom caused by the temporary rise in agricultural prices, and following massive deforestation and the monopolisation of land the small independent tenant farmer is squeezed out of business.

The economic process has its political counterpart with the post-war eruption of the Labour Party as a major force which finds its way into the Lowland community *via* the schoolteacher Jean Gordon organising the union for her own father's ploughmen and the reforming zeal of Robert Colquohoun, the ex-army minister who has been gassed in France. His impassioned speech at the memorial stone sounds the socialist note which he will struggle to maintain during his tenancy of the Kirk:

> "Let us believe that the new oppressions and foolish greeds are no more than mists that pass. They died for a world that is past, these men, but they did not die for this that we seem to inherit. Beyond it and us there shines a greater hope and a newer world."[14]

It is the main political purpose of *Cloud Howe*, the second part of the trilogy, to develop this theme. When Chris marries Colquohoun they move from Kinraddie to the town of Segget, whose economy is based on jute mills and large numbers of working-class operatives. This gives Gibbon the opportunity to show the state of hostility which exists between the working class and petty bourgeoisie, polarising around what have become the two principal political parties – Tory and Labour.

Following the rumbling years of the early twenties which are given over to the personal experiences of Chris and her marriage to Colquohoun the point of continuity is taken up over a confrontation at the local war memorial just before the General Strike. After the broken promises of the post-war period the obvious bankruptcy of the 'Homes fit for Heroes' slogan, and the beginning of a slump which was to get far worse, the working

class realise that they have been cheated, and when the Spinners
arrive at the memorial service on armistice day both carrying a
red flag and singing about it, John Cronin, their leader, puts the
case in forthright political terms:

> "WE went to the war, we know what it was, we went to lice and
> dirt and damnation: and what have we got at the end of it all?
> Starvation wages, no homes for heroes, the capitalists fast on our
> necks as before. They're sacking men at the mills just now and
> leaving them on the bureau to starve—that's our reward . . . .
> Come over and join us, the Labour Party. You first, Mr Col-
> quohoun, you were out there, you've sense."[15]

Robert has both sense and sympathy with the Spinners' cause,
but his objective social position as part of the petty bourgeoisie at
first prevents him from coming out in open support. Instead, he
has to endure the complaints and outrage foisted upon him by the
local headmaster, shopkeepers, and landowners' agents. They
bleat out the clichés of conservative fear of 'mob rule', 'anarchy',
and 'violence' from the upstart working class, and to their voice is
added that of the young Laird who has returned from English
university and the Grand Tour filled with his mindless prescrip-
tion for the nation's ills:

> The thing that was needed everywhere was Discipline, hwaw?
> and order, and what not. The hand of the master—all the Jahly
> old things. He had been down in Italy the last few months and
> had seen things there, Rahly amazing, the country awakening,
> regaining its soul, its old leaders back—with a new one or so.
> Discipline, order, hierarchy—all that. And why only Italy; why
> not Scotland? He'd met other men, down from the 'varsity of
> late, who were doing as he did, going back to their estates.
> Scotland a nation—that was the goal, with its old-time civiliza-
> tion and culture, Hwaw?[16]

So fascism gets its representative in the Lowlands, but Chris
rebuffs him with her reminder that the notion of peaceful good
old days is a romantic upper-class myth and she spells out the
realities of torture and bloodshed she knows from her materialist
grasp of history.

All these political forces come into head-on collision during
the General Strike. By this time Colquohoun has joined in active
support of the Labour Party, has been making collections for the
miners, working in conjunction with John Cronin who, it is
important to note, is not a 'Spinner' himself but a railway porter.

The detail is significant because Cronin and Colquohoun, acting
as spearhead for the Labour Party, are instrumental in restraining
the Spinners who during the strike set out to blow up a railway
bridge so as to stop the running of strike-breaking trains. Cronin
and Colquohoun see such positive action as too drastic and
persuade the men to set off their stolen dynamite as a 'test
blasting'.

But when the Trades Union Congress and Labour leaders sell
out and the strike collapses this dewy-eyed act of 'moderation' is
seen for the betrayal of leadership that it is. Colquohoun is
morally and spiritually shattered by the downfall of everything he
believes in and retreats into religious morbidity and visions of
Christ, whilst Cronin turns a political blind eye to the events of
1926 and becomes a full-time Labour Party bureaucrat, touring
the country preaching class alliance and the 'good sense' of a
coalition government whilst his own father is dying of poverty
and starvation. Gibbon is quite unsparing of the Labour Party as
a betrayer of working-class initiative – a feature of the trilogy
which no doubt reflects the left-wing policies of the Communist
Party (under orders from the Comintern) during the years when
the novel was being conceived and written, but also the more
personal leftist militancy of Gibbon, a man who had joined
enthusiastically in the 'Glasgow Soviet' and, as his close friend
Hugh MacDiarmid has claimed, had always been very much to
the left:

> From the political angle, the principal criticism to be levelled
> against him is that which the Communist Party themselves
> levelled when they expelled him as a Trotskyist . . . . Gibbon
> shared this theoretical inadequacy—this anti-intellectualism and
> Left-Wing Infantilism—to the full.[17]

though deciding whether this formulation is either just or accurate
is a problem compounded by the difficulty of assessing Mac-
Diarmid's own political attitudes, which have shifted around
notoriously through the years.

The period which follows the General Strike sees the effect of
1929 and its economic aftermath biting deep into working-class
living standards. Men are thrown out of work onto the dole, mills
are mismanaged into a state of bankruptcy, the small shopkeepers
begin to suffer from lack of trade, and the vicious cruelties of
evictions result in families sleeping in hovels built for animals.

'MacDonald was in with the Tories, and said they were fine',[18] and meanwhile the establishment tries to whitewash its disasters with a blether of triviality:

> the *Mearns Chief* . . . said week by week we were fine, and Scotland still the backbone of Britain, and the Gordon Highlanders right gay childes, not caring a hoot though their pay was down, and Progressives just the scum of the earth that planned to take bairns out of the slums and rear them up in Godless communes . . . . Ay, the *Mearns Chief* was aye up-to-date, and showed you a photo of Mrs MacTavish winning the haggis at a Hogmanay dance.[19]

Superb, crippling irony, which repays Gibbon's courage in narrating long passages through the confused and gullible viewpoint of some 'unknown warrior' of the class war and what David Craig calls the 'collective voice'[20] of an entire people.

It is the degradation of the early Thirties which adds the death stroke to Colquohoun's wounded condition. Awakened from his spiritual escapism and melancholia by the harshness of events, he throws himself anew into aiding the oppressed and sees through the limitations of his former views. But too late: he expires at the pulpit preaching a sermon which summarises post-war history and calls for a new vision:

> "Against ignoble oppressions and a bitter tyranny the common people banded themselves at last . . . . And the leaders of the great Nine Days . . . looked into their hearts and found there fear . . . . There is no hope for the world at all . . . but a stark, sure creed that will cut like a knife, a surgeon's knife through the doubt and the disease—men with unclouded eyes may yet find it."[21]

But where is that new creed to come from? Certainly not from religion; for Colquohoun has suggested that it be abjured: 'forget the dream of the Christ, forget the creeds they forged in His shadow'.[22] The gentry, the aristocrats, and the owners of productions have got their Toryism, plus its Nationalist and Liberal variants, but what is there for the majority of the people, the working class, if not trades unionism and the Labour Party?

Yet there is a further stage to go. Both the political and the artistic continuity of the trilogy are maintained as attention moves on from the small mill town of Segget into the city of Duncairn, with its fisheries, factories, and heavy industry. After Colquohoun's death Chris and her now-teenage son Ewan are forced to move to the fictionalised amalgam of Aberdeen and Glasgow, and Gibbon's focus, pivoting about Chris as an a-political axis, swings onto the development of the young man's consciousness. The process of urbanisation and change in the principal means of production from agriculture to heavy industry thus continue to be reflected in a natural manner as the result of the social experiences of his main characters and are not imported arbitrarily just to support the exposition of Gibbon's own opinions. The extension of the novel's political viewpoint is revealed through the process of Ewan's social life, his response to the experience of historical change, and the stages of his own personal maturity.

With the mills of Segget ruined by bankruptcy, he is forced into the city to find a job, taking with him his literate education, his archaeological interest, and his deep sense of pride and independence. These attributes at first keep him spiritually separate from and bring him into conflict with his workmates. The pride is eventually lowered, however, and he joins in a unity with the working class whose bonds are strengthened as the novel develops. Having inherited his mother's sense of history and added to his own well-developed radicalism, he is thus perfectly placed to join in the political struggles which surround him and are presented in the full state of complexity which existed in the early Thirties. The National government is in its fully Tory swing; the rising Scottish Nationalists are represented by their candidate 'Hugh MacDowall, the chap who wrote in "Synthetic Scots" ': [23] the Communists have their representatives; there are fashionable absurdities like the Douglas Scheme: 'the only Plan to Save Civilization by giving out lots and lots of money to every soul whether he worked for't or not';[24] and the Labour Party is still trying to convince the workers that they must trust its leaders.

Ewan's aloofness to all this network of class forces is shattered when he sees the police beat a young boy unconscious and trample an old man to death under their horses whilst they are breaking up a demonstration against the Means Test. This arouses his anger and his dormant class allegiances, but it also provides him with a political lesson when the local council is forced into raising the assistance rates. He passes beyond the fear of direct action which had inhibited his stepfather Colquohoun.

In this new state of consciousness (which is reinforced by his

relationship with Ellen Johns, the socialist girl from England)
his first activity is to try organising the apprentices amongst
whom he works:

> Ewan and some others were getting up a party for the young in
> Duncairn, neither Labour or Communist, nor yet in opposition,
> but to try and keep the two of them working in harness for the
> general good of the working class, get rid of the cowardice and
> sloth of Labour and cut out the nonsensical lying of the Com-
> munists.[25]

The classic Popular Front strategy – though being posed in 1933
and 1934; yet Ewan is still very sceptical about the Communists:

> their tactic of rioting for rioting's sake was pure insanity, it got
> nowhere, if a revolution were properly organised it should be
> possible for a rising class to take power with little or no violence.[26]

But when he leads the apprentices in a strike against the speed-up
in production times and armament manufacture he is given
another painful lesson concerning action, violence and their use
by the supposedly 'impartial' state forces. He is beaten and tor-
tured by the police and only manages to be dragged from their
hands due to the blackmailing of a corrupt council leader. This
experience gives him the feeling of solidarity with History's down-
trodden:

> lost and be-bloodied in a hundred broken and tortured bodies all
> over the world, in Scotland, in England, in the torture dens of
> the Nazis in Germany, in the torment-pits of the Polish Ukraine,
> a livid, twisted thing in the prisons where they tortured the Nan-
> king Communists, a Negro boy in an Alabama cell while they
> thrust the razors into his flesh, castrating with a lingering cruelty
> and care. He was one with them all, a long wailing of sobbing
> mouths and wrung flesh, tortured and tormented by the world's
> Masters while those Masters lied about Progress through Peace,
> Democracy, Justice, the Heritage of Culture.[27]

And after discussing the lessons of the strike with Jim Trease, a
Communist organiser, he moves further left:

> the Communists were right. Only by force could we beat brute
> force, plans for peaceful reform were about as sane as hunting a
> Bengal tiger with a Bible. They must organise the masses, make
> them think, make them see, let them know there was no way they

could ever win to power except through the fight of class against class, till they dragged down the masters and ground them to pulp.[28]

This decision is backed up by continuing a bitter criticism of the press as a reactionary force – 'the *Daily Runner,* a fine big paper, the pride of Duncairn, and awful useful for lining your shelves'[29] – and of the Labour Party as deceitful class collaborators.

Ewan becomes quite uncompromising, almost ruthless, and what might now be called a doctrinaire communist. When poison gas cylinders explode in the workshops he doesn't hesitate to turn the event to the Party's advantage by spreading the rumour that the gas was deliberately allowed to escape to test its effect on crowds. This is probably the moral and political crux about which the whole of the book's political development hangs. It is the point at which the liberal reader would probably lose sympathy with Ewan. No, creating lies, that's going too far! One can see what he has suffered, but . . . .

Ellen Johns, his lover and political soul-mate, reacts this way: she has joined him in the Communist Party but never really given herself to it in the way which Ewan has. Seeing him reach this degree of commitment, she reverts to her Labour Party past by offering him the soft option, tempting him to sell out:

> "I'm sick of being without decent clothes, without the money I earn myself, pretty things that are mine, that I've worked for" . . . .
> She leaned forward and told him all that she planned: he would get away from ridiculous jobs . . . . They could save up like anything and get married in a year or so, have a dinky little flat somewhere in Craigneuks . . . you couldn't have any fun without money.[30]

Ewan resists this temptation and carries on with his commitment to the working-class movement. Yes, he has spread a lie; but then the landowners, the government, the factory owners, the press, the church, and the police are spreading lies *every day,* and robbing and oppressing the working class at the same time. Ewan has taken up his position against them in a *class war,* and he will use any methods to assist the deprived majority to defeat the privileged minority. He is not acting in self interest (except as he himself is a member of the working class) and as the novel ends he has given up everything to lead the hunger marchers on their 500-mile trek down to London. He sees his political activity as a matter of necessity, and quite happily collects money for the marchers' boots with the police on his tail, under no illusions about the difficulty of the political tasks which face him or the nature of the class whose battles he is leading. As far as he's concerned it's a simple matter. Men and their families are starving to death in the Scottish slums, and nobody is helping them: society must be radically changed to achieve the justice which is missing, and the oppressed class must overthrow their oppressors to do it.

Thus the trilogy ends on a militant note: it makes a concrete and very specific case for the necessity of a revolutionary party and Gibbon offers no comforts as a reward for joining the fight. But the case is made with consummate artistic skill by always having the explicitly political lessons arise out of the normal activity of man within society, which is not to claim that Gibbon wrote a nineteenth-century novel out of which arose twentieth-century conclusions. On the contrary, the novel is probably the best example in the British tradition of committed writing – expressing a militant proletarian point of view without becoming overtly propagandist. In fact Gibbon proves that it is not necessary for the literary traditions of the eighteenth and nineteenth centuries to be abandoned in favour of modernist techniques in order to express a proletarian point of view: on the contrary, he makes a very good case for those who, like Trotsky, Victor Serge, and Georg Lukács, have argued that modern proletarian writing must grow out of the traditions created by the middle class and cannot hope to snatch a tradition of its own out of the air.

Unlike those writers of the left whose sectarian and vulgar Marxist opinions led them to reject bourgeois culture as 're-actionary' and worthless, Gibbon, writing in 1935, showed great respect for its achievements and its still living strength:

> Capitalist literature, whether we like it or not, is not in decay
> . . . . Towards the culmination of a civilization the arts, so far
> from decaying, always reach their greatest efflorescence (the
> veriest tyro student of the economic process knows this). That
> efflorescence is now in being. It is not a decayed and decrepit
> dinosaur who is the opponent of the real revolutionary writer,
> but a very healthy and vigorous dragon indeed.[31]

His own work flows out of the traditions of the eighteenth and nineteenth centuries even whilst going beyond them to establish a significant claim for the creation of a new type of novel which expresses a working-class point of view of the world. As a writer he works from the classically Marxist position of transcending bourgeois culture from a position of strength, having mastered its techniques and put them to full use in the interests of a new objective.

He is not misled by the naive and sectarian delusion that a highly developed and completely separate culture is being held back from self-expression by the economic and cultural oppression of the working class and refuses the temptation to sentimentalise and glorify working people which many other writers of pro-letarian sympathies are still unable to resist.

But unlike those writers who had Utopian views of the work-ing man breaking off his chains and gaining political power in a blaze of glory and *bonhomie,* asserting the inherent superiority of their proletarian culture in the process, yet who express this view in the language and the literary conventions of the middle class, Gibbon has confidence enough in the richness of the *spoken* word as used by that oppressed majority to use it as the base for his *literary* expression. He taps into the rich, complex, and heterogeneous verbal life of everyday intercourse and is not afraid to use it as a base for his literary creativity, without ever plunging into the disasters and excesses of naturalism.

There is thus a logic and coherence between his apprehension of reality, his commitment to revolutionary politics, and his linguistic choices and skill which not only raise him way above all the inter-war generation of British writers but put him on a level with the greatest of his European and American contemporaries. Although he is still relatively neglected, there will undoubtedly come a time when *A Scots Quair* will find its place regularly alongside such works as *U.S.A., The Case of Comrade Tulayev,* and *La Condition Humaine.*

NOTES

1 Kurt Wittig, *The Scottish Tradition in Literature* (Oliver and Boyd, 1958), p. 330.

C

2 *A Scots Quair* (Hutchinson, 1946); second edition, 1967, p. 15. All subsequent page references are to the second edition.
3 *Ibid.* p. 101.
4 *Ibid.* p. 406.
5 *Ibid.* p. 97.
6 *Ibid.* p. 97.
7 *Ibid.* p. 174.
8 *Ibid.* p. 149.
9 *Ibid.* p. 481.
10 *Ibid.* p. 67.
11 *Ibid.* p. 144.
12 *Ibid.* p. 148.
13 *Ibid.* p. 157.
14 *Ibid.* p. 193.
15 *Ibid.* p. 268.
16 *Ibid.* p. 275.
17 Hugh MacDiarmid, 'Lewis Grassic Gibbon', 1946, reprinted in *The Uncanny Scot* (MacGibbon and Kee, 1968), p. 160.
18 *A Scots Quair*, p. 339.
19 *Ibid.* p. 341.
20 David Craig, 'Novels of Peasant Crisis', *Peasant Studies*, Vol. 2, No. 1, October 1974.
21 *A Scots Quair*, p. 349.
22 *Ibid.* p. 349.
23 *Ibid.* p. 378.
24 *Ibid.* p. 392.
25 *Ibid.* p. 413.
26 *Ibid.* p. 439.
27 *Ibid.* p. 451.
28 *Ibid.* p. 457.
29 *Ibid.* p. 365.
30 *Ibid.* p. 490.
31 *Left Review*, February 1935, p. 179.

'Letters from Iceland': Going North

Tom Paulin

For anyone born after the Second World War the 1930s can seem to take shape as just another literary period, the object of scholarly interest, packaged and safe. If this happens, then the poetry, with its deliberate relevance to politics and society, must cease to affect us in some of the ways which it, often provocatively, aims to.

What I want to argue is that *Letters from Iceland* offers a response to history, politics and society which is not only still valid, but which has still to be followed. For me, the response, in the 1970s, is less to the European situation Auden and MacNiece were writing about, and more to society in Britain, to landscape, and to Ireland. It involves an effort to apply what MacNeice meant by 'The obscure but powerful ethics of Going North', and to understand what Auden meant by telling Byron that

> Parnassus after all is not a mountain,
> Reserved for A.1 climbers such as you;
> It's got a park, it's got a public fountain.

For Auden, Byron was 'the right person I think, because he was a townee, a European, and disliked Wordsworth and that kind of approach to nature, and I find that very sympathetic'. The dislike is sympathetic because, as Auden says elsewhere in *Letters*, 'Landscape's so dull' – the admiration of landscape as significantly beautiful in itself is both boring and anti-social. And an ostensibly apolitical admiration is itself a political act because its rejection of civic life is dangerous and irresponsible. There is a clear continuity between the post-war statement in 'Mountains':

> And it is curious how often in steep places
> You meet someone short who frowns,
> A type you catch beheading daisies with a stick:
> Small crooks flourish in big towns,
> But perfect monsters—remember Dracula—
> Are bred on crags in castles . . . .

and Auden's mockery in *Letters*:

> The mountain-snob is a Wordsworthian fruit;
> He tears his clothes and doesn't shave his chin,
> He wears a very pretty little boot,
> He chooses the least comfortable inn;
> A mountain railway is a deadly sin;
> His strength, of course, is as the strength of ten men,
> He calls all those who live in cities wen-men.

And yet for all Auden's reiterations of the obvious fact that nature is stupid (for example, in 'Their Lonely Betters'), pastoral poetry is not only still being written but acclaimed.

It is Auden's and MacNeice's deliberate intention to present their voyage to Iceland as being apparently escapist, like pastoral poetry – 'And North means to all: "Reject!" '; 'For Europe is absent. This is an island and therefore/Unreal.' But, just as with Marvell, this offered rejection conceals a serious political intention. As MacNeice says: 'We are not changing ground to escape from facts/But rather to find them.' And what they found was, for example, Goering's brother taking breakfast at Holar, parties of Nazis visiting Iceland because they had a theory that 'Iceland is the cradle of the Germanic culture.' More than this they confronted the possibly antisocial forces within their own culture and their own imaginations – a fact which Auden states directly when he says that his name 'occurs in several of the sagas':

> In fact I am the great big white barbarian,
> The Nordic type, the too too truly Aryan.

MacNeice dramatises this in 'Eclogue from Iceland' where, as Craven and Ryan, he and Auden confront the ghost of Grettir who is the enemy of society, an outlaw, a gangster, an Aryan Romantic hero. Through Grettir, MacNeice warns us that

> Men have been chilled to death who kissed
> Wives of mist, forgetting their own
> Kind who live out of the wind.

The formulation is carefully Yeatsian: men's hearts have become hardened by their dedication to extreme political fantasies – in Germany by following Hitler, in Ireland by worshipping political martyrs, and in Europe generally by electing heroes of the imagination who, once elected, have become dictators. Byron, like Wordsworth, is one of those dictators, because Auden's attitude to his Romanticism is essentially the same as Bertrand Russell's. For Russell, the influence of Byron and Napoleon (whom Byron admired and compared himself with) exercised a profound and terrible influence on the nineteenth-century imagination. Their cult of the aristocratic hero and satanic rebel and leader resulted, for Russell, in twentieth-century Fascism. The Romantic rebellion, which is the revolt of 'unsocial instincts' against 'social bonds' (an aristocratic philosophy of rebellion), inspired Hitler's 1933 coup.

So when Byron describes landscape, what we must consider is its effect upon us:

> The roar of waters!—from the headlong height
> Velino cleaves the wave-worn precipice;
> The fall of waters! rapid as the light
> The flashing mass foams shaking the abyss;
> The hell of waters! where they howl and hiss,
> And boil in endless torture.

In many ways this, like much of Byron's poetry, has the effect of a rousing speech delivered by a politician to a massed audience. The excited descriptions of thunderstorms, rushing rivers and wild seas in *Childe Harold* all appeal to our sensations, to our wish to be carried along and away in an excited experience of total liberation. Byron's praise of freedom becomes an imaginative tyranny:

> Yet, Freedom! yet thy banner, torn but flying,
> Streams like the thunder-storm *against* the wind;
> Thy trumpet voice, though broken now and dying,
> The loudest still the tempest leaves behind.

This is great rhetoric, but its appeal, like that of one of Byron's favourite cadences, 'the young, the beautiful, the brave', is to all that is simple, heroic and inhuman. We are being asked to worship a hero of the imagination, someone greater than ourselves who has thought and suffered deeply and in doing so has learnt terrible truths.

This, it seems to me, is a distinctively protestant idea. It's clearly present in *Childe Harold* when Byron, praising solitude, says 'alone—man with his God must strive'. Protestantism's ingrained individualism, particularly in its Calvinistic form, is one important influence on the pseudo-Romanticism of *Childe Harold*. It emerges again in our culture in Carlyle's hero-worship, a late form of Calvinistic Romanticism, and it attempted to dominate English culture in the 1920s and 1930s in the person of Lord Reith (Churchill's scornful dismissal of him as 'old Wuthering Heights' was exactly right). Here, one would be tempted to argue that landscape is responsible for authoritarianism – the barren mountains of Scotland and Ireland produce an extreme politics and religion. But by this argument Switzerland, where Calvin was born and Rousseau lived – it is the setting for *Manfred*, James's 'The Private Life' and Auden's *Elegy for Young Lovers* – ought not to be the safe democracy it so unassumingly is. And yet mountains do embody an imaginative authoritarianism which it is Auden's effort throughout his career to resist. A few years after writing *Letters from Iceland* he was teaching a university course called 'Romanticism from Rousseau to Hitler', and it is important to notice how necessary he felt it was, in 1936, to answer the kind of criticism of Byron which Russell was later to make in *The History of Western Philosophy*:

> Suggestions have been made that the Teutonic
>   Führer-Prinzip would have appealed to you
> As being the true heir to the Byronic—
>   In keeping with your social status too
>   (It has its English converts, fit and few),
> That you would, hearing honest Oswald's call,
> Be gleichgeschaltet in the Albert Hall.

> 'Lord Byron at the head of his storm-troopers!'
>   Nothing, says science, is impossible:
> The Pope may quit to join the Oxford Groupers,
>   Nuffield may leave one farthing in his Will,
>   There may be someone who trusts Baldwin still,
> Someone may think that Empire wines are nice,
> There may be people who hear Tauber twice.

> You liked to be the centre of attraction,
>   The gay Prince Charming of the fairy story,
> Who tamed the Dragon by his intervention.
>   In modern warfare though it's just as gory,
>   There isn't any individual glory;
> The Prince must be anonymous, observant,
> A kind of lab-boy, or a civil servant.

> You never were an Isolationist;
>   Injustice you had always hatred for,
> And we can hardly blame you, if you missed
>   Injustice just outside your lordship's door:
>   Nearer than Greece were cotton and the poor.
> To-day you might have seen them, might indeed
> Have walked in the United Front with Gide.

The acquittal doesn't ring quite true – one feels that Auden half-believes that Byron might have been a blackshirt, and that the line: 'Nothing, says science, is impossible', evades, in its witty development, the real issue.

If Byron is often imaginatively authoritarian, so is Wordsworth. For example, in the famous boating episode in the *Prelude* the 'huge peak, black and huge,' becomes like the ghost of Hamlet's father – that 'guilty thing' which advances with a 'martial stalk' and pours poison in his son's ear. It is this implantation of guilt which is the basis of Wordsworth's mystical experience:

> I struck and struck again,
> And growing still in stature the grim shape
> Towered up between me and the stars, and still,
> For so it seemed, with purpose of its own
> And measured motion like a living thing,
> Strode after me.

Auden's resistance to this is cultural rather than personal: Parnassus must be colonised and tamed by deliberately changing it from a grim empty peak above a lake to a public park with fountains, cafés and ice-cream vans. The dominating mountain must be dominated and made social, humanist and democratic. If this has largely been accomplished in England, in Ireland it is only beginning. So, when MacNeice describes the Icelandic landscape he is implicitly writing about Irish politics and landscape:

> Houses are few
>   But decorous
> In a ruined land
>   Of sphagnum moss;
>
> Corrugated iron
>   Farms inherit
> The spirit and phrase
>   Of ancient sagas

> Men have forgotten
>   Anger and ambush,
> To make ends meet
>   Their only business.

Gaunt mountains, the stock properties of Romanticism and of the Irish tourist trade, must now be industrialised:

> But the people themselves
>   Who live here
> Ignore the brooding
>   Fear, the sphinx;
> And the radio
>   With tags of tune
> Defies their pillared
>   Basalt crags.

That word 'basalt' was, for MacNeice, inescapably associated with Ireland. It is a stone which dominates Co. Antrim where he grew up, and he identifies it with the protestant character in an early poem, 'Belfast':

> The hard cold fire of the northerner
> Frozen into his blood from the fire in his basalt
> Glares from behind the mica of his eyes
> And the salt carrion water brings him wealth.

Here, the volcanic political landscape has not been defied: it has hardened the character of its inhabitants, incarnating in each of them the Old Testament God of Justice.

Here and in *Autumn Journal* ('Free speech nipped in the bud,/ The minority always guilty') MacNeice exactly defines the North of Ireland, but there are moments when he adopts a Yeatsian scorn of industrialism and fails to apply the discoveries and lessons of *Letters*:

> Ourselves alone! Let the round tower stand aloof
>   In a world of bursting mortar!
> Let the school-children fumble their sums
>   In a half-dead language;
> Let the censor be busy on the books; pull down the
>   Georgian slums;
>   Let the games be played in Gaelic.
> Let them grow beet-sugar; let them build
>   A factory in every hamlet;
> Let them pigeon-hole the souls of the killed
>   Into sheep and goats, patriots and traitors.

If this is in many ways a fair attack on the Republic of Ireland, it blurs certain issues: would he prefer people to live in Georgian slums rather than new council estates? Also, the attack on De Valera's introduction of sugar beet and industrialisation is reactionary because it views Ireland from the point of view of an aesthetic tourist. Anyone who has observed the difference which a factory, or a local co-operative movement, can make to some of the more impoverished rural areas of Ireland must have no doubt that the more mess there is for conservationists to deplore the more prosperous the actual inhabitants are.

It is in this context, and in that of Auden's considered dislike of mountains, that one of the finest photographs in *Letters* becomes an important political and cultural statement: it shows a petrol pump in the foreground, a pair of corrugated iron houses, a group of human figures, some washing on a line, and then, tucked away at the edge of the photograph and only faintly visible, two mountain peaks which appear tiny in comparison with the petrol pump and houses. It expresses, with grey subtlety, all that Auden means by this attack on landscape poetry:

> For now we've learnt we mustn't be so bumptious
>   We find the stars are one big family,
> And send out invitations for a scrumptious
>   Simple, old-fashioned, jolly romp with tea
>   To any natural objects we can see.
> We can't, of course, invite a Jew or Red
> But birds and nebulae will do instead.
>
> The Higher Mind's outgrowing the Barbarian,
>   It's hardly thought hygienic now to kiss;
> The world is surely turning vegetarian;
>   And as it grows too sensitive for this.
>   It won't be long before we find there is
> A Society of Everybody's Aunts
> For the Prevention of Cruelty to Plants.
>
> I dread this like the dentist, rather more so:
>   To me Art's subject is the human clay,
> And landscape but a background to a torso;
>   All Cezanne's apples I would give away
>   For one small Goya or a Daumier.
> I'll never grant a more than minor beauty
> To pudge or pilewort, petty-chap or pooty.

c*

The poetry of natural objects is sterile and politically suspect: there are certain people who aren't invited to read it. Here, a description Auden includes of a volcanic eruption which took place in 1727, ceases to be a merely interesting piece of historical detail and assumes a contemporary relevance: the mountain erupts and lava and boiling water hurtle down towards the church and village. The inhabitants, who were in church when the mountain began to burn, flee with great difficulty to safety, but their crops, livestock and many of their houses are destroyed. This is an image of a community threatened by war (reports of the Spanish Civil War began to reach Auden when he was in Iceland) and it is also an image which attributes the destruction of a culture and a community to a mountainous Romantic landscape. The volcano was a favourite symbol for Byron and Shelley of both personal and revolutionary energies (a 'worn-out figure' Byron calls it in *Don Juan*), and for Auden it represents all those anti-social tendencies in Romanticism which then threatened European culture. The Icelandic landscape becomes clearly symbolic:

> Until indeed the Markafljöt I see
> Wasting these fields, is no glacial flood
> But history, hostile, Time the destroyer
> Everywhere washing our will, winding through Europe
> An attack, a division, shifting its fords.

Here, the 'glacial flood' becomes history, armies moving along the autobahns, crossing frontiers and destroying cities.

Though Auden, throughout his career, placed the highest possible valuation upon civic life, his attitude towards the city in *Letters* is sometimes Romantic, anti-Hobbesian and optimistic – that is, revolutionary. He describes modern man as outwardly conformist, but inwardly revolutionary like the clerk in Davidson's 'Thirty Bob a Week':

> Turn to the work of Disney or of Strube;
>   There stands our hero in his threadbare seams;
> The bowler hat who straphangs in the tube,
>   And kicks the tyrant only in his dreams,
>   Trading on pathos, dreading all extremes;
> The little Mickey with the hidden grudge;
> Which is the better, I leave you to judge.

Man, in contemporary society, is dominated by the 'Ogre', a

variation on Shelley's 'One shape of many names' – that is, the
reification of an idea of power and authority that most men are
too timid, too conformist, to challenge. In not challenging it they
are potential followers of, say, Mosley's blackshirts who will
replace one Ogre by another. If they were to challenge it then
they might, as Byron possibly would, 'have walked in the United
Front with Gide'. The formulation is too simple, as Auden
recognises and evades:

> I know, too, I'm inviting the renowned
> Retort of all who love the Status Quo:
> 'You can't change human nature, don't you know!'

Between the smugness of the right and that of the left there is
little difference. It's no wonder, therefore, that in his post-war
work Auden becomes Hobbesian in his political thinking. Re-
luctantly Hobbesian it's true (unlike Dryden), but nevertheless
firmly on the side of law and order. We have to take seriously the
post-war challenge of:

> Guard, Civility, with guns
> Your modes and your declensions:
> Any lout can spear with ease
> Singular Archimedes.

For anyone who sees a culture and a community, however
imperfect, threatened by violent louts, Auden's poetry, with the
valuation it places on civic life, sounds crucially right.

In *Letters*, however, he appears to dismiss Hobbes as the
consoling policeman of the failed and disenchanted:

> Banker or landlord, booking-clerk or Pope,
>   Whenever he's lost faith in choice and thought,
> When a man sees the future without hope,
>   Whenever he endorses Hobbes' report
>   'The life of man is nasty, brutish, short,'
> The dragon rises from his garden border
> And promises to set up law and order.

Though Auden, to my mind, always believed in law and order,
one of the interesting features of his attitude to it is his sense of
the forces which a stable polity cannot accommodate. This is not
to say that he indulges any view of man as being, once or
potentially, a noble savage: Byron sometimes does this in
Don Juan where he discovers this archetypal figure in Daniel

Boone and then immediately and confusingly socialises him by comparing him to 'the Man of Ross run wild'. Rather, Auden is aware of certain dionysiac forces which can become dangerous if the city takes no account of them. (For Auden, one of the central myths of our culture is the *Bacchae* for which he wrote a libretto, *The Bassarids*.) Here, an unpublished pre-war poem, ' "Sweet is it", say the doomed,' demonstrates this:

> For first the civil space by human love
> Upon the unimaginative field imposed
> Destroyed that tie with the nearest which in nature rules,
>
> Built in its stead a world of comfortable answers
> With some asylum safe for every sufferer,
> In which a host of workers, famous and obscure,
>
> Charitable men, kind fathers, pillars of the churches,
> Meaning to do no more than use their eyes,
> Each from his private angle, then sapped belief.
>
> At dusk across our windows fell no longer
> The shadow of the giant's enormous calves,
> The kobbold's knocking in the mountains petered out;
>
> The dateless succession of midsummer dances broken,
> The mounds of green turf were unfairied; in marsh after marsh
> The sterile dragon died a natural death.[1]

Auden values the 'civil space' highly and therefore he has no wish to be overshadowed by the sterile mysticism of a giant mountain, but he's also showing that conformity and stability, however necessary, involve a loss. It's this feeling which is explored in the post-war sequence, *Horae Canonicae*, where the cruel justice of the crucifying city is set against a 'squalid existence' in a Hobbesian state of nature; and it's there again in the conclusion to Auden's essay on Mayhew:

> Even when I was a child, the streets were still full of vendors, musicians, Punch-and-Judy men, and such. Today they have vanished. In all modern societies, the public authorities, however at odds politically, are at one in their fear and hatred of private enterprise in the strict sense; that is to say, self-employment. The fiscal authorities hate the self-employed man because he keeps no books to audit, the health authorities hate him because it is easy for him to avoid their inspectors, etc. Aside from crime and

prostitution, the only contemporary alternative for the poor is either to be the employee of a firm, a factory, or the municipality, or to be on relief. Perhaps this is inevitable, perhaps it is better, but I have yet to be convinced that it is.

Though Auden is lamenting one of the disadvantages of sophisticated social organisation, he is in no sense attacking or dismissing the state as Yeats did. There is a peculiar vigilance in Auden's treatment of other writers which seeks out and recommends stability and *civilitas*. So, reviewing Eliot's selection of Kipling's verse in 1943, he calls Kipling 'the poet of encirclement', and one feels the pressure of self-identification in everything he says: 'Poem after poem, under different symbolic disguises, presents this same situation of danger without, the anxiety of encirclement – by inanimate forces, the Picts beyond the Roman Wall.' What makes Kipling so extraordinary, he suggests, is that 'while virtually every other European writer since the fall of the Roman Empire has felt that the dangers threatening civilisation came from *inside* that civilisation (or from inside the individual consciousness), Kipling is obsessed by a sense of dangers threatening from *outside*'. Auden, in his criticism of Romanticism, is discovering the dangers within civilisation and the individual consciousness, and when he quotes this couplet of Kipling's as an example of external danger: 'Once and again as the Ice came South/The glaciers ground over Lossiemouth', there is a clear parallel with the glaciers in Iceland which symbolise both inner spiritual dangers and the moving armies which make up history. There is no sufficient explanation, Auden says, for the 'terror of demons, visible and invisible, which gives his work its peculiar excitement, any more than the English Civil War expresses Hobbes's terror of political disorder'. No one can particularly like Hobbes, but his political philosophy, as Auden shows, is the only weapon a society has against those forces which threaten it. The post-war bucolic, 'Islands', states this:

> Once, where detected worldings now
> Do penitential jobs,
> Exterminated species played
> Who had not read their Hobbes.

And in the next stanza he describes that Romantic cult-figure, Napoleon, exiled on St Helena where he has 'five years more/To talk about himself'. Auden is only interested in the political issues which islands raise, and I suspect that if he ever went for a walk in the country and saw, say, a beech tree, he paid much less attention to the tree itself than he did to the squirearchical culture it embodies.

This extraordinary sensitivity to politics means that while Auden and MacNeice may at times present their voyage to Iceland as being possibly escapist and solipsistic they are actually raising that criticism in order to insist on their political subject. They are not writing a travel book – they are writing about European culture by focusing on a democratic community which works under the physical shadow of its landscape and the spiritual shadow of its heroic past. Deliberately, then, both poets refuse to describe landscape in isolation from its inhabitants or some of its sinister tourists. Their book is packed with statistics, jokes and photographs which ignore the landscape – photographs of herring factories, a new concrete school, corrugated-iron farms, sports galas – anything but a barren mountain. Because, Auden says, 'it is the strictly relevant I sing', he has constantly and wittily to defeat our conventional expectations of picturesque descriptions, praise of solitude, etc. He recalls us to the English landscape, to the condition of England:

> There on the old historic battlefield,
> The cold ferocity of human wills,
> The scars of struggle as yet unhealed;
> Slattern the tenements on sombre hills,
> And gaunt in valleys the square-windowed mills
> That, since the Georgian house, in my conjecture
> Remain our finest native architecture.

This is the real North of *The Road to Wigan Pier* and *The Condition of the Working Class in England*.

What Auden and MacNeice are so importantly saying is that the artist has social responsibilities. He must do everything in his power to avoid 'kissing wives of mist' because, if he doesn't, he will become a Grettir, an enemy of society, a terrorist. The artist 'must differ from the crowd'

> And, like a secret agent, must keep hidden
> His passion for his shop. However proud,
> And rightly, of his trade, he's not allowed
> To etch his face with his professional creases,
> Or die from occupational diseases.

Auden's analysis of the development of European culture from the civility of Augustanism to the irresponsibility of the Romantic artist elaborates this:

> Those most affected were the very best:
> Those with originality of vision,
> Those whose technique was better than the rest,
> Jumped at the chance of a secure position
> With freedom from the bad old hack tradition,
> Leave to be sole judges of the artist's brandy,
> Be Shelley, or Childe Harold, or the Dandy.
>
> So started what I'll call the Poet's Party:
> (Most of the guests were painters, never mind) –
> The first few hours the atmosphere was hearty,
> With fireworks, fun, and games of every kind;
> All were enjoying it, no one was blind;
> Brilliant the speeches improvised, the dances,
> And brilliant, too, the technical advances.
>
> How nice at first to watch the passers-by
> Out of the upper window, and to say
> 'How glad I am that though I have to die
> Like all those cattle, I'm less base than they!'
> How we all roared when Baudelaire went fey,
> 'See this cigar,' he said, 'it's Baudelaire's.
> What happens to perception? Ah, who cares?'
>
> To-day, alas, that happy crowded floor
> Looks very different: many are in tears:
> Some have retired to bed and locked the door;
> And some swing madly from the chandeliers;
> Some have passed out entirely in the rears;
> Some have been sick in corners, the sobering few
> Are trying hard to think of something new.

What Auden objected to, as he says in 'The Greeks and Us', was how

> In the nineteenth century and in our own the individual artistic genius has sometimes claimed a supreme importance and even persuaded a minority of aesthetes to agree with him; but only in Athens was this a universal social fact, so that the genius was not a lonely figure claiming exceptional rights for himself but the acclaimed spiritual leader of society.

The artist, therefore, has a duty to be responsible both in the content of his work and in his relation to society where he is a private citizen.

The social responsibility of the artist is a virtually obsessive theme in Auden's criticism: he praises, unexpectedly, Poe and Van Gogh for it, also Goethe, and he can conclude an essay on Wagner, whom he calls 'the greatest of the monsters', with the statement that Wagner was 'unknowingly, on the side of Reason, Order and Civilization'. Mittenhofer, the 'great Poet' in Auden's libretto, *Elegy for Young Lovers,* is a mythical figure based on 'the myth of the Artistic Genius' created by the European Romantics. It was Auden's effort throughout his career to attempt to exorcise this myth. Both he and MacNeice are aware of the attractiveness which the myth has for them, and this comes through in their dialogue with Grettir:

> Grettir: Brought up to the rough-house we took offence quickly
> Were sticklers for pride, paid for it as outlaws—
>
> Craven: Like Cavalcanti whose hot blood lost him Florence.
>
> Ryan: Or the Wild Geese of Ireland in Mid-Europe.
> Let us thank God for valour in abstraction
> For those who go their own way, will not kiss
> The arse of law and order nor compound
> For physical comfort at the price of pride:
> Soldiers of fortune, renegade artists, rebels and sharpers
> Whose speech not cramped to Yea and Nay explodes
> In crimson oaths like peonies, who brag
> Because they prefer to taunt the mask of God,
> Bid him unmask and die in the living lightning.
> What is that voice maundering, meandering?

The irony is only partial, for though the 'Voice from Europe' dismisses this 'renegade' pose as 'Blues . . . blues', there is more commitment to it than criticism of it. But the Eclogue ends with Grettir telling them to return to England and be responsible:

> Minute your gesture but it must be made –
> Your hazard, your act of defiance and hymn of hate,
> Hatred of hatred, assertion of human values,
> Which is now your only duty.

This is the situation of 'The Sunlight on the Garden': the sirens calling to duty; grace and freedom being abandoned for responsibility:

Holidays should be like this,
Free from over-emphasis,
Time for soul to stretch and spit
Before the world comes back on it,

Before the chimneys row on row
Sneer in smoke, 'We told you so'
And the fog-bound sirens call
Ruin to the long sea-wall.

And the book ends with a sombre commitment to the
European situation:

Our prerogatives as men
Will be cancelled who knows when;
Still I drink your health before
The gun-butt raps upon the door.

This commitment is felt throughout *Letters* because in
choosing to organise it as a series of letters to friends and relatives
in England Auden and MacNeice selected a pre-eminently *social*
form. They approached their apparently Romantic terrain with
essentially Augustan equipment, without the egotistic cadences of
Wordsworth or the self-indulgent rhetoric of *Childe Harold*. In
writing his *Letter to Lord Byron* (obviously the outstanding
feature of the book) Auden hit upon exactly the right literary
form and personality: he was able to simultaneously evoke the
Napoleonic and the Augustan Byron. It was as deliberate an act
of civilisation as the building of a community in a wasteland. One
feels this in that very fine early poem, 'Missing', which anticipates
Auden's rejection of a fascist Romantic heroism in *Letters*:

From scars where kestrels hover,
The leader looking over
Into the happy valley,
Orchard and curving river,
May turn away to see
The slow fastidious line
That disciplines the fell,
Hear curlew's creaking call
From angles unforeseen,
The drumming of a snipe
Surprise where driven sleet
Had scalded to the bone
And streams are acrid yet
To an unaccustomed lip;

The tall unwounded leader
Of doomed companions, all
Whose voices in the rock
Are now perpetual,
Fighters for no one's sake,
Who died beyond the border.

Heroes are buried who
Did not believe in death,
And bravery is now,
Not in the dying breath
But resisting the temptations
To skyline operations.
Yet glory is not new;
The summer visitors
Still come from far and wide
Choosing their spots to view
The prize competitors,
Each thinking that he will
Find heroes in the wood,
Far from the capital,
Where lights and wine are set
For supper by the lake,
But leaders must migrate:
'Leave for Cape Wrath to-night',
And the host after waiting
Must quench the lamps and pass
Alive into the house.

That word 'disciplines' shows how this Romantic landscape is political – it appeals to a militaristic heroism, it is made for the lonely genius who leads others to destruction. Notice, too, how the couplet – 'But resisting the temptations/To skyline operations' – introduces into the bleak wasteland scenery those feminine comic rhymes so characteristic of both *Don Juan* ('romantic/frantic' for example) and Auden's letter to Byron. This witty criticism of heroism prepares us for the vision of a civilised life which, importantly, is only possible near the capital city and far from Cape Wrath – the setting for heroism, anger and extreme politics. It anticipates the Horatianism of *About the House* and *City Without Walls*.[2]

*   *   *

The question for us now is where Auden's and MacNeice's initiative leads. For me, the total effect of their work, and especially of *Letters from Iceland*, is to make it impossible to read a volume of nature or rural poetry (especially by any poet writing after the Second World War) without being affected by a peculiar feeling of emptiness. Without human or political content nature means very little, and to describe it in isolation from that content is to abdicate the responsibility to be relevant which Auden and MacNeice impose on themselves and us – indeed it is to recommend, however unconsciously, such an abdication. The country is an annex of the city, not an alternative to it. There is much recent English poetry which ignores this, but it is even truer of Irish poetry, for pastoralism is the enemy of Irish poetry, just as autobiography and puns are the enemies of Irish prose. 'Landscape', by Kevin Faller, shows this:

> Where painted women
> in the neons pass
> hid by a smile
> I lift my glass
>
> to that grey lady,
> the western sky,
> embracing Corrib
> with a sigh –
>
> trailing her veils
> in the mourning gleam
> where castle and church
> entomb a dream.

Why should the pathetic fallacies of a rain-soaked landscape be more a subject than women in lounge bars? Religion and political mysticism (Ireland symbolised as Cathleen ni Houlihan) are the probable reasons, for behind these slight quatrains there lies a complex tradition of sexual repression and Gaelic nationalism. It's a very minor example of the way in which a man may kiss a wife of mist, but the rejection of the real world which it makes is still very much a part of Irish culture – as, for example, in the introduction to a recent collection of essays called *The Irish World* which speaks admiringly of 'the streak of violence which flashes like quicksilver across the placid island'. Again, a minor example, but the point importantly is that the effect of an aesthetic of landscape is to make violence and dubious political ideas acceptable. Insidiously they become part of a culture and so condition people's responses to art and politics.

These are just two instances of the contemporary relevance of Auden's and MacNeice's achievement. Another is the questions raised by Auden's admiration for the novelist which he states near the beginning of *Letters* when he says that novel writing is a 'higher art than poetry altogether'. And he returns to this subject three years later when he identifies the poet with heroism and military uniforms:

> Encased in talent like a uniform,
> The rank of every poet is well known;
> They can amaze us like a thunderstorm,
> Or die so young, or live for years alone.
>
> They can dash forward like hussars: but he
> Must struggle out of his boyish gift and learn
> How to be plain and awkward, how to be
> One after whom none think it worth to turn.

And although Auden never put his sympathies with the novelist into practice, either by writing novels or narrative poetry (his early ballads are only a partial exception), he does offer another initiative here. Perhaps the humanism he advocates is too consciously a creed, but it does open up an imaginative possibility which can be treated either in poetry or prose.

So, finally, we discover in *Letters from Iceland* something which looks very like a poetic. If there's nothing particularly new about it that is because it's an initiative that is obvious but which hasn't been sufficiently explored. Both Auden and MacNeice suggest that poetry should be responsible, relevant and, at times, narrative – it should not be about the unimaginative fields.

NOTES

1 It is included in *The English Auden* (Faber, 1977).
2 In revising this essay I've begun to realise that 'Romantic heroism' is one of its more inadequate simplifications. A better term for what Auden is rejecting would be 'authenticity'. Lionel Trilling's *Sincerity and Authenticity* and Richard Sennett's *The Fall of Public Man* (a sociological application of Trilling's argument) are two devastating critiques of that ethic of authenticity which pervades European

culture. It sets intimate personal feeling above impersonal social relations and codes of behaviour, and its intense narcissism – to give one example – finds an extreme contemporary expression in Ingmar Bergmann's dreary accounts of desperate affairs on isolated Nordic islands. In 'Missing' Auden is rejecting or at least qualifying that northern territory of puritan authenticity, and as in his late 'Ode to Terminus' he is celebrating a social god 'of walls, doors and reticence'. He is firmly in favour of those civil barriers which control chaotic, anti-social, personal feelings. His point of view is, and always was, essentially conservative and pessimistic (and also very deliberately English) – he adheres to a neo-classical ideal of propriety, tact and civility, and it is this ideal which is brilliantly and persuasively advocated by Trilling and Sennett.

Christopher Caudwell's Illusions

Michael Draper

Christopher St John Sprigg – who took the pen name Christopher Caudwell for his serious writing – was born in Putney, London, on 20 October 1907, heir to a family tradition of versatile journalism. After a childhood spent in the Berkshire Downs, he attended a Roman Catholic school in Ealing, where he is said to have bemused his contemporaries by his ability to argue in support of any belief. He left school before he was fifteen and became a cub reporter and novel reviewer on the *Yorkshire Observer*, for which his father was at that time literary editor, then moved to London in 1925 to become editor of the trade journal *British Malaya.* The following year he and his elder brother founded a firm of aeronautical publishers, for which he edited a technical periodical.

Over the next ten years, while continuing his journalism, he acted as a press agent, invented an infinitely variable gear (the designs for which were published in the *Automobile Engineer*), read widely in the London Library and published several books. Five of these were popular aviation works: *The Airship* (1931), *Fly with Me* (in collaboration with Henry D. Davis, 1932), *British Airways* (1934), *Great Flights* (1935) and *Let's Learn to Fly* (1937). Seven were detective novels: *Crime in Kensington* (1933), *Fatality in Fleet Street* (1933), *The Perfect Alibi* (1934), *Death of an Airman* (1934), *Death of a Queen* (1935), *The Corpse with the Sunburnt Face* (1935) and *The Six Queer Things* (1937). He also edited and introduced a volume of *Uncanny Stories* (1936).

At the same time he was writing poetry – which he liked to consider his true vocation, although only one piece was published during his lifetime (in *The Dial* for March 1927) – stories, plays and even aphorisms. He was, it scarcely requires saying, a fluent and prolific writer, turning out thrillers at his brother's home, where he was resident, unperturbed by background noise. In 1936 appeared his one serious novel, *This My Hand*, which was

the first of his works to be published under the pen name of
Caudwell, his mother's maiden name.

The history of the period between the two great wars is too
well known to require re-telling here. But the following quotation
is a sharp reminder of its contemporary impact:

> the War at last survived, there come new horrors. The eating
> disintegration of the slump. Nazism outpouring a flood of bar-
> barism and horror. And what next? Armaments piling up like an
> accumulating catastrophe, mass neurosis, nations like mad dogs
> . . . . Against the sky stands Capitalism without a rag to cover it,
> naked in its terror. And humanism, leaving it, or rather, forcibly
> thrust aside, must either pass into the ranks of the proletariat or,
> going quietly into a corner, cut its throat.[1]

Such was Caudwell's reckoning of the situation. Amid the suffering and demoralisation, Russian-style Communism seemed to
many the great red hope. The Stalin purges, the Russo-German
pact and the betrayals in Spain were all shocks still to come,
Khrushchev's denunciation of Stalin and the suppression of the
Hungarian revolt twenty years in the future. 'We both need a
religion, but what religions are there to have nowadays? Communism remains, I suppose . . . .' So the ex-Catholic Caudwell
noted in an unpublished autobiographical story.[2]

He'd begun to read the principle Marxist texts at the end of
1934. In the summer he moved to Porthleven, Cornwall, where
he began work on *Illusion and Reality, A Study of the Sources
of Poetry*. Back in London, he moved in November to lodgings
in working-class Poplar and shortly afterwards joined the local
branch of the Communist Party.

To his friends Paul and Betty Beard he wrote:

> Seriously, I think my weakness has been the lack of an integrated
> Weltanschauung. I mean one that includes my emotional, scien-
> tific, and artistic needs. They have been more than usually dis-
> integrated in me, I think, a characteristic of my generation
> exacerbated by the fact that, as you know, I have strong rational-
> ising as well as artistic tendencies. As long as there was a
> disintegration I had necessarily an unsafe provisional attitude to
> reality, a somewhat academic superficial attitude, which showed
> in my writing as what Betty described as the "lack of baking".
> The remedy is nothing so simple as a working-over and polish-
> ing-up of prose, but to come to terms with myself and my
> environment. This I think during the last year or two I have

begun to do. Naturally it is a long process (the getting of wisdom) and I don't fancy I am anywhere near the end. But 'I. and R.' represented a milestone on the way, and that, I think, was why it seemed sincere, free from my other faults, and, with its necessary limitations, successful.[3]

Through the next year he pressed on, both with his theoretical writings and with his, now freelance, commercial output, breaking off at 5 p.m. each day to take up the burden of party activities: fly-posting, slogan-chalking, speaking at street corners or selling the *Daily Worker*. He visited Paris to study the Popular Front and started to teach himself Russian. With the outbreak of the Spanish Civil War, the Poplar branch of the Communist Party began raising funds to buy an ambulance for the Republic. Caudwell was chosen to drive it across France.

On 11 December 1936, having handed it over to the Spanish Government, he joined the International Brigade. 'You know how I feel about the importance of democratic freedom', he wrote home. 'The Spanish People's Army needs help badly; their struggle, if they fail, will certainly be ours tomorrow, and, believing as I do, it seems clear where my duty lies.'[4]

From Albacete on 24 January he wrote:

> We expect to draw better arms than No. 1 Company which went straight up with old rifles and suffered fairly heavily. I am No. 1 on a machine-gun, or strictly speaking a 'fusil mitrailleuse'; quite a handy little weapon but out of date and none too reliable . . . . I'm a group political delegate . . . instructor to the Labour Party faction and joint-editor of the Wall newspaper.[5]

Caudwell's brother decided to try to get him recalled to England, on the grounds that he was more valuable to the cause as a writer than a soldier, a difficult task since Caudwell was unknown to party intellectuals either through personal contact, which he had never cultivated, or publication. Advance proofs of *Illusion and Reality* were procured and, on the strength of these, a recommendation of immediate recall was cabled to Spain. But it was already too late. Caudwell had been killed on 12 February, his first day in action, defending a retreat in the Battle of the Jarama River.

The books on which his reputation rests all made their appearance posthumously: *Illusion and Reality* (1937), *Studies in a Dying Culture* (1938), *Poems* (1939), *The Crisis in Physics*

(1939), *Further Studies in a Dying Culture* (1949) and *Romance and Realism* (1970). At the time of his death Christopher Caudwell was 29.

*   *   *

Although it's the work of Caudwell, rather than Sprigg, that concerns us here, it may be helpful to glance initially at a sample of the latter's detective fiction.

Crime in Kensington is a tolerable diversion. Sprigg overcomes the potential awkwardness of having to write down from his real interests by the strategy of coupling brisk, efficient storytelling with an element of burlesque – his monocle-sporting hero Charles Venables musing in the first chapter, 'When one hears a bloke threaten to kill his wife and then immediately afterwards meets a sinister and mysterious Oriental, it is time to move somewhere else, for one has obviously walked into the plot of a thriller of the vulgarest and most exciting description.' The characters carry improbable names such as Miss Sanctuary and the Rev. Septimus Blood (an eccentric curate who's introduced the Mozarabic rite to a church in Houndsditch).

Beneath the superficialities of C. St John Sprigg, however, the volcanic tremors of the emergent Caudwell can be detected. Venables writes the 'society' column for a newspaper whose

> public had brains with linings so corroded and crusted by jazz, sentimental films and cheap literature that the most earth-shaking events of the world had to be predigested and peptonized before they could be absorbed. A paper whose political policy had been invariably allied with the most reactionary and anti-social elements of English life.

There are allusions to Donne and Shakespeare; an autopsy report is described, for example, as 'Macbeth . . . reduced to the terms of a butcher's shop'. A Scotland Yard detective, showing an unexpected recourse to scientific concepts, considers 'criminal investigation was in essence a reconstruction of the crime . . . in four dimensions – in the space-time continuum'. Venables approaches a seance with psychoanalytic expectations: 'The Unconscious, given complete liberty of action in a dark room, might play some revealing pranks.' His editor opines that a criminal betrays himself when anxiety 'conjures up phantoms that plague him'. The action is dominated by Nemesis, moving 'as irrevocably

as in a Greek play'. Most prophetically of all, Venables, having
spotted a fake suicide note from its style, exclaims, 'How typical
of the police attitude to evidence! You will recognize a science
of graphology, but not one of literary criticism.'

Caudwell's work as a thriller writer, his interest in psychology
and the desire to discover some meaningful correlation of the
two seem to have shaped his venture into the novel proper, *This
My Hand*. 'We are all the innocent-guilty', one character declares.
'Our very interest in a murderer is due to our feeling that the
murderer is bound to us in this very way. He is atoning for our
wicked thoughts.' *Macbeth* and T. S. Eliot's *Waste Land* (1922)
are Caudwell's implicit points of reference as he depicts universal
spiritual malaise. The central character is even described, when
he leaves a prostitute, as groping 'his way down the badly-lighted
stairs' (virtually a quote of l. 248 of *The Waste Land*).

Caudwell presents a world of unlovable characters trying to
orient themselves anew, who form a definite postwar generation. The style he employs is restrained, mannered even; and
channelled through an omniscient narrator who, without passing
judgment on them, expounds the characters' inner feelings. That
the novel anticipates Albert Camus' *The Outsider* (1942) to an
extent, suggests a sympathy for modernist apprehensions rather
at odds with the views developed by Caudwell as a critic.

Behind the action loom both the Great War, which is mentioned
around twenty-five times, and psychological determinism. Salmon,
the pacifist commercial traveller, speculates that guilt is

> the modern disease. Indeed there is a system of psychology which
> assumes that practically all mental phenomena are based on it.
> For all I know it may be true of the modern soul. The War was
> perhaps only a large-scale voluntary expiation. Hence the eager-
> ness with which we all rushed into it. If so, it will, of course, be
> followed by one on a much larger scale. Not until the modern
> soul does penance . . . not until it has also received an absolution
> in which it believes (though God knows where that will come
> from)—not till then will it be at peace.

This passage calls to mind the very un-Marxist reference to 'mass
neurosis' which Caudwell was to include in the description of the
atmosphere between the wars quoted earlier. Another character is
described by her doctor as 'suffering from what we all suffer from
more or less – the difficulties of adjustment to life, of squaring our
dreams with reality'. Illusion and reality: here the title, and prem-

ise, of Caudwell's major work is beginning to come into focus.

Ian Venning, the novel's principal character, commits murder but, in discarding the sense of guilt, seems paradoxically to become more substantial than the weak, conventional characters around him. Graham Greene's *Brighton Rock* (published two years later) is perhaps an analogue, but Caudwell, in contrast, had abandoned Roman Catholicism. Any hope of salvation from the unappetising world he portrays would have to be in keeping with a scientific world-view. After his second murder, Ian

> did not feel frightened or horrified. He felt as if a great mechanical arm which had been waiting to work had come round and hit him. The wheel had come round full-circle mechanically and its task was accomplished. He had done what he was bound to do.

Salmon's mysticism is the only element of the book that even begins to challenge such negativity. Though Ian

> had acquired toughness and indifference it was only at the price of a cold poison which he could feel invading every part of his life. But when he talked to Salmon, he talked to a man who had cut up the phenomena of life into entirely new divisions. It was exciting.

The proletariat are present only (to borrow a term Caudwell would soon be using) as the most suffering class. The conditions of the Fowling district, 'a huddle of lightless back-to-backs', are luridly described through the eyes of a middle-class do-gooder, but the only action to take place there is a father's rape of his daughter and her consequent suicide. Socialism is only mentioned as a fad one character takes up whilst in her teens.

Like the less ambitious *Crime in Kensington*, *This My Hand* is a competent piece of work but rather thin. The characters, situations, themes and language all deserve greater development, although that's obviously a promising feature in an author's early endeavours. Perhaps the most remarkable quality the novel displays to one coming to it from the better-known Caudwell, however, is its sheer unexpectedness. The verse, the theoretical writings and this piece of fiction are so different in sensibility they could have been produced by three different people. Caudwell was clearly still experimenting, grilling both himself and the Zeitgeist, switching the mode of discourse in search of a positive answer.

According to D. E. S. Maxwell, the Great War reappears

prominently in the unpublished verse, principally in two sequences called 'The Requiem' and 'The Canon'. Within the latter, 'Requiescat in Pace' considers the possibility of personal involvement in future carnage:

> We (it may be) to greater wars,
> To murder done for purer stars
> Making more wives and mothers weep.[6]

The published poems are for the most part prentice-work lit up by flashes of achievement. The influences of Donne and T. S. Eliot are a little too apparent, the former often used to sanction a would-be vigorous, but actually inept, scansion. But Caudwell's basic approach – to adapt old conventions to a modern sensibility, at the same time exploring a parallel dichotomy between Man's lofty ideals and grubby practice – results in some fairly accomplished exercises on love, art and death, with peaks that mark him out as a poet of genuine potential.

Consider, from 'Twenty Sonnets of Wm. Smith' XIII, the weary objectivity of:

> The various over-valued orifices;
> The sense-receptors love is moulded on.

Or the sudden, but wholly appropriate, reversal of perspective in the last line of no. IV:

> And tired of roses, eyes, superfluous stars
> I praise you with the filthy rags of time,
> With universes, galaxies, those tracts
> Of death that wait to drink our limbs and acts.

Only the conspicuous cadging of 'rags of time' from Donne's 'The Sun Rising' drops this back towards the level of pastiche.

The outstanding achievement of the *Poems,* however, is 'Orestes', Caudwell's forty-page re-rendering of the Orestean tragedy as a madcap psychoanalytical burlesque (Auden now his model). Apollo, descending to Dr Tape's consulting room, laments:

> Once I could damn straight out the gods on high
> But now the gods are subject till they die
> To God knows what; the wheel of living gleams
> And new mutations upset old *régimes*—

Bits of artistic and philosophical apparatus are salvaged from various cultural traditions and the resulting assemblage sent trundling at high speed through Caudwell's concerns. There are some ingenious and fluent changes of register, particularly in the speeches of the chorus which even draw on popular song and limerick. The Furies claim responsibility for the War, individual psychological disturbance and the final decay of all civilisations, and proclaim Orestes doomed.

> He'd be O.K. if he had had no parents
> And could refrain from eating tasteful food
> Or the sly bliss of talk or reproduction
> But as it is, we fear that he must go.

> Three thousand years upon the plank of death
> He's tottered dangerously but kept his grip;
> Now he's unsafer than he ever was
> Because he's seen at last what lies below him.
> Christ told him God had hung a net down there;
> Muhammed mentioned magnets in his toes;
> Huxley suggested gravity was with him,
> But now he knows one slip will break his neck.

> Each night I have descended into hell.
> Which is like Brighton on a larger scale.

But to repudiate the Furies, as Ian does in *This My Hand,* is to become inhuman,

> A fag-end thrown
> Contemptuously upon earth's foul floor
> Whom God's angelic chars disdain to salve

The drama ends with the intervention of Athene/Dr Tape, who supplies a few facile psychoanalytic remarks which prove insufficient to prevent Electra drowning herself and Orestes getting run over by a tank.

Political commitment appears in the published verse only by implication. Proletarian revolution is mentioned only once and then as a metaphor for neurosis.

*   *   *

Plainly there is a world-wide conflict between the instincts and the environment and all the tremendous and elaborate super-structure of society—religion, art, laws, science, states, patriotism, ethics, political aims and aspirations, liberty, comfort, peace, life itself—all these things tremble and collapse in ruins; yet it was just this splendid edifice that man constructed to *sublimate,* in Freudian nomenclature, to *resolve,* in ours, the contradiction between his environment and his instincts. This immense decaying superstructure fills with awe the mind even of the revolutionary who sees the cause of its collapse and the still more complex structure which will supersede it; but as a substitute for it the psycho-analysts solemnly offer the meagre constructs of Freudian philosophy and Jungian mythology, tattered scraps expected to heal the conflict which a whole Europe of human achievement cannot resolve.[7]

Dr Tape having failed, Caudwell turned to Dr Marx.

As may be inferred from the Marxist *Modern Quarterly's* 'Caudwell Discussion',[8] Caudwell was a somewhat unorthodox Communist for his day. Although he toiled sincerely at day-to-day Party work, what excited his imagination seems to have been not so much the class struggle in its own right as a seemingly remote philosophical problem he perceived through it: that of the subject-object relation.

Caudwell believed that human understanding and action, in all areas of life, were bedevilled by phoney dualisms. Bourgeois thought had structured itself around contradictory extremes of objectivity and subjectivity: mechanical materialism and idealism, matter and mind, causality and free will. The challenge of synthesis had hitherto been evaded because fragmentation of consciousness into specialised fields had concealed the actual chaos, permitting inconsistent eclecticism or dishonest positivism which 'smuggles another reality (usually the mind) into the system in order to organise it and provide some standard of validity . . . concealed under some such name as "convenience" or "probability" '.[9]

The same was true of bourgeois practice. The crises in the economy and physics were two sides of the same coin. Indeed theory and practice were sundered in consciousness just because of the class division in society. Free will and the free market were both misconstructions rooted in the increasingly unviable division of labour between bourgeoisie and proletariat.

> Only finally the contradiction shatters its own categories and emerges in a synthesis: in economy, communisms, in ideology, dialectical materialism.[10]

The former would cancel all forms of alienation, the latter

resolve the sort of philosophical cruxes Caudwell tackles in his *Studies* and *Further Studies in a Dying Culture*. Dialectical understanding would also rescue art from the status of an insignificant illusion based on aestheticism or formalism, and restore it to its proper, fundamental, place in human life.

Prudence wasn't Caudwell's strong point. Brief summary belies the intricacy of his thought less than the uninitiated might suppose. Rather, it tends to overemphasise his coherence, since he commonly presents impossibly neat accounts of life, persuasive in general terms but on reflection demanding endless specific qualifications. For now we might question just how far in twentieth-century England

> *one class is the conscious, contemplative, directing, and therefore ruling class and the other is the unconscious, active, directed and ruled class* . . . [the former becoming] less functional, and more parasitic, contemplative and idealistic, and the exploited class more and more . . . the sole controllers of the productive forces of society at the same time as they become more and more divorced from its products.[11]

especially as it's admitted elsewhere that,

> The proletariat is . . . able for a time to identify itself with the extension of the Empire, for this extension brings it increased wages and increased employment.[12]

Caudwell tends, in fact, to set up simplified oppositions, in order to then unsheath dialectical materialism and part cleanly a Gordian knot that wouldn't have taken too much weight anyway. He continually fights shy of coming to terms with sustained tensions, presumably because he was himself experiencing several and trying, under the pressure of apparently terminal crises in society, to transcend rather than explore them.

As David N. Margolies has emphasised,[13] Caudwell's central affirmation concerning literature is that it performs a social function. This he endeavours to show by a description of its economic origin and subsequent history, with the suggestion that poetry's importance to society in 'primitive communism', severely diminished by later divisions of labour, will be restored with the setting up of sophisticated communism but enriched by the range of techniques developed in between times (a conclusion which surely has as much to do with verbal symmetry, and wishful thinking, as with reason).

Poetry being language and language a social product, poetry's sources must be social, Caudwell argues. Indeed, in primitive society the poetic form is that of all literature. It is usually associated with music and dance, constitutes public as opposed to private speech and is a central part of the social awareness and adaptability which distinguishes Man from other animals. The function of poetry in primitive society is to harness the instincts to collective tasks such as preparation for harvest, war or winter:

> poetry, combined with dance, ritual, and music, becomes the great switchboard of the instinctive energy of the tribe, directing it into trains of collective actions whose immediate causes or gratifications are not in the visual field and which are not automatically decided by instinct . . . .
> Words, in ordinary social life, have acquired emotional associations for each man. These words are carefully selected, and the rhythmical arrangement makes it possible to chant them in unison, and release their emotional associations in all the vividness of collective existence. Music and the dance co-operate to produce an alienation from reality which drives on the whole machine of society . . . .
> Thus the developing complex of society, in its struggle with the environment, secrete poetry as it secretes the technique of harvest, as part of its non-biological and specifically human adaptation to existence.[14]

To master reality, man creates and commits himself to illusions, which he then struggles to realise. In more Marxist terms, being determines consciousness, freedom is secured through 'recognition' of this necessity and the point is not to merely interpret the world but change it.

With the development of society through the division of labour, there is an increasing specialisation of consciousness involving the separation out of literature into various forms. Ceremonies and work songs are joined by such genres as epic and tragedy (their contents reflecting the tensions of various transitional periods) and eventually language branches out into lyric verse, the novel, the sciences, history, theology, law, economics 'and other appropriate divisions of cultural capital'.[15]

Caudwell's account of the relationships between magic, myth, religion and art is rather scrambled, but the main point to be taken is that, whereas art's illusion receives only a qualified assent, reflects contemporary tensions in its form and content and leads to renewed involvement in reality, full-blown religion is far more rigid and tends merely to reinforce the 'inverted world' of existing class divisions. But even art is limited in its function by the existence of a class structure. Both 'high culture' and 'folk culture' degenerate as the former grows remote from real life and the spontaneity required for the latter is crushed by mechanical tasks.

The same constriction afflicts the individual. Although civilisation increasingly offers the potential for elaborate personal development, class divisions arbitrarily restrict the individual's growth, this imperfect fit giving rise to anxiety and neurosis. The poet, now that work and art are divorced, becomes a solitary maker of lyrics, though his art still depends on 'the complex history of emotions and experience shared in common by a thousand generations'.[16]

In its individualism modern literature reflects the great liberal fallacy that freedom is simply the absence of restraints – a reflection, in turn, of the development of the bourgeoisie as a ruling class dependent on an apparently free and natural market, actually a front for state-enforced exclusive ownership of the means of production. By this sham freedom – a denial of the very social relations that could make genuine freedom possible – 'man has enslaved himself to forces whose control is now beyond him, because he does not acknowledge their existence'.[17]

> Millions are forced to go out and be slaughtered, or to kill, and to oppress each other. Millions are forced to strive with their fellows for a few glittering prizes, and to be deprived of marriage, and a home, and children, because society cannot afford them these things. Millions and millions of men are not free.[18]

Finally, however, the proletariat, 'led by a conscious political party . . . imposes on the bourgeoisie the final "freedom" of release from ownership of private property' and 'with the disappearance of the bourgeoisie the last coercive relation rooted in the necessities of economic production disappears, and man can set about becoming genuinely free'.[19]

This is reflected in literature, particularly since a progressive element among the bourgeois intellectuals (including Caudwell) goes over to Communism and helps to lead the struggle.

> The working out of the bourgeois illusion concerning freedom . . . is a colossal movement of men, materials, emotions and ideas, it is a whole history of toiling, learning, suffering and hoping

D

men. Because of the scale, energy, and material complexity of the movement, bourgeois poetry is the glittering, subtle, complex, many-sided thing it is . . . . And the consciousness of social necessity which is the condition of freedom for the people as a whole in classless, communist society, will be realised in communist poetry because it can only be realised in its essence, not as a metaphysical formula, but by living as men in a developing communist society, which includes living as poets and readers of poetry.[20]

I must emphasise again that Caudwell's own expositions are more complex and richer than my brief summary, but not necessarily more sophisticated.

While there is much that is convincing in Caudwell's analysis, and more the sympathetic reader might find it easy to accept, inspection reveals both simplification of reality and spurious reasoning built on it.

On the positive side, there are his attack on evasively vague usages of the term 'liberty' (a rebuke that certainly hasn't ceased to be topical), the concomitant assertion that all the specifically human elements in life (literature included) rest on communal resources, and the use of a perspective that attempts to transcend deadening compartmentalisations of knowledge and experience in one invigorating overview.

On the negative side, though, the primitive function of literature as Caudwell understands it is taken as a norm without adequate assessment of later developments, and poetry is classed as having been a distinct entity at a stage when it had obviously still not fully differentiated out from dance and music and is then, by the imposition of a crude dialectical formula, declared to be a use of language which will become increasingly important after the revolution, without there being any consideration of how far fragmentation of communal consciousness is due to society being large and complicated, rather than merely class-based. The latter omission also calls heavily into question the millenial vision of contradictions overcome toward which Caudwell's political stance points, an ultimately counter-productive attitude in that it sets up unrealistic expectations and idealises contemporary politics so as to lead almost inevitably to a loss of heart.

Caudwell continually makes simple linear assumptions about the course of events, past and future, which at times, coupled with God-on-our-side moralising, almost reduce the complex history of mankind to melodrama. His declarations concerning the intensification of class division seem in retrospect part of the tension brought about by its comparative diminution. His generalisations that popular culture is increasingly worthless and that slaves cannot produce art require, to say the least, some amendment in view of the overwhelming influence of American negro culture throughout the world this century. (Caudwell, of course, dismisses jazz categorically.) He treats base/superstructure determinism as virtually a one-to-one process, never allows for complexity brought about by feedback and accident (which, even for those convinced that the economic structure of society is the ultimate foundation of social consciousness, must throw severe doubt on the value of this model in the appreciation of particular works of art), espouses 'laws of association in society' which surely cannot be scientifically formulable because there are always too many variables, and looks forward to a millenium envisaged in the most abstract and unfathomable terms.

These distortions can, needless to say, be related back to his own 'social being'. When he writes that people are forced to specialise according to 'one psychic function – that most marked genetically' so that 'a marked bent for a slightly remunerative occupation (such as poetry) will be sacrificed to a slight bent for a markedly remunerative occupation'[21], he's clearly thinking of the frustrations of fully developing his own extensive talents. Most people's allocations have been, and still are, quite arbitrary. Nor, for that matter, could there be any question of complete (rather than more) satisfaction through socialism, since each person has only vague potential abilities and desires which are conditioned by experience, and the intricacies of living must preclude any absolute fit that could ensure total absence of irritation. The proletarianisation of the bourgeoisie and the breakdown of culture are also concepts likely to call forth over-response from a middle-class journalist who had left school early and taken to writing thrillers.

This combination of a liberating breadth of perspective and a constrictingly narrow access to it based on the uncertainties of one young English writer in 1937 is again prominent in Caudwell's history of English literature. Poetry is covered in chapters IV, V and VI of *Illusion and Reality*, literature in general in *Romance and Realism* and Shaw, Wells and the two Lawrences

(D. H. and T. E.) are scrutinised in *Studies in a Dying Culture*. Caudwell's account of the rise and fall of 'bourgeois' literature has often been highlighted by his friends and enemies alike as his most immediately interesting achievement, distracting attention from the full range of his work. Stanley Edgar Hyman, in a chapter of *The Armed Vision*[22] dropped from subsequent editions, hails the chart depicting 'The Movement of Bourgeois Poetry' as the best thing in the book when related to the text, whereas Raymond Williams, in his acute critique of Caudwell in *Culture and Society 1780-1950*[23] laments that Caudwell's discussion is rarely even specific enough to be wrong.

Caudwell is not, however, attempting to examine particular works of literature in depth, but to clear the decks for future raids on the inarticulate, particularly his own. The historical sketch is part of a greater perspective he's seeking to establish, not an end in itself, and is necessarily therefore somewhat cursory and patchy in nature. This, I think, excuses the rather restricted approach Caudwell adopts, though not the glib, one-to-one decoding of art into caricature economic history into which he frequently lapses.

The provocative mixture of inanity and insight achieved is exemplified by his comments on Shakespeare. On the one hand, he tries to show that Shakespeare's plots symbolically express the contradiction of capitalism and dubs *The Tempest* 'a bizarre forecast of communism'[24] on the grounds that it contains white magic and therefore nature harnessed to man's service. (In fact, *The Tempest* does refer to communism explicitly – in Gonzalo's description of his ideal commonwealth, in 2.i., and Sebastian and Antonio's derisive commentary, which prophetically seizes on the problem of the dictatorship of the proletariat.) On the other hand, he notes that the drama of the period can call on 'a language of great range and compass' because it precedes 'the elaborate division of labour, to which the elaborate complexity of culture corresponds', proposes that it blends individual orientation and collective expression ultimately 'because of the alliance of the monarchy with the bourgeoisie',[25] and observes that Shakespeare couldn't have written after his retirement from the theatre because his 'magic wand was a collective one',[26] that is, dependent on the cultural apparatus of the court.

A lapse back toward inanity is the assertion that Tennyson's deeply-felt meditation on 'Nature, red in tooth and claw' in *In*

Memoriam 'only reflects the ruthlessness of a society in which capitalist is continually hurling down fellow capitalist into the proletarian abyss'.[27] That little word 'only' is enough to put into eclipse the latent sensible suggestion that capitalist society did produce some disposition to construe nature in this way.

Four of Caudwell's sounder observations are as follows:

> Miltonic blank verse . . . does not seem to us revolutionary; but then we forget against what he was revolting—against the easy fluent glitter of the Court, the sweetness and corrupt simplicity of a Suckling or a Lovelace.[28]
>
> Robinson Crusoe on his island, absolutely alone and completely free, yet calls into existence a bourgeois world. Even the exploited proletariat is there in the person of the ignorant, good-natured Man Friday, and as the bourgeois always dreams, there is no overt domination in their relationship—Friday is exploited quite in the best paternal manner.[29]
>
> Wordsworth's 'Nature' is of course a Nature freed of wild beasts and danger by aeons of human work, a Nature in which the poet, enjoying a comfortable income, lives on the products of industrialism even while he enjoys the natural scene 'unspoilt' by industrialism.[30]
>
> This source of all happiness and woe is the disparity between man's being and man's consciousness, which drives on society and makes life vital. Now all this tension, everything below the dead intellectual sphere, is blotted out in Shaw . . . heroes appear to him as the neat little figures of a bourgeois history book, quite inhuman, and regarding their lives as calmly as if they were examination papers on the 'currents of social change'.[31]

There is much that is of value in Caudwell's criticisms, especially in such shrewd iconoclasm as the essay on Shaw. He illuminatingly introduces the writer's economic position for consideration. Pope, for instance, dependent on patrons, 'writes for an audience he has directly in mind',[32] whereas the Romantic poets, confronted by the cash-nexus and an increasingly peripheral status, declare themselves heroic outsiders and their verse an end in itself. The surrealists react against society's neglect by pursuing skill-fetishism into complete subjectivity:

> When poetry has become completely personal and completely non-social, it is then no longer art, nor, since language is social, is it language. It is a kind of indistinct swearing.[33]

He also has some stimulating things to say on the 'epistemological problem of the observer' in the modern novel, which he connects with 'the discovery of the relativity of bourgeois norms, hitherto taken as absolute, whether in art, society, or physics'[34] and which has therefore been tackled with greatest success by writers 'in some way alien to the culture they describe'. And his remarks on Byron as a revolutionary provide, incidentally, a penetrating gloss on the potential contradictions he himself risked, closely anticipating Raymond Williams' retrospective strictures on the literary Marxists of the 'thirties.[35]

The weaknesses of the Caudwellian history of English literature are fairly predictable. He pursues genuine insights into crass overstatement and, sick of his own hack work, writes off all popular culture as 'mere massage', generalising that 'the man who writes for money is not an artist'.[36] He tries to cram the richness of individual experience into simplified class pigeonholes and, despite the observation that 'in language reality is symbolised in unchanging words, which give a false stability and permanence to the object they represent . . . till we arrive at the Platonic Ideas, Eternal and Perfect Words',[37] is himself content to describe capitalism as a distinct entity conjuring itself out of subordinate prior conditions and to bandy about such hopelessly capacious terms as capitalist poetry and bourgeois culture.

As the question of literature's future development begins to come into view, Caudwell returns to the discussion of its mode of operation and its social function.

Words have both connotative and denotative significances, he points out, reflecting the elements of feeling and reason in our lives.

> But these do not exist in the word-as-itself, in contemplation, any more than a pound note exists in itself as paper and print. They exist only in the word as a dynamic social act, just as a pound note only exists in exchange.[38]
> Truth is individual man's experience of the connections of phenomena, become organised by homologation with millions of other such experiences.[39]

Common worlds of feeling and perception are built up in society, through which new experience is assimilated, thus modifying and developing them toward greater, though never absolute, understanding. Art and science are the prongs of this activity:

both are conscious of the necessities of their worlds and can change them—art the world of feeling or inner reality, science the world of phenomena or outer reality . . . .[40]
Consistency is the virtue of science, beauty of poetry—neither can ever become pure beauty or pure consistency, and yet it is their struggle to achieve this which drives on their development. Science yearns always towards mathematics, poetry towards music.[41]

Science strips perception of all personal qualities in so far as is possible, producing an objective observer. Art, transfiguring perception along lines laid down by feeling, produces a subjective world.

This mock ego of science and this mock world of art are both necessary because object and subject are never parted in experience . . . . But science and art do not when fitted together make a complete concrete world: they make a complete hollow world —an abstract world only made solid and living by the inclusion of the concrete living of concrete men, from which they are generated.[42]

More fundamental than propaganda, they do not persuade but show – a point singled out in W. H. Auden's brief but enthusiastic review of *Illusion and Reality*.[43] As Samuel Hynes comments, Caudwell in so saying had provided a theoretical defence for art against the Agitprop mentality.[44]

Caudwell checks any drift of art into total subjectivity, on the other hand, by distinguishing it from dreams, madness and mere 'surrealism', all of which lack art's social component. That is, they do not enrich consciousness and thus emancipate man from mechanical determinism (the function of consciousness being to secure a more flexible adaptation to existence than simple reflex actions can provide). Not aware of necessity, they stay stuck in the grooves of compulsion and are thus barren illusions. Art, however, 'is no more neurosis than thought is dream'.[45] Art and science only distort reality to sharpen man's experience of it, their emphases complementary, the former correcting the latter's reductionism.

Poetry restores life and value to matter, and puts back the genotype into the world from which it was banished.[46]
Art tells us what science cannot tell us, and what religion only feigns to tell us—what we are and why we are, why we hope and suffer and love and die.[47]

Caudwell discusses the different strategies embodied in different art forms and in the various branches of literature and relates their development to social history. Poetry, for example, is 'an organised emotional attitude to a piece of reality'[48] and the novel 'an objective slice of subjective reality',[49] while the varying stress on individual character in the drama of different eras is traced to the changing division of labour, and the industrial revolution, which made men's lives unprecedently interweave, is credited with, in so doing, fathering the novel, the symphony and the evolutionary sciences.

Caudwell seizes on any number of suggestive points, but typically damages his exploration of them by confusion, over-statement and fanciful antitheses. Two major specific objections should be made to his description of art's function.

One, first made by Montagu Slater,[50] is that art and science are not quite the simple complementary pair he claims. The function that Caudwell allocates art – mediation between the genotype and social existence, accommodating the natural man to the civilised man – is fulfilled by the entire apparatus of civilisation as such, including disciplines like philosophy and politics, so that the whole art/science antithesis is more nebulous than its presenta-tion suggests.

The other objection, quite centrally damaging, is that the adaptation to new experience of, on the one hand, an individual and, on the other, a whole civilisation are scarcely interchange-able. Tension between productive forces and social relations will in many cases find reflection in tensions in the individual's experience, but only as one component of the material art deals with. Caudwell would probably have replied that in a period of revolutionary crisis it becomes the overwhelming component, but even if that were in a sense true, it's the human experience, not the economic analysis, that art must embody. Pointing to the means of production, Caudwell is suggesting a fallacious short-cut to artistic creativity.

The cry he puts into the mouth of the bourgeois theoreticians has its personal application too.

> "Give me," they all cry, "absolute truth, absolute justice, some rule-of-thumb standard by which I can evade the strenuous task of finding the features of reality by intimate contact with it in action. Give me some logical talisman, some philosopher's stone, by which I can test all acts in theory and say, this is right . . . ."[51]

Although he puts his faith in the dialectic of theory and practice, Caudwell tends to steer his practice by theory understood as a panacea.

His negative comments on the 'Auden group' are excellent up to a point. He accuses them of operating from 'an obscure bourgeois base, on which is imposed a mechanical pseudo-Marxist revolutionary formula' which 'sometimes has quite an unpleasant air, as of a bourgeois trying to "cash in" on the revolution'.[52] But, for all his sincere attempt to subordinate himself to the greater good, Caudwell is clearly at a loss for corresponding constructive suggestions.

He recognises that 'communist poetry' could only come to exist through a 'communist consciousness', but attempts to fabricate one rather than allow it to accrue naturally while pursuing his political convictions. He cannot accept that poetry containing ideological contradictions might be worth writing in the meantime. The ironic upshot of his attempt to find a world-view that would give shape to his art, then, is a journey into silence alleviated only by theorising:

> ... the poet can successfully endeavour to change poetry, to make it social and public again. But a prerequisite is to attain a world-view that will become general .... Having achieved that world-view, the poet, when he has a new experience that necessitates expression in poetry, can then project it into the new world struggling to be born and become a poet of the future.[53]

For the present, however: silence.

His ability to rorschach patterns out of reality till it's hard to tell true correspondence from mere analogy reaches its extreme in his glib avowal that 'whatever methods are necessary for a social transformation must be necessary in art',[54] which is in effect a defence of censorship. However, the supposedly reactionary reservations of artists and scientists are surely correct this time. Following Caudwell's own analysis, true art and science express consciousness, not consciousness minus components which the authorities (or anybody else) disapprove of. It might be necessary on social grounds to prohibit sensationalist films, or to restrict free speech during a period of political conflict such as a civil war, but this ought to be affirmed openly in its own right and not with such oblique ingenuity.

For the rest Caudwell, the middle-class Marxist, delivers a

D*

ventriloquial speech to 'bourgeois revolutionaries' in the name of the 'conscious proletariat'[55] – the real proletariat presumably being occupied with more immediate worries than the future of poetry – who insist on their making a straight choice between denying social determinism altogether or leading proletarian art. Caudwell speaks vaguely of a future of 'collectivism and integrity . . . consciousness and freedom shared by all . . . the development of broadcasting', enriched language, the return of poetry to the drama, film coming into its own[56] and gestures toward a 'socialist realist' programme for the novel which would somehow encompass 'a definite world-view' while showing 'the relativity of all value and the change of all being'.[57]

*   *   *

Caudwell's faults are obvious and make it easy to dismiss his critical writings as a cul-de-sac not worth visiting. He is blatantly over-hasty in making specific connections and in drawing general conclusions from them. His narrow programmatic approach to literature results in severe distortions in his appreciation of it. He considers abstract ideology as a substitute for concrete technical discussions of what writers have done and what they should be doing. His arguments are almost exclusively negative. Indeed he clears the decks for action until they're entirely dismantled (if there was an element of flippancy and opportunism in the work of Auden and his followers, at least they were trying to produce poems, not declaring them impossible), and he tends to denigrate the cultural achievements of the past in favour of those that might exist some time in the future. By crudely equating the new human experience art absorbs and new developments in the economic base, he tries to evade the unfortunate home truth that artists can't necessarily produce what they want, only what they're able to, and seems to be implying that all good art must be politically progressive. His arguments are organised messily and his prose is often slapdash.

His style does have a compensating vigour, on the other hand, contains memorable turns of phrase and is on occasion the vehicle for a sly humour (something that tends to get lost in summary). And the very reason his thoughts lack manoeuvrability – that he's articulating a novel vision, and to stop and qualify it would be to risk letting the whole thing slip out of focus – perhaps renders that drawback an inevitable accompaniment to the qualities of energy and audacity that make his work so exciting.

As his arguments briskly take shape, you begin to feel that he really has got the drop on all the big names and ideas he proposes to sort out. But the sense of exuberance resulting from this is born not of Caudwell's frivolity, but his responsibility. He honestly does care about a terrifically broad range of human activities and his heroic determination to bring them into a meaningful relation leads, however imperfectly, to a creative fusion of the sciences and arts in one humanist culture which may be termed genuinely post-Romantic – and genuinely inspiring. When his age and educational background are considered, the achievement is quite amazing. Moreover, though in practice he often fails to judge works as they operate rather than as ideological exempla, his stress on function is a sturdy and refreshing counter-attack on literature's trivialisation, whether into light entertainment or propaganda. It is perhaps significant that, although Raymond Williams is comparatively critical of Caudwell in *Culture and Society 1780-1950,* when he comes to discuss creativity in *The Long Revolution*[58] he nevertheless resorts to quotation from Caudwell to make himself clear.

> Born with the possibilities of being a great Elizabethan or a dignified Augustan, Donne was by his age forced into the mould of a tortured metaphysical.[59]

So Caudwell revealingly wrote of his hero, John Donne, another young intellectual who had attempted to stir all the ingredients of life into one heady brew.

Not content with simply pursuing his art, Caudwell, maturing in a time of crisis, felt it necessary to relate the uncertainty of the age and his inner uncertainty as a writer, to clarify the world-view with which his art would necessarily be involved and to describe and encourage the new philosophy that he felt was emerging from the moribund culture around him. Despite his remarkable achievements, Caudwell's was not the kind of eloquent gift that flowers early, however. His was a broader, and perhaps deeper, talent for the final unfolding of which he was still acquiring resources when his sense of responsibility led him to Spain.

Caudwell will go on being read, as a fascinating minor figure with the capacity to excite and inspire, especially in times of economic and cultural insecurity. But it's important that he is done the honour of being read critically – neither as a name to cite vaguely in support of radical assumptions about the arts nor as a quaint autodidact to be patronised by his more sophisticated successors, but a man who lived as thoroughly as he could on all fronts and who left a body of writing valuable to posterity both for its shrewd observations and its dauntless spirit.

It is Caudwell's misfortune to have had two distinct literary careers – one under his real name, one posthumously under his pen name – both offering a misleading view of his real talents. A hack in his lifetime, remembered now as something of an intellectual curiosity, he was essentially a creative writer who turned to theory to get his bearings, but died before his imagination could become properly focused. It's thus, and with all the complexity of response which that view demands, that he deserves to be remembered.

The problem of the subject-object relation – the need to find some sort of accommodation between the extremes of idealism and materialism – remains a cardinal one, on the other hand. Although Caudwell's near-total abandonment of a 'provisional attitude to reality', under the pressures of social crisis and his religious upbringing, betrayed him into attempting a premature synthesis of various kinds of knowledge under the banner of Marxism, the issues he raised and the answers he proffered nevertheless constitute a vision from which sustenance can still be drawn.

The enduring loss to the republic of letters, of course, is that the man who achieved it never had the opportunity to build on it himself.

NOTES
1 *Studies in a Dying Culture*, III.
2 Quoted in Samuel Hynes's excellent Introduction to Caudwell's *Romance and Realism*, Princeton University Press, New Jersey, 1970, p. 6.
3 *Ibid.* p. 13.
4 Quoted in John Strachey's Introduction to *Studies in a Dying Culture*.

5 Quoted in D. E. S. Maxwell's *Poets of the Thirties* (Routledge & Kegan Paul, 1969), p. 67.

6 Quoted by Maxwell, *op cit.*, p. 72.

7 *Illusion and Reality*, IX, 1.

8 A discussion on the validity of Caudwell's approach, including contributions from Maurice Cornforth, George Thomson, Montagu Slater, Alick West, G. M. Matthews, Margot Heinemann and J. D. Bernal—Vol. VI, Nos. 1 (Winter 1950-51), pp. 16-33; 2 (Spring 1951), pp. 107-34; 3 (Summer), pp. 259-75; and 4 (Autumn), pp. 340-58.

9 *Illusion and Reality*, Introduction.

10 *Crisis in Physics*, II. 10.

11 Caudwell's italics, *Further Studies*, III.

12 *Romance and Realism.*

13 In his book *The Function of Literature: A Study of Christopher Caudwell's Aesthetics* (Lawrence & Wishart, 1969).

14 *Illusion and Reality*, I. 4.

15 *Ibid.* I. 3.

16 *Ibid.* I. 4.

17 *Studies in a Dying Culture*, Foreword.

18 *Ibid.* VIII.

19 *Illusion and Reality*, III. 1

20 *Ibid.* III. 3.

21 *Ibid.* I. 2.

22 Knopf (New York, 1948), ch. 7.

23 Chatto & Windus, 1958, part III, ch. 5.

24 *Illusion and Reality*, IV. 1.

25 *Ibid.*

26 *Ibid.* IV. 3.

27 *Ibid.* VI. 1.

28 *Romance and Realism.*

29 *Ibid.*

30 *Illusion and Reality*, V. 2.

31 *Studies in a Dying Culture*, I.

32 *Illusion and Reality*, IV. 5.

33 *Romance and Realism.*

34 *Ibid.*

35 Williams, *op cit.*

36 *Illusion and Reality*, VI. 2.

37 *Studies in a Dying Culture*, III.

38 *Illusion and Reality*, VIII. 2.

39 *Ibid.* VIII. 1.

40 *Ibid.*

41 *Ibid.* VII.

42 *Ibid.* VIII. 4.

43 *New Verse* 25 (May 1937), pp. 20-22.
44 In his book *The Auden Generation* (Bodley Head, 1976), p. 258.
45 *Illusion and Reality*, X. 6.
46 *Ibid.* X. 4.
47 *Ibid.* XI. 5.
48 *Ibid.* X. 4.
49 *Romance and Realism.*
50 *Modern Quarterly*, Vol. 6, no. 3 (Summer 1951), pp. 262-5.
51 *Studies in a Dying Culture*, V.
52 *Romance and Realism.*
53 *Ibid.*
54 *Ibid.*
55 *Illusion and Reality*, XII. 2.
56 *Ibid.* XII. 3.
57 *Romance and Realism.*
58 Chatto & Windus, 1961, part 1, ch. 1. v.
59 *Romance and Realism.*

Potential Recruits: Evelyn Waugh and the reader of 'Black Mischief'

William Myers

It seems that Evelyn Waugh 'came to denigrate Decline and Fall,'[1] perhaps because, though brilliantly funny, it doesn't add up to much. Its critics think differently. Frederick J. Stopp, for instance, believes that the prison governor, 'with his rationalist dogmatism, . . . bears the responsibility for unleashing the force which destroys Prendergast'. But, he argues, 'events cannot deny their Providential origin'.[2] That, however, is exactly what they do deny: if the issues or the people were real, Prendy's decapitation would not be funny. *Decline and Fall* stifles, quite systematically, almost every serious response. Its few portentous passages are embarrassing, notably Paul's Noel Cowardish meditation on 'the *impossibility* of Margot in prison'[3] and Professor Silenus's superficial solemnities. It is not a novel which will stand systematic interpretation.

Vile Bodies is more overtly moralistic; but the 'Masked parties, Savage parties' parenthesis,[4] which climaxes in the phrase that gives the book its title, has no bearing on its source in the Prayer Book, and the wording of Father Rothschild's meditation on impermanence – 'perhaps it is all in some way historical' – is painfully slack. So too is the suggestion that the Catholic Church has been preaching platitudes about doing things well 'for several centuries'. Mad parties and flimsy conspiracy do not provide an adequate base for pontifications about 'the instability of our whole world order', nor even for poor Agatha Runcible's nightmare. The surprisingly clumsy ending is evidently an attempt to give these philosophisings, which Waugh later regretted, concrete form; nor on the evidence of the brilliant first six chapters were they part of the book's original impulse. The later comedy is somewhat strained, so perhaps Waugh only moralised when invention flagged.

In one respect, however, these first two novels do achieve a very real seriousness. Waugh's urbane reductiveness is consistent with moral intelligence and literary poise in personal matters. Nina's feelings for Adam, in *Vile Bodies*, when he dances alone in the hall, Adam's sale of her to Ginger, and their Christmas adultery mark out clear and tense antitheses between sophistication and innocence. Waugh's style makes it easy to laugh and difficult to judge. Even better is Peter Beste-Chetwynde, later Lord Pastmaster, in *Decline and Fall*. Peter is both beautifully poised and touchingly vulnerable, notably when he goes 'deadly white'[5] at Paul's arrest. He remains impeccably worldly – he 'makes' Margot retreat to Corfu while he arranges Paul's release and the return of Margot's gifts – but in his last scene he is drunk and unexpectedly childish, blaming Paul for his mother's marriage to the newly ennobled Lord Metroland – 'What a name! What a man!' (Epilogue) – and 'comforting' himself with the thought of her liaison with Alistair. In *Vile Bodies* he tells Metroland to go to hell, as they stare, equally miserably, at Alistair's hat and umbrella. The allusions to Peter's inner life are as sparse and elliptical as those to Lord Tangent's death-agony, but they raise questions as deftly as the latter dispose of them and point forward to the graces of *A Handful of Dust*.

On the whole, however, the first two novels dance with such irresponsible skill round serious issues that their final effect is to disconcert and delight rather than to shock and teach. *Black Mischief* is easily read as a similar kind of book. A spirit of heartless, morally feather-weight farce, for instance, ensures that Mr Youkoumian's bland indifference to his wife's atrocious sufferings is simply funny. Equally disarming is the imposition of European social and political institutions on a primitive society. Waugh has great fun distributing titles among his Africans and the humour works both ways. When the Earl of Ngumo threatens 'to dismember any man on his estates' who uses contraceptives[6] the 'loud grunts of disapproval' from his peers are notably reminiscent of the noises made by middle-aged dominant males in English county families. Again, like its French counterpart, the Nestorian Church has its little nest of fascists, 'Nestorian Catholic Action' eager for 'a whack at the modernists and Jews' supposed to be responsible for the birth-control programme. All this blends admirably with the farcical triviality of life at the British Legation, the machinations of M. Ballon, and the adventures of Dame Mildred and Miss Trim. If Waugh had wanted to write serious satire, it could be argued, he would have given these ladies an interest in the abolition of prostitution and the drug-traffic, like their originals in *Remote People*. On the contrary, for much of the novel he seems to deliberately keep the serious potentialities of his subject and setting happily in check.

Nevertheless there are intimations of a serious concern with issues in *Black Mischief* not to be found in *Decline and Fall* and the best part of *Vile Bodies*. A character most effectively calculated to catch the liberal reader off-guard, for instance, is General Connolly, the 'stocky Irishman in early middle age who [has] seen varied service in the Black and Tans, the South African Police and the Kenya Game Reserves before enlisting under the Emperor's colours'.[7] The tough, unimaginative, unintellectual mercenary officer in Africa is, on the face of it, an unattractive figure. For a joke Waugh named him after Cyril Connolly, but he also made him Irish so that his service in the Black and Tans, quite apart from his subsequent record, is likely to produce a quick reflex of dislike. But cutting right across the cliché is Connolly's affection for Black Bitch. Waugh does a very thorough job of presenting her as a kind of likeable monkey:

> She was in the yard in front of her house laundering some of the General's socks (for she could not bear another woman to touch her man's clothes) chewing nut and meditatively spitting the dark juice into the soap-suds, when a lancer dismounted before her in the crimson and green uniform of the French Legation.
> "Her Grace the Duchess of Ukaka."
> She lifted her dress so as not to soil it and wiped her hands on her knickers.
> "Me" she said.
> The man saluted and handed her a large envelope; she squatted on her heels and examined it, turning it this way and that, holding it up to her ear and shaking it, her head sagely cocked on one side.

Connolly's easy and deep affection for Black Bitch, however, makes it very difficult for us to protest against such a monstrously wicked piece of writing: we cannot, after all, allow ourselves to be shocked by personal habits, however crudely drawn, which can rouse a man like Connolly to real tenderness. Mr Youkoumian's marriage places us in a related dilemma. If we object too strongly to Waugh's gleeful descriptions of his domestic tyranny, we are in danger both of seeming humourless and of trapping ourselves in a culturally arrogant and so illiberal misreading of foreign manners and customs. And our embarrassment is all the greater because Waugh is obviously not being all that serious. He hasn't attempted to penetrate the complexities of Connolly's inner life, nor of Black Bitch's, nor of the Youkoumians'. He has on the contrary plainly arranged their marriages as a joke; and if we protest about that too strongly, we will disqualify ourselves from joining in his sharp indignation at the insolent mean-spiritedness of the Colonial administrators who finally take over Azania and justify Connolly's expulsion on the grounds that 'he's married to a wog'.[8]

The temptation is to see Waugh's treatment of Seth in similar terms merely as a trap for unwary modernity. Seth has the hope-less task of representing personal decency in Africa, of embodying the notion of the human individual of intelligence and good will on which the softened twentieth-century version of liberalism is based. 'I have seen the great tattoo at Aldershot,' he declares, 'the Paris Exhibition, the Oxford Union. I have read modern books – Shaw, Arden, Priestley . . ., at my stirrups run woman's suffrage, vaccination and vivisection.'[9] This touchingly absurd speech im-plies either that 'the African' cannot really understand the complexities of Western thought, or that in an African context our comfortable assumptions about human order are as naive and superficial as Seth makes them sound. Either way we are cleverly trapped. But though a booby and a virgin, Seth isn't just a joke. His loneliness is serious and symptomatic.

> Seth lay awake and alone, his eyes wild with the inherited terror of the jungle, desperate with the acquired loneliness of civiliz-ation. Night was alive with beasts and devils and the spirits of dead enemies; before its power Seth's ancestors had receded . . .; between them and night only a wall of mud and a ceiling of thatched grass; warm naked bodies breathing in the darkness an arm's reach apart, indivisibly unified, so that they ceased to be six or seven blacks and became one person of more than human stature . . . Seth . . . was alone, dwarfed by the magnitude of the darkness, insulated from his fellows, strapped down to mean dimensions.

The last phrase decisively reverses our view of Seth. It is sharp, precise and powerful in its indignation at the way he and Africa have been humanly diminished by civilisation. It is as if Waugh were scathingly opting for barbaric terrors and barbaric com-munion.

The other source of moral unease in *Black Mischief* is, of course, Basil Seal. Seth and Basil are very well matched – both exhibiting not the same kind, but the same degree, of charming immaturity. Basil is the reverse of Peter Pastmaster in *Decline and Fall*. Where Peter was a vulnerable adolescent with the manners of a debauched worldling, Basil is a debauched worldling with the heart of a ruthlessly invulnerable adolescent:

> He stood in the doorway, a glass of whisky in one hand, looking insolently round the room, his head back, chin forward, shoulders rounded, dark hair over his forehead, contemptuous grey eyes over grey pouches, a proud rather childish mouth, a scar over one cheek.[10]

The bland incapacity of Lady Seal and Sir Joseph to admit the truth about Basil is justly rewarded by Basil's theft of his mother's emerald bracelet, but our pleasure in his wickedness becomes rather less comfortable when he moves in on the innocent Seth. Connolly, however, seems to offer some assurance that Seth will survive Basil's depradations, and our fears are further allayed when he is distracted by the affair with Prudence whose absurd Legation life and hilarious prose style act as apparent guarantees of the novel's continuing harmlessness. The reader should take warning, however, from the celebrated love-scene in Basil's room which so astutely anticipates the seediness of Graham Greene's Africa:

> The atmosphere of the room was rank with tobacco smoke. Basil, in short-sleeves, rose from the deck-chair to greet her. He threw the butt of his Burma cheroot into the tin hip-bath which stood unemptied beside the bed; it sizzled and went out and floated throughout the afternoon, slowly unfurling in the soapy water. He bolted the door . . . . Prudence stood isolated, waiting for him, her hat in her hand. At first neither spoke. Presently she said, "You might have shaved," and then "Please help me with my boots"[11]

Like Peter Pastmaster's moment of intimate humiliation with his step-father, Prudence's pathos and dignity in this little scene remind us with disconcerting brevity – the flawless surface of the comedy is not to be disturbed – of the reality of personal experience which in the main Waugh's writing succeeds in smoothly ignoring. The possibility that his vivid little cardboard characters might actually come alive is functionally unsettling.

The main threat to the novel's tonal equilibrium remains, of course, its dangerous flirtations with barbarism, and it is this

which makes *Black Mischief,* for better or worse, a far more
serious problem for the reader and critic than either of its predecessors. Waugh himself said as much. In the open letter he
planned to address to the Archbishop of Westminster in defence
of the novel against the strictures of the editor of *The Tablet,* he
wrote: 'The story deals with the conflict of civilisation, with all
its attendant and deplorable ills, and barbarism. The plan of my
book throughout was to keep the darker aspects of barbarism
continually and inobtrusively present.'[12] The book is certainly full
of flippantly brief allusions to cannibalism, public executions,
nudity and slavery. Always giving an additional *frisson* to the
comedy is our awareness that contraceptive users in Azania may
indeed be dismembered by a laughing Earl of Ngumo, and while
the comic tone and inventiveness are adroitly sustained during the
trip to the monastery, the shambling son of the great Amurath,
who has been kept chained and naked in a cave for decades by
astute Nestonian monks until it becomes politically expedient to
dethrone Seth, is, to say the least, disconcerting. Even our
unanxious delight at the solipsistic idiocies of Lady Seal, Sir
Joseph, Sir Samson, and Dame Mildred becomes in hindsight
less morally innocent than we thought: like them we have found
safety in blinkers.

The notorious masterstroke by which Waugh removes those
blinkers after Seth's death and Prudence's disappearance is all
the more appalling for the vivid economy of his prose:

> Basil shook him violently. "Speak, you old fool. Where is the
> white woman?"
> The headman grunted and stirred; then a flicker of conscious-
> ness revived in him. He raised his head. "The white woman?
> Why, here," he patted his distended paunch. "You and I and the
> big chiefs—we have just eaten her."
> Then he slumped forward into a sound sleep.
> Round and round circled the dancers, ochre and blood and
> sweat glistening in the firelight; the wise men's headgear swayed
> above them, leopards feet and snake skins, amulets and neck-
> laces, lions' teeth and the shrivelled bodies of bats and toads,
> jigging and spinning. Tireless hands drumming out the rhythm;
> glistening backs heaving and shivering in the shadows.
> Later, a little after midnight, it began to rain.[13]

This, then, is the humanising communion from which poor Seth
tried to shield himself with the emasculating milk-and-water

liberalism of Europe. Yet it is not Seth that we have to worry about at this juncture, but Evelyn Waugh, and his ruthless pursuit of stylistic and narrative effect at the expense, apparently, of every conceivable human value. It is this which evidently upset the editor of *The Tablet*.

It has confused, if not upset, Waugh's later critics. Malcolm Bradbury praises the assured handling of 'disparate materials, tones and events' in the novel, but finds Waugh's approach so 'tangential . . . that it is difficult to find the centre of the action and be sure of the effect he is trying to produce'.[14] David Lodge, on the other hand, identifies 'dogmatic Christian anti-humanism' as the 'consistent point of view' lying 'behind Waugh's fictional world', but he sees sympathy with it – and by implication even awareness of it – as irrelevant to the reader's enjoyment of the novel's satirical comedy which he describes as 'a mosaic of local comic and satiric effects.'[15] These remarks, it seems to me, would be perfectly justified in connection with *Decline and Fall* and *Vile Bodies*, but they cannot be advanced in defence of *Black Mischief*. My reason for saying this is that the eating of Prudence is morally a different kind of event from the decapitation of Prendergast. Once Prudence has confronted, however fleetingly, the sordid implications of her affair with Basil, she has become too whole a person to fit into a mere mosaic of macabre comic effects. It is as if Waugh had killed off Peter Pastmaster instead of little Lord Tangent. Of course one doesn't expect Waugh to offer us 'a simple didactic framework' which Lodge rightly regards as unsuitable to any serious fiction, but if there is no intelligible, complex and coherent artistic purpose in *Black Mischief*, then the novel is exactly what the editor of *The Tablet* said it was, nasty, insolent and wicked. It is with trying to see it as an aesthetic and moral whole and not as a mosaic of local effects that I am at present concerned.

This can only be done if we take seriously its central preoccupation with barbarism and civilisation. It was a subject that Waugh repeatedly returned to. One of his favourite images is of civilised society under siege. In *Helena* Constantius sees the imperial frontiers in just such terms: 'inside, peace, decency, the law, the altars of the Gods, industry, the arts, order; outside, wild beasts and savages, forest and swamp, bloody mumbo-jumbo, men like wolf-packs'[16]. The whole framework of Waugh's political ideas is founded on a basic commitment to reason and order, from which even religion could benefit. While recognising the sacramental validity of the Coptic liturgy, he found its huddled and befuddled mystery-mongering distasteful: he preferred 'the great open altars of Catholic Europe' which he saw as 'a great positive achievement . . . consciously accomplished'.[17] And he knew civilisation was vulnerable: 'the anarchic elements in society' called for strong government.[18] But the divisions between savage and civilised was not simple. In *Edmund Campion* he praises the saintly rule of Pope Pius V, yet notes that during his reign prostitutes were 'turned loose on the Campagna to be massacred by bandits',[19] and when Campion goes to Dublin, the siege image is interestingly reversed: 'the cosy colonial world of the Pale' is surrounded by 'the tumultuous tribal life of the Irish people',[20] yet it is the latter, not the former, who will remain faithful to 'the great open altars of Catholic Europe'. As Lodge rightly emphasises, 'in Waugh's historical scheme there is no point at which all was right with the world'.[21] Bradbury argues, also correctly, that in Waugh's work 'anarchy has to triumph, for its persistence is the real basis of faith'.[22] His conservatism therefore can never hope for outright victory.

> A conservative [he wrote] . . . has positive work to do. Civilization . . . is under constant assault and it takes most of the energies of civilized man to keep it going at all . . . . Barbarism is never finally defeated; . . . men and women who seem quite orderly, will commit every conceivable atrocity . . . . we are all potential recruits for anarchy . . . . Once the prisons of the mind have been opened, the orgy is on. There is no more agreeable position than that of the dissident from a stable society. There are all the solid advantages of other people's creation and preservation, and all the fun of detecting hypocrisies and inconsistencies.[23]

This is an important statement. Waugh is evidently and consciously describing himself when he writes of the dissident as well as of the conservative. Indeed he changes sides emotionally even as he writes and becomes himself virtually a fifth columnist for anarchy at the heart of civilisation. The siege image is transformed. There are enemies within as well as without.

Exactly the same tensions can be seen in what he has to say about art and artists. Again his starting points are reason and order. His preference is for the artist who approaches his work deliberately and dispassionately, even if this involves him in apparent superficiality. Novels, he wrote in 1962, are 'mere shadows compared with the real world',[24] but shadows sufficed him. He saw the world of the pre-war novels as an 'absurd little humble of antagonising forces', and he set out to record it with no more than the scrappy, half-educated 'sense of period' which he shared with his contemporaries.[25] But he believed that 'superficial acquaintance' was 'one of the materials of the writer's trade',[26] the artist responded to 'the amorphous, haphazard condition in which life presents experience' like a carpenter who wants to put 'a rough piece of timber' into shape.[27] Like Constantius in *Helena* he preferred 'representational work' which exhibited 'technical virtuosity' rather than 'vision';[28] and, like Charles Ryder in *Brideshead Revisited*, he thought modern art was 'bosh'.[29]

But, as in society, so in the art-work, there is an enemy within. In *Work Suspended*, the narrator uses the siege metaphor to describe his reactions to his father's death. He confesses to having relied on conventional phrases to control his emotions, but he concedes that such 'dependence on verbal forms . . . saves us nothing in the end'. Feelings use words as a disguise; they dress themselves in 'the livery of the defence . . . [they] pass through the lines; . . . [and] there is always a Fifth Column among the garrison ready to receive them . . . – that is how the civilised man is undone'.[30] This takes us to the centre of Waugh's conception of his own work. In 1946, he made the famous and surprising declaration that he was not a satirist. Satire, he maintained, needed a society with 'homogeneous moral standards'.[31] This statement helps to define his literary ancestry. It places him among writers like Swift, Thackeray and Shaw, who all achieved considerable rapport as entertainers with a very large public, but who felt, like Waugh, morally estranged from the world that applauded them. Such writers use their gift to lure the reader into what promises to be a relatively irresponsible and undemanding game with deliberately superficial, though obviously witty, descriptions of the human situation; but they know the game will go wrong, that witty, verbal strategies, apparently designed to protect the civilised man from being undone, invite infiltration and betrayal by dangerous emotions. They know also, precisely because the world lacks 'homogeneous moral standards', that every man's breaking point in this process is different. A harmless superficial game with words thus becomes a contest between author and reader to see who can bear the most reality. The art of Evelyn Waugh is not one of representation but of confrontation. Whether it should be called satirical or not is irrelevant. It is based on the universal capacity of men to use reason to open up the prisons of the mind.

As in politics and art, so in religion Waugh's starting point is an apparently impregnable logical rigour. According to Fr. D'Arcy he was a remarkably cool convert. At 'the root of all Catholic apologetics' he observed in *Edmund Campion* is the claim 'that the faith is absolutely satisfactory to the mind'.[32] All Catholics felt assured, he wrote later, that there were grounds 'in logic and in historical evidence . . . for accepting the Church',[33] and he was confident also that 'the clarity of Western reason' had made theology 'intelligible and exact'.[34] He sometimes gives the impression that just as he was attracted to the novel because it was like cabinet-making, so he was attracted to the life of Christ simply because it happened 'at a particular geographical place, as a matter of plain historical fact'.[35] Certainly *Helena* is explicitly about 'the opposed faces of history and myth'.[36] But there is an enemy within in religion, as in society and literature. The historical is constantly yielding to the mythical as the wild proliferation of relics in Helena's baggage illustrates. Reason too has its limitations: it is the heretics after all who want to make the doctrine of the Trinity intelligible and exact, while the philistine Western bishops are rightly content simply to declare it a mystery 'as if that explained everything'[37]. 'Oh books' Helena exclaims – with justified impatience,[38] since, as Pope Sylvester remarks, 'Nothing stands to reason with God.'[39]

The standing of reason is especially problematical in the field of ethics. Again Waugh's starting point is uncompromisingly rational. Without reason, in his view there can be no true acts of the will. True mortal sin, for instance, requires, in addition to grave matter, a clear sense of the consequences of acting and a freedom from all compulsion, internal or external, to do so. 'I hope it is dipsomania' Brideshead remarks of Sebastian's drinking in *Brideshead Revisited*[40], humanly an appalling remark, but logical if sin really is more serious than sickness. The same logic applies to the forgiveness of sin. The penitent has to recall and judge his actions, confess them exactly, and repudiate them from clear and appropriate religious motives. Moral responsibility is thus predicated on man's capacity to know and obey an objective, rationally comprehensible moral law. Hence Waugh's hatred of psychoanalysis which challenged the concept of clearly motivated and responsible choices. Yet he also knew that Brideshead's rigorous logic was absurd, that men sin like men not like angels, and as men are forgiven. 'The Church', Pope Sylvester remarks in *Helena*, 'isn't a cult for a few heroes. It is the whole of fallen mankind redeemed'.[41] The average penitent, Waugh observes in the next chapter, does not examine his conscience scientifically; he notes 'merely the few big fishes' and blurts out 'an emotional inaccurate tale of self-reproach'.[42] This is inevitable since the whole of fallen mankind redeemed includes 'the barrowman . . . the fuller . . . the lawyer [and] the lawyer's clerk', as well as Helena herself.[43] The central Christian doctrine of the Redemption calls in question, therefore, much that Waugh cherishes, class differences, clear thought, responsible action, even the claim of civilisation to be superior to savagery. There were two enemies within – Barbarism and the Forgiveness of God. The Christian who loves order – and he must if he loves the moral law – has to cope with both.

These were not a set of neatly ironic dialectical ambivalences for Waugh. 'The novelist', he wrote in the Preface to *Helena*, 'deals with experiences which excite his imagination' and much of what he found exciting he knew to be ugly and unlawful. He had been an active homosexual; between his marriages he fornicated freely; he was an appalling bully, a drunkard and a snob. Equally integral to his personality, of course, were his love of order, friendship, reason, good workmanship, honour and purity of life. He was in fact at odds with himself temperamentally to an extreme degree, just as he was at odds with the values and beliefs of most of his contemporaries; and certain issues seem to have made him acutely aware of the tensions and contradictions inside himself. Of these one of the most potent was racialism.

Waugh was never a racialist in principle. In *Labels* he pointedly fails to read Spengler and he deplores the attitude of his English hosts in Port Said to the 'gyppies'. In *Robbery under Law* there is an especially scornful attack on a notably racialist sneer at Mexican Catholicism. Both his reason and his religion demanded racial tolerance. Nevertheless he was evidently excited by racialist vocabulary, by racial dominance and subservience, by barbaric insolence and cruelty. In Paris in 1925 he hoped to watch a boy 'dressed as an Egyptian woman' being 'enjoyed by a large negro'.[44]

He liked to savour native life in brothels; in *Labels*, he writes of 'a stud of negroes' repopulating Portugal after the earthquake.[45] There is 'a fascination', he wrote elsewhere, 'in distant lands and barbarous places, and in particular in the borderlands of conflicting cultures and states of development'.[46] At times, the fascination seems to have had a strong erotic charge; yet it was on this dangerous compromising ground that he chose to confront his new co-religionists and his old liberal enemies almost immediately after his conversion.

One explanation for this is that he simply wished to demonstrate with studied impiety that he was not going to allow his comic gift to be sanctimoniously diluted by the Church. Yet the celebrated young literary lion's sudden conversion after a sudden divorce remains even now a potent factor in one's reading of his book. Waugh must have calculated on the reader's need to understand how laughter of such an intimidating kind on issues as emotionally charged as those of race and cannibalism could be reconciled with Christian values and perspectives, but he airily refuses to explain. Part of the book's potency, indeed, is this relentless holding of his religion in reserve. In this he is remarkably unlike Graham Greene. The novel's triumph is that it refuses to be didactic; but if it lacks an ideological framework, it has none the less a powerful unifying principle. Waugh is doing nothing less than putting himself on record, his fascination with nudity and barbarity, his urbanity, cynicism and graceful selfishness; his preoccupation with anarchy and death; his love of order, verbal elegance, structural deftness, his capacity for complex and humiliating feelings of envy and lust; his moral sensitivity and respect for innocence; his cold-heartedness; his exact sense of moral principle; and his utterly unprincipled capacity for cruel glee. A perversely negative capability of being in the midst of flagrant contradictions without reaching inelegantly towards ways of resolving them, of being shamelessly and wittily in need of redemption, is what constitutes his challenge to the reader of *Black Mischief*. Waugh had lived with contradiction for long enough. It fuelled his art. Part of the fascination of *Decline and Fall* is that in so elegantly formed a work, one of its main characters should have his head *sawn* off. What Catholicism gave Waugh, however, was the certainty that such contradictions were not freakish, but built into the eternal scheme of things. God affirmed reason, order, authority and choice – and He forgave worldlings, adventurers, racists, cannibals and fools. There was no need for men to hide their natures from themselves or each other. Evelyn Waugh, at any rate, was quite unwilling to do so.

Black Mischief marks a decisive advance in his progress as an artist because it has a coherence and seriousness qualitatively different from its two predecessors. It is not a 'Catholic' work, but its power and purpose are intimately connected with that sense of himself and of fallen mankind redeemed which the Church gave him. I find it a brave book, and I think it wrong-headed of Malcolm Bradbury to suggest that 'Waugh's Catholicism [was] not big enough to contain the world'.[47] Waugh was not the kind of artist to try to 'contain' anything. But by careful and economic allusion he did take moral and aesthetic bearings on the extremes of worldly experience. In this, he had an inclusiveness and courage comparable with Swift's.

NOTES

1 Christopher Sykes, *Evelyn Waugh. A Biography* (1975), p. 87.
2 Frederick J. Stopp, *Evelyn Waugh. Portrait of an Artist* (1958), p. 67.
3 *Decline and Fall*, 3, iv.
4 *Vile Bodies*, ch. 8.
5 *Decline and Fall*, 2, vi.
6 *Black Mischief*, ch. 5.
7 *Ibid.* ch. 1.
8 *Ibid.* ch. 8.
9 *Ibid.* ch. 1.
10 *Ibid.* ch. 3
11 *Ibid.* ch. 5.
12 Quoted by Stopp, p. 32.
13 *Black Mischief*, ch. 7.
14 Malcolm Bradbury, *Evelyn Waugh* (Writers and Critics, 1964), p. 55.
15 David Lodge, *Evelyn Waugh* (Columbia Essays on Modern Writers, 1971), p. 12.
16 *Helena*, ch. 3.
17 *Remote People* (1931), pp. 88-89.
18 *Robbery under Law* (1939), p. 17.
19 *Edmund Campion* (Penguin Books ed., 1953), p. 55.
20 *Ibid.* p. 34.

21 David Lodge, *Evelyn Waugh*, p.8.
22 Malcolm Bradbury, *Evelyn Waugh,* p. 13.
23 *Robbery under Law,* pp. 278-9.
24 'Evelyn Waugh's Private Diaries', *The Observer Magazine* (13 May 1973), p. 50.
25 *Labels* (1930), p. 40.
26 *Robbery under Law,* p. 1.
27 *Ninety-Two Days* (1934), p. 13.
28 *Helena,* ch. 8.
29 *Brideshead Revisited,* 1, 6.
30 *Work Suspended,* 1, 4.
31 'Fan-Fare', *Life* (6 April 1946), p. 60.
32 *Edmund Campion,* p. 101.
33 *Robbery under Law,* p. 207.
34 *Remote People,* p. 85.
35 *The Holy Places* (1952), p. 12.
36 *Helena,* ch. 10.
37 *Ibid.* ch. 8.
38 *Ibid.* ch. 5.
39 *Ibid.* ch. 8.
40 *Brideshead Revisited,* 1, 6.
41 *Helena,* ch. 9.
42 *Ibid.* ch. 10.
43 *Ibid.* ch. 8.
44 'Private Diaries', *The Observer Magazine* (1 April 1973), pp. 26 and 29.
45 *Labels,* p. 203.
46 *Ninety-Two Days,* p. 13.
47 Malcolm Bradbury, *Evelyn Waugh,* p .13.

The Saloon Bar Society: Patrick Hamilton's Fiction in the 1930s

P. J. *Widdowson*

As with most 'thirties writers', Patrick Hamilton's work begins to appear in the 'twenties and continues into the 'forties and 'fifties. Nevertheless, the timbre of his writing is indelibly of the inter-war years,[1] and his best works are certainly those of the late 'thirties. Hamilton, like so many others of his generation, registers in the private, personal crises of individuals and small groups, the inner stagnation and decay of his own class in the twentieth century, and its responsibility for the hag-ridden condition of contemporary civilisation. Just as the airless and corrupt orthodoxy of middle-class families and attitudes, the sickening stench of decaying genteel, incubates the individual neurosis, so, cumulatively, it is seen to engender the public crisis. Such a metaphorical correlation informs the early poems of Auden, the early fiction of Edward Upward, the seedy world of Graham Greene's novels, the obsessed tone of Orwell's *Coming Up for Air* and *Keep the Aspidistra Flying*, and Christopher Isherwood's early novels of a private hell. And Patrick Hamilton, almost totally disregarded now,[2] also offers ingress to the physical and mental landscape of that ugly and neurotic world.

Hamilton was both novelist and playwright – best known, in fact, for his theatrical thrillers *Rope* (1929) and *Gaslight* (or *Angel Street*) (1939). The focus of this essay, however, is on his novels and especially *Hangover Square*, set in the context of other fiction in the 'thirties. In particular, I want to suggest that Hamilton, at his best, does for pre-war England what Isherwood's 'Berlin' novels do for Germany. Hamilton, like Isherwood, can at times reveal the meaning of ostensibly trivial lives.

* * *

The world of Hamilton's books is enclosed within a radius of roughly fifty miles of London. It is composed mainly of interiors: of guest-houses, boarding-houses, Lyons cafés, cheap hotel rooms, and, pre-eminently, of pubs. Think of Hamilton's work and one thinks of dingy saloon-bars in Earls Court or of mock-Tudor roadhouses on arterial roads in the Home Counties. The atmosphere is obsessively drink-laden: the preoccupation with opening-time, with the *mores* of drinking, with the drinkers themselves; the warmth and ephemeral security of the pub ambience, the wild euphoria of drunkenness, the sick depression of the hangover; the bottle on the mantelpiece, the bottle in the suitcase, the bottle in the wardrobe, the first drink of the day. Alcohol is the symptom, the motif, in Hamilton's world, of the personal crisis, of irresponsibility, of failure, of fear and break-down, of an inability to cope with the world, and of decline and inadequacy. Occasionally, it transcends itself and becomes a metaphor for some wider malaise. This drunken, deracinate world is peopled by a curiously homogeneous set of characters: weak young men of good family who have a small legacy or an indulgent mother, viciously attractive and amoral women who prey on their dog-like adorers, minor-public-schoolboys who have become brutal young men, ex-First World War officers – more or less bogus, 'resting' actors and actresses, failed writers, old Edwardians who have survived into the alien, servantless, world of the 1920s and 1930s, brash and prosperous commercial men, and all those failing members of the middle class from whom 'gentility' remains a principle without substance – if indeed it ever had any. It is a shabby, depressed world, often depicted in raw, wet weather, but with sporadic excursions into the bright, cold, exhilaration of winter days in the country or by the sea – precarious moments of vitality and freshness which actually deepen the smoke-filled alcoholic misery of the pervasive interior fug. Little of any overt significance happens here: people do their jobs if they have them and return to bleak rooms and uncom-fortable meals in their boarding-houses; they wait for people – who usually fail to turn up – on cold city corners; they arrange abortive jaunts to Brighton or drive very fast in open motors; and always there are the endless rounds of drinks.

To write about these novels as I have done here may seem to suggest that they approach caricature. And indeed, although that would not be the whole truth, it is not entirely unfair. Hamilton is concerned with a particular milieu, which begins to take on a mythic status all its own. And his manner of presenting it is imbued with strong elements of caricature. This is overt in the fantasy *Impromptu in Moribundia* (1939), but it is also apparent in the inescapably Dickensian manner of an early novel like *Craven House* (1926), and in later works like *The Slaves of Solitude*

(1947) or the 'Mr Gorse' novels of the early 'fifties. Generally, however, it is floated in a realistic medium of sharply-observed gesture
and scene, reinforced by a brilliant ear for dialogue. One is persuaded that the scenes and characters have solid and credible
existence, are not merely hackneyed type-images or caricatures.
Indeed, at its best, the depressed world of Hamilton's books bears
down on one with a force and actuality that is hard to evade. And
it is precisely in the pressure exerted by his synthetic form, I
suggest, that the 'mythic' import or the resonance of his decayed
and insignificant-seeming enclave is located.

In his ambivalence of modes – between the empirically
observed and the self-consciously fictive – Hamilton also proves
to be a man of his period. So many of the younger novelists of the
'thirties evince a similar irresolution about form, oscillating
between the realistic depiction of the palpable world and the
fabulation of contrived worlds, the use of fable, allegory, satire
and the dystopia. The pressure to expand the novel form seems
to represent an attempt, not, as the modernists had done, to
penetrate and express the shifting inner realms of individual
consciousness as a way of comprehending the world, but to find a
strategy for commenting directly on the large forces and movements of society that form and control the individuals in it. A
primary concern with the large-scale and more abstractly defined
factors of twentieth-century existence is likely to lead either to
the boldly-simple outline of the fable and cartoon, or to a type of
realism in which such forces are located solidly and specifically in
particular, 'real', social situations while still retaining their status
and integrity. We can see the oscillation – or the conflict – in
much of the work of the period: in the fantasies and allegories of
Upward's *Railway Accident* and *Journey to the Border*; in
Wyndham Lewis's 'externalist' satire in *The Revenge for Love*
and *The Vulgar Streak;* in Rex Warner's allegories; in Aldous
Huxley's progression to the pure novel of ideas or the dystopia of
Brave New World; in the uncertainty of Orwell's fiction in the
late 'thirties, and its resolution in the fabular *Animal Farm* and
1984. Nevertheless, despite – indeed because of – these uncertainties and experiments, there remains an insistent residual
sense of the novel trying to regain a direct engagement with the
crucial public issues of its time: in the painstaking attempts at
accurate reporting, in the powerful flights of allegory and fable –
and in the tensions between them. Any reconciliation of these

approaches, in the English fiction of the 1930s, lies in the work of Greene, Isherwood and, I would claim, Patrick Hamilton's *Hangover Square*, where a particular focus and a particular manner create a circumscribed but resonant metaphor for the larger issues. And while their novels, admittedly, offer no positive vision for the future, they nevertheless look inwards only to reveal the sickness of the world out there. There is an interesting passage in Hamilton's *Impromptu in Moribundia* where he attacks the modernistic literature of 'Moribundia' (England); (amongst others, he refers to Toile, S.T., Ecyoj, Yelxuh and Esnerwal!):

> they are for the most part hopelessly and morbidly turned in upon themselves, and sterile in consequence. But where else are they to turn save upon themselves? In a world which is unchangeable and inexpandable, where is there to gaze save inwards? . . . . Obviously, in doing so, they must become self-conscious to an ever more tormented degree, and paralysed for effective action accordingly. Finally, a stage must be reached when the mind can only look at ever-receding reaches of the mind, and an art on the border line of madness or idiocy must be reached . . . .
>
> For these reasons art, literature, and poetry in Moribundia take on a more and more painfully subjective aspect, more and more the character of meaningless masturbation, there being no future which they can fertilize.[3]

This is interesting if only because it indicates the slant of Hamilton's thinking about literature in the late 'thirties. One might argue, of course, that the obsession with drink and the depressed mentality of most of his characters is only one more example of such futile introspection. But it is possible to retort, I think, that the obsession and the consciousness *in themselves* are not of principal interest – only insofar as they express or reveal a public condition. Hamilton's novels, modulating from the simple denotative manner of *Twenty Thousand Streets Under the Sky* (1935) to the uncompromisingly fabular in *Impromptu in Moribundia*, and reaching synthesis in *Hangover Square*, represent an attempt to locate the crisis of his period in a fully-realised and convincing fictional world.

*   *   *

Craven House (1926) is a very remarkable early novel. Like Isherwood's *The Memorial*, it spans the First World War,

beginning in the mellow years of Edwardian security and ending
in the middle 'twenties, and it too is concerned to place responsibility for the war and the post-war society with the middle
classes. Although the sense of the parents' liability for the
crippled lives of the younger generation is less bitter than in *The
Memorial*, the heroine, Elsie, is only just rescued from the
ferocious cleanliness of her mother's moral piety, and, by the end,
Craven House has been revealed as the hollow sham it is. The
house, which takes paying-guests of the phoney or decayed
genteel variety (under the patina of 'friendship'), is a microcosm
of middle-class England – a sort of symbolic reverse of what
Forster's house, Howards End, represents. And indeed, one may
read the whole book in such allegoric terms: the movement from
Edwardian security to post-war break-up; the house passive,
unchanging, apparently secure until the final smash; the various
characters acting out aspects of the middle-class way of life –
snobbery, insensitivity, prudery, hidden sexuality, cowardice,
moral flaccidity, prejudice, complacence, under the skin of genteel
correctitude; the lower orders (the domestics) in the basement –
lumpen, but increasingly less 'manageable' as time passes; the two
principal young people struggling to maturity in, and finally
rebelling against, the potent but insubstantial repressiveness of
the past. It is a deeply schematic book, and the Dickensian
manner of the narration reinforces this. Hamilton draws with a
heavy line and an overt and inescapable irony:

> Mr Spicer returned to domesticity with a quantity of Little
> Stories (touching or otherwise); a vivid and unutterable sense of
> the lurid bestiality of his short experience in France, but no sense
> whatever of it being in any way other than righteous, seemly,
> eternal, and cumulatively expressive of the highest glories
> achievable by men.[4]

But Hamilton's intrusive manner is by no means ineffective. It
is, in fact, the art of caricature at its best, where the *features* of
the victim are extrapolated:

> Mr Spicer soon began to peer to the extent of downright Nosi-
> ness: that his peering was directed towards the numerous young
> ladies seated, with crossed legs, upon the chairs lining these
> avenues: that the difficulties arising from an attempt to combine
> (1) the intense function of peering sideways, with (2) the perfectly
> nonchalant function of strolling forwards, reduced Mr Spicer's
> stride to something uncommonly resembling the crab's.[5]

E

The observed characteristics of a character or scene are exaggerated and reified by the narrative manner, so that their *meaning*, rather than their being, is revealed.

Nevertheless, in this early work, where so many of Hamilton's characteristic gestures are apparent, and despite his chill revelation of the middle class's inner obliquity and dangerous power, the tone remains relatively light-hearted and there is a happy ending. The young people escape, and step into a world which has the potential for action and happiness. There is an interesting ambiguity here, since the unwholesome stagnation and fecklessness of Craven House/England is strong enough in the texture of the novel to suggest that logically they should be trapped and crippled. But at this point – for Hamilton writing in the mid-'twenties – the middle-class malaise can still be thwarted by youth and hope. In this respect, the novel may accurately enact the ambivalent stance of Hamilton's generation, with its sense of two presents and two futures locked in tense irresolution: promise and rebuilding or decay and disaster. By the mid-'thirties that ambivalence had passed.

There are two points about *Craven House* I wish to emphasise. Firstly, that Hamilton had already identified the moribund middle-class world-view as his focus; and secondly that he was developing a particular manner for presenting it. *Craven House* is in no sense a descriptive novel, and in the end it is not really concerned with the *mores* of the middle class in themselves. It is what they mean, rather than what they are, which interests him, and they are already perceived and treated as symptomatic, as metaphors of social dissolution. And yet, at the same time, they have a particular and recognisable social existence. Hamilton's manner, here, is a good instance of what one might call 'interpretative' or 'synthetic' realism. And in it one can feel the pressure – present in all his work – to find a way of making the decadent middle class enact, in the actual forms of their individual, day-to-day, social being, their own quintessence and their own responsibility for the world they have made. It was a question of where to put the emphasis in the manner of presentation.

Twenty Thousand Streets Under the Sky, A London Trilogy (1935)[6] represents one approach, and, for a large book which is clearly intended to establish a solid and extensive image of the loneliness at the centre of London in the post-war years, an unsuccessful one. Made up of the interlocking stories of three young people – Bob, the barman, Jenny, the prostitute, and Ella, the barmaid – the novels are composed of an unfocused 'realism' and authorial commentary. Parts of them evince Hamilton's characteristic virtues: vivid dialogue and speech gestures, fine grotesquerie of characterisation (Ella's appalling lover, Ernest Eccles, in the third volume for example), and occasionally the suffocating decay of the Edwardian household lingering on into the new world of the 'twenties (the house in which Jenny goes into service in the second volume). But generally the texture of these novels is impoverished; and it is precisely in the absence of a rich and enveloping atmosphere that their weakness lies. The pub, for example, the 'Midnight Bell', which should be a focal image of a non-home in the wastes of London, of a phoney warmth and security, remains no more than a punctiliously observed pub. The crux of this failure lies in the modes of narration Hamilton employs. The bare utilitarian prose, the literal descriptiveness, and the author's 'wise' voice *telling* us what it all signifies, straining to reveal the diagnostic of loneliness in modern urban society, fail to create the concrete, self-supporting 'world' which can imply the pervasiveness of a particular symptom. These novels stick at the individual and the specific; the stories seem inconsequential; and the author's voice, with little support from its own fictional world, merely remains one individual's voice with an observation to make, pointing up significances we cannot verify:

> In all the teeming, roaring, grinding, belching, hooting, anxious-faced world of cement and wheels around her it really seemed as though things had gone too far. It seemed as though some climax had just been reached, that civilisation was riding for a fall, that these days were certainly the last days of London, and that other dusks must soon gleam upon the broken chaos which must replace it.[7]

This passage is neither securely enough lodged in the character to be dramatised consciousness, nor so reinforced by the world created in the texture of the book that it becomes the focus of many analogous rays. It is merely a strained and arbitrary deduction.

Perhaps it is because Hamilton's characters in this novel are the victims of society, rather than responsible for it, which leaves them as instances rather than representatives. But there is no doubt that Hamilton's reliance on reportage and commentary is more culpable for the ultimate inconsequentiality of these novels. It is possibly significant that here even drinking – Hamilton's most suggestive expanding metaphor – fails to transcend the jottings, precise and detailed as they are, of an individual who spends much time in its vicinity and therefore believes that it contains, intrinsically, a common metaphorical significance. In *Twenty Thousand Streets* . . . the bottle of Haig in the suitcase means alcoholism. Nothing more.

A diametrically different approach is employed in the highly-amusing, and even less well-known, *Impromptu in Moribundia*, a fantasy or dystopia published in 1939. This is a significant novel for two reasons: firstly because it lays on the table Hamilton's conviction that in the stagnancy and stupidity of the English middle-class way of life resides the sickness of his society; and secondly because it employs an uncompromisingly fabular mode to expose it. Hamilton's brilliant strategy in this book is simply to make his fictive Moribundia an enactment of the stereotypes and myths of the English middle-class culture and consciousness. Hence the visitor from 'Earth', on his arrival in Moribundia, finds himself actually watching the cricket-match from Henry Newbolt's poem 'Clifton Chapel'. And the apparently confused chronology is no accident – the Edwardian ethos, for Hamilton, still informs society in the 'thirties and is central to its sickness. Thus, 'Moribundia'. During the course of his visit, the narrator experiences most aspects of the Moribundian life, continually expressing his 'surprise' at their difference from their English counterparts. Different they may appear – inasmuch as the images, pre-conceptions and tacit assumptions of the English middle class are here the reality – but in fact they are a *literal* enacting of its 'mind'. This is

> the land in which the ideals and ideas of our world, the striving
> and subconscious wishes of our time, the fictions and figments of
> our imagination, are calm, cold actualities.[8]

Moribundians are so conditioned that they generally think and talk in the clichés of popular and mass expression – hence the incidence (one of Hamilton's great comic inventions) of 'balloon-ing':[9] which means that in the middle of a conversation a balloon will automatically appear out of the top of a Moribundian's head in which are inscribed the words of an advertisement of the 'Thinks' variety. In addition, the inhabitants are often reified into the images of popular culture: people walk down the road with dripping taps in place of noses, or, if suffering from indigestion, with little devils scrabbling round their waists poking them with forked instruments; husbands and wives out shopping *become* the amazonian viragos and diminutive hen-pecked males of the comic picture-postcard, just as drunken men are invariably in evening dress, hiccough, cling to lamp-posts, have bright red noses, pronounce all their 's's' as 'sh's', and are observed by amiable policemen. More seriously, the vast mass of the population is composed of two groups which exist exactly in terms of their type image. Firstly there are the working classes who think and act just as the middle class (through its press) believes they think and act:

> the Moribundian working man is utterly happy and contented, and this in spite of the fact that Moribundians admit, in fact *insist*, that he is 'always grumbling' . . . . [But] this 'grumbling' is merely a charming affectation on the working man's part, by which he attempts to screen, but actually reveals his inner feelings. He grumbles in the same way as one might growl at a child one loved, in excess of affection.[10]

In this world, the working classes *do* buy new grand pianos every week and smash them up for firewood, they *do* keep coal in the bath, and they do know their place:

> 'It's no good, there's nothing to be done about us. We're hopeless. We don't even try. Things aren't what they used to be. Why, in my grandfather's day a man was proud to do a job of work . . . . You don't get that nowadays. All we think of to-day is how we can *avoid* work—how we can scamp a job and get more money for it . . . . We're thoroughly spoiled, that's what the matter is. Look at all these modern luxuries . . . .' etc.[11]

The other group are the 'little men', all identically little, bowler-hatted and be-suited, who are the self-appointed guardians of the moral law of society. In a frightening scene at the end of the novel, a mob of 'little men' hounds the narrator out of Moribundia for contravening its small-minded, petit-bourgeois code:

> Instead of the harmless, helpless, friendly, tolerant, duty-doing little business men . . . I saw cupidity, ignorance, complacence, meanness, ugliness, short-sightedness, cowardice, credulity, hy-

steria and, when the occasion called for it , . . . cruelty and blood-thirstiness. I saw the shrewd and despicable cash basis underlying that idiotic patriotism, and a deathly fear and hatred of innovation . . . .[12]

In addition to such grotesque expressions of the stereotypes of middle-class consciousness are deftly-handled exposures of the Moribundian ideology. The key concept here is 'Unchange'. Moribundia (and, it must never be forgotten, England in the 'thirties) 'was ideal because it could not change: it could not change because it was ideal'.[13] Its science, religion, politics and culture, all reinforce this idea. (These sections are fine parodies of contemporary attitudes and developments.) Politically, of course, this means that anything which envisages change is anathema; hence the 'tsinummoc' and the 'tsixram' are Moribundia's sworn enemies, and 'Ehtteivosnoinu' is its Hell.[14] There is also a mordant section on the Moribundian ability to emasculate its critics and opponents by indulging them as spoilt pets or by corrupting them with its own values: Shaw, Wells, trades unionists and communist agitators are variously implicated here. The final cumulative image is that of a society which is literally acting out the world-view of the English middle class, an ideal society in which 'Unchange' – mental and physical – is its diagnostic, and in which the narrator feels an 'insidious sort of despair . . . the feeling as that of being *half-dead*'[15].

Hamilton's use of the satirical fable is perhaps pre-figured in the bold caricatures of *Craven House*; but in between comes the Priestleyan 'realism' of *Twenty Thousand Streets* . . . , lacking precisely that resonance which a novelist concerned with connotation would demand. How, then, to make a frontal assault on a class whose 'gigantic temperamental dullness'[16] was both a protection against the oblique thrust and the centre of the very malaise the novelist wishes to expose? Other writers in the period, who saw the novel's function in its strategic social force, to propagate or pillory a system of ideas, glanced in the same direction. In the context of Hamilton's remarks (quoted earlier, p. 120) on the stagnant, self-regarding obsessions of the inward turned art of modernism, it would seem that the fable or fantasy presented itself as an outward-turned form through which to explore public issues in terms not absolutely those of the polemic. It is a useful strategy because the ostensibly comic and 'unreal' presentation helps to control the obsessive, almost hysterical, subjective response activated by loathsome values. It is a way of objectifying hatred. Furthermore, the *discrete* system of the fabular world can accommodate all the essential abuses of a system without the diffusion of effect incident on situating them in a more obviously phenomenal location. They are synthesised, synthetic. (A negative analogy is Orwell's confused and finally unconvincing attempt to combine the essential and the topically 'real' in *Keep the Aspidistra Flying*: clearly Orwell can't abide his own spokesman/anti-hero as a person, so do Comstock's pronouncements have the status they seem to be given? That Orwell later uses the fabular mode in *Animal Farm* and *1984* is not without point.) In *Impromptu in Moribundia* Hamilton identified and exposed the enemy by denuding it of its specific and multifarious forms of being and self-expression.

But for the novelist with a strong sense of the rich specificity of social behaviour, it is exactly here that the disadvantage of the dystopic fable lies. Will the fable stick? Certainly it has internal coherence – indeed *must* have – since its own type of suspended credibility lies in the fable's *donnée*, 'the willing suspension of disbelief', being consistently sustained in its texture. And the satire on 'real life' is overt. But is the point gained by shooting a sitting-duck – especially one which is purpose-built of straw, cardboard and glue? Paradoxically it is precisely in the systematic and exclusive coherence of the fabular world that its limitation lies: if the reader refuses to play ball, he can escape unscathed. And the novelist who is not primarily a polemicist will look for a mode in which he can locate the essential in the particular without apparently endangering the integrity of either. *Impromptu . . .* seems to me to be a clearing of the decks for Hamilton's finest achievement, *Hangover Square*.

* * *

Whether or not it was a strange kind of luck that allowed Hamilton to write *Hangover Square* just as the Second World War was beginning, it encapsulates his principal themes and characteristic virtues in a context which allows them to resonate. It is not too much to claim, I think, that this novel represents an equivalent achievement to Isherwood's 'Berlin' novels – although here, of course, it is London in the late 'thirties which is the symptomatic tea-table.

At its top level, *Hangover Square*[17] is a fine recreation of a small, seemingly trivial and irresponsible, world centred in Earls Court between Christmas Day 1938 and 4 September 1939. The life of its central characters is aimless, seedy and drunken:

> the wet winter nights when the door was closed; the smoke, the noise, the wet people: the agony of Netta under the electric light: Mickey drunk and Peter arguing: mornings-after on dark November days: the dart-playing and boredom: the lunch-time drunks, the lunch-time snacks, the lunch-room upstairs: the whole poisoned nightmarish circle of the idle tippler's existence.[18]

Three people are focused upon: George Harvey Bone, a 'battered boozer', big, shy, clumsy, diffident, job-less, but with a real charm and sensitivity, a gentleman adrift in an alien world who suffers from accelerating schizophrenia, his 'dumb moods', which totally disconnect him from his 'normal' personality. He has been sucked into the Earls Court world because he is deracinated and because he is obsessed by Netta Longdon. Netta is a spoilt middle-class girl, a 'resting' actress, hard, callous, careless – a bitch who exploits, and consequently despises, George. In his 'dumb moods' George realises that he has to kill Netta Longdon. Netta's closest ally is Peter, one of Hamilton's flashy 'new men' of the roadhouse and the car-salesroom. He, too, is hard and superficial; and George recognises, as the novel develops, that he must kill Peter too.

Not very much happens for most of the book: there are George's sporadic attempts to go away with Netta; occasional attempts to break free of the Earls Court life; endless drunks followed by remorseful promenades round 'hangover square'; plans by George in his 'dumb moods' to kill Netta and Peter, and then escape to Maidenhead – a dream of the past which is the still point in George's sickeningly turning world; a false attempt at the killing; and finally the killing itself, followed by a disenchanting visit to Maidenhead and suicide. Much of the novel's impact, in fact, springs from the solid sense of a sordid, futile and irresponsible world, which is conveyed as much by the cheap hotels, cornerhouses, cinemas, pubs and streets as by the sleazy self-indulgence of the characters and the drink-sodden atmosphere.

But there are other structures within the novel which expand the significance of this trivial and depressing world. One is the faint, but insistent, sense of the coming war: the references to

Munich; Peter and Netta's binge on the strength of it; and, conversely, George's sense of 'disgrace':

> He just couldn't stand Munich. Somewhere at the back of his mind it was weighing on him: it had become part of his general feeling of disgrace, of the shame in which he in particular, and the world generally, was steeped. He still couldn't get over the feeling that there was something *indecent* about it—Adolph, and Musso and Neville all grinning together, and all that aeroplane-taking and cheering on balconies.[19]

There is the occasional passing mention of Hitler and of the doom to come, out on the fringes of the focal world of Earls Court or Brighton: 'Fine for the King and Queen in Canada . . . . Fine for the West Indian Team . . . . Fine for Hitler in Czechoslovakia . . . . You couldn't believe it would ever break, that the bombs had to fall':[20] 'he wondered what it was all about – the pounding sea, the beach, the rain, the stars, the lights, the piers, Brighton, Hitler, Netta, himself, everything';[21] 'He passed the King Edward Peace statue (a fat lot of peace with Hitler about!) and walked along by the Hove lawns.'[22] Finally there is the killing of Netta and Peter with the radio simultaneously broadcasting Chamberlain's declaration of war, and George's suicide the day afterwards. It becomes apparent that this is not merely topical detail, but that there is a definite relationship between George's private tragedy and the enormous public tragedy of Europe (see the quotation above: 'he in particular, and the world generally') – a sense partly conveyed by the reiterated phrase, late in the novel, 'the summer had crashed', which at one and the same time describes the weather, refers to the deepening crisis of George's life, and catches up the impending crash of the war. But, more importantly, it is the cumulative effect of the book as a whole. Given the persistent encapsulating structure of the coincidence of the public and private catastrophes, the nature of the main characters, and the relationships between them, begin to take on other dimensions, and the raddled backwater of Earls Court becomes sinister.

Peter is especially important here. He is first introduced merely as an unpleasant type with his 'nasty fair face, with its nasty fair "guardsman's" moustache'.[23] Gradually these features begin to take on a sullen significance of their own (like Carker's teeth in *Dombey and Son*); they define a type – just as his habitual grey

E*

check trousers and polo-neck sweaters become a 'uniform', and
Peter, 'a scornful, ultra-masculine man who desired to single
himself out from the herd and wear a "uniform" '.[24] At the same
time he is more precisely located in the culture of his period: he
exudes the atmosphere 'of Great Portland Street, of transactions
with secondhand cars, of dubious deals with men, of persuasions
in public houses, borrowings and post-dated cheques'.[25] But this
recognisable Hamilton 'type' is given a further dimension in
Hangover Square: much earlier, in a passing reflection on the
Munich binge, George thinks: 'They *liked* Hitler, really. They
didn't hate him, anyway. They liked Musso, too. And how they
cheered old Umbrella! Oh yes, it was their cup of tea all right
was Munich . . . . (Peter, of course, *was* a fascist, or had been at
one time—used to go about Chelsea in a uniform.)'[26] 'They', of
course, are part of the 'disgrace' George feels in the world and in
himself. By the middle of the book, we know that Peter has been
in jail twice, once for assaulting and wounding 'a certain left-
winger' at a political meeting, and once for killing a pedestrian
while driving under the influence (a recurrent motif of Hamilton's
– always the same general type driving).[27] By the end of the book
he is referred to simply as 'the blond fascist'.[28] Clearly this type
of 'new man' is Hamilton's type of the English fascist also. I will
return to this in a moment, having first glanced at Netta – for
she is implicated, and it is she more than Peter who relates to
George Harvey Bone and his destruction.

Netta is a spoilt-middle-class girl: 'he could see her as she
must have grown up, encouraged in her insolence, hardness and
tyranny by the power of her beauty and the slavishness in others
it inspired: he could see her later, with a cold decision to exploit
this power to the full in a material way'.[29] George, of course, is
one of the slavish ones who underwrite her materialistic careless-
ness. Netta is a product of the inter-war years – the 'waves' she
sends out are, pointedly, those of 'a small amateur wireless
station'[30] – and George is significantly both attracted and repelled
by her. Emancipated – but more promiscuous than free – her
values are those of a world in which human flesh is merely a
commercial proposition – the world of films, 'stardom' and the
director's couch. (Hence George's recognition that she is really
nothing but a prostitute.) Her hatred of George springs from their
difference: 'unlike herself . . . he had a curious but inerasable
streak of providence'.[31] But what makes Netta more than a simple

bitch is her relationship to Peter: George, in one of his 'dumb moods', suddenly realises that they are both part of the same evil that is destroying him: 'surely it was Netta and Peter, surely it had been Netta and Peter all along! . . . . You could no more kill Netta without killing Peter than you could kill Peter without Netta.'[32] And this leads me back to Hamilton's central statement in the novel. (It is, for once, the author's voice and not George's consciousness, and it *is* almost exactly in the middle of the novel – the Fifth Part, Chapter Four.) Netta is 'stimulated' by Peter because his acts of violence provide him with a 'halo' of 'something bloody, brutal, and unusual', and by her understanding of 'his intense, smouldering, revengeful social snobbery':

> She knew how, behind that pallid, sullen, Philip-the-Fourth-like face, his soul winced when people of the moneyed class, when titled or rich people, were merely mentioned. She knew of the horror, the diseased fury, he harboured in his heart against his own upbringing, the fact that he had not been to a mentionable public school. She knew with what a passion, behind a studied manner of indifference, he clung to each of his few contacts with what were to him the right sort of people. She knew how his political activities, his practical 'fascism' in the past, were derived from this sickly envy and passion. Banished, by reason of his birth and lack of money, from the class of which he had so fanatical a secret desire to be a member, he had not turned in anger against that class, or thrown in his lot with any other. That would have been an admission of defeat. On the contrary, he sought to glorify it, to buttress it, to romanticize it, to make it more itself than it was already—hoping thereby, in his ambitious, twisted brain, to gain some reward from it at last, have some place or even leadership in it under the intensified conditions he foresaw for it. Netta knew all this and instead of repelling her it had a decided appeal for her. This was because, in her fish-like way, she had much the same social ambitions and snobbery as he did.[33]

The forms of Netta's social snobbery are slightly different – those of the society column of *The Tatler* or *Vogue*, 'but she was all the same . . . at one with him in spirit'.

> And to this was added something else—a feeling for something which was abroad in the modern world, something hardly realized and difficult to describe, but which she knew Peter could discern as well as herself.
> This something, which she could not describe, which was probably indescribable, was something to do with those society

columns and something to do with blood, cruelty, and fascism—a blend of the two. It had the same stimulus and subtle appeal for her as the fact of Peter having been in jail. It was not the avowed ideology of fascism; she was supposed to laugh at all people who had any strong opinions of any sort. On the other hand it was, in all probability, one aspect of the ideology of fascism. She was supposed to dislike fascism, to laugh at it, but actually she liked it enormously. In secret she liked pictures of marching, regimented men, in secret she was physically attracted to Hitler: she did not really think that Mussolini looked like a funny burglar. She liked the uniforms, the guns, the breeches, the boots, the swastikas, the shirts. She was, probably, sexually stimulated by these things in the same way as she might have been sexually stimulated by a bull-fight. And somehow she was dimly aware of the class content of all this: she would have liked to have seen something of the same sort of thing in this country. She was bored to distraction by the idea of war, of course, and hence arose her glorious joy (perceived by George) at the time of Munich, when, at one stroke, war was averted and the thing which she was supposed to dislike and laugh at, but to which she was so drawn in reality, was allowed to proceed with renewed power upon its way.

It might be said that this feeling for violence and brutality, for the pageant and panorama of fascism on the Continent, formed her principal disinterested aesthetic pleasure. She had few others.[34]

It is important to emphasise one point here: a passage of this sort is unique in *Hangover Square,* and its uniqueness is a crucial aspect of its significance. Like Isherwood's very occasional breaks into public reportage in *Mr Norris Changes Trains,* this is a sudden – and easily forgotten – revelation of the wider context in which the sordid little world, disproportionately treated, exists. But it illuminates the trivial focus and imbues it with an expressiveness greater than the sum of its particularised parts. Peter and Netta are indeed symptomatic of a society which engenders the Second World War – in much the same way that Mr Norris, Fraulein Schroeder, Anni, the Nowaks, Sally Bowles, even William Bradshaw and Herr Ishyvoo, Isherwood's 'passive' observers, are responsible – as part of the corporate consciousness – for Hitler's rise to power. As individuals, of course, they are not; but as symptomatic enactments of facets of the middle-class 'mind', they very definitely are.

And what does that make George Harvey Bone? I should be careful here not to turn the novel into an unsubtle symbolic or allegoric construct: George Harvey Bone is George Harvey Bone, 'a battered boozer from Earls Court',[35] and he exists inextricably in the texture of a credible fictional world as that and no more. But part of his solid and organic existence resides in his cultural credentials. George's values are those of the past – or at least they are not those of the alien present. Despite his familiarity with the features of the post-war world – its cinemas, cornerhouses, freedoms of behaviour – George is ill-at-ease, a lonely, unrelated figure. He adores Netta, who rejects him time and again (they are 'unlike'); he drinks frantically, and hates his own improvidence; he is spending his inheritance – by indulging images of the present like Netta – and he dies literally penniless,[36] having spent up. He has a certain charm – for those who can perceive it – the charm of the pathetic and the innocent in a world which exploits and denigrates such ambiguous virtues.[37] And occasionally he has a sense of the world he has lost: it is glimpsed briefly through Johnnie (a good man from his past, who has come to terms with the modern world) – 'it was the feeling that he had a friend now . . . that *he* had a background;[38] but more importantly it appears in his 'dumb moods' when he thinks of escaping to Maidenhead, always *after he has killed* Peter and Netta. And 'Maidenhead' is described in a way that establishes it as an image of the Edwardian past:

> Maidenhead, peace, the river, an inn, a quiet glass of beer, and safety, utter safety . . . . Maidenhead, where he had been with poor Ellen, the river in the sun, in the shade of the trees, his hand in the water over the side of the boat, the sun on the ripples of the water reflected quaveringly on the side of the boat, his white flannels, tea in a basket, the gramophone, the dank smell at evening, the red sunset, sleep![39]

(It is significant that George only remembers Maidenhead in his 'dumb moods', and that he vows to abjure anything alcoholic except beer.) Rather like George Bowling in Orwell's not unsimilar, but less certainly-handled, novel, *Coming Up for Air*, George Bone wishes to return to an idyllic pre-war world (of childhood, and *therefore* idyllic, never objectively real). But to do so he has to kill Netta and Peter – the types, for better or worse, of the actual contemporary world. George, at this level, is a sympathetic instance of the 'Unchange' mentality of Moribundia. And as such, sympathetic though he may be, he is as organically responsible for his own society as Netta and Peter are – indeed his passivity, his indulgence and his abdication of responsibility fundamentally engender theirs. (Just as William Bradshaw's and Herr Ishyvoo's 'objective' detachment and sense of superiority actually contribute to the Berlin situation.) George, after all, courts and indulges Netta, tolerates Peter, and, significantly, in his 'dumb' or dream-like moods, can make no connection at all between the coming war and himself, between the personal and the public crises. His final point of breakdown only comes with the recognition (again rather like George Bowling) that 'Maidenhead' does not exist – the past, 'unchange', has no substance:

> .... Maidenhead was no good at all.
> It was just a town with shops, and newsagents, and pubs and cinemas. It wasn't, and never could be, the peace, Ellen, the river, the quiet glass of beer, the white flannels, the ripples of water reflected quaveringly on the side of the boat, the tea in the basket, the gramophone, the dank smell at evening, the red sunset, sleep . . . .
> It ought to have been, but it wasn't. He had made a mistake. In fact he could hardly recognise it. It had let him down, like Netta. But as there was no Maidenhead, there was no anywhere, and he had got rid of Netta and Peter, and now of course he must get rid of himself.[40]

And at this point, the war – partly at least a product of that 'dream' – has begun, and George kills himself, its avatar.

Three other structures or metaphors, which reinforce this pattern, remain to be explored. First of all there is the drink motif. This is a subtle example of duality of purpose: at one and the same time it defines and conveys in concrete terms the way of life of the characters, and, within the other structures we have noticed, it becomes a metaphor for the wider irresponsibility and decay of society. This is not, of course, to suggest that all pre-war England was alcoholic, merely that as the private world expands into a symptomatic correlative for society at large, so its key features expand too, and George, Peter and Netta's drinking, as an instance of the retreat from responsibility and consciousness, implies a wider malaise. This is further underpinned by George's schizophrenia which acts both as a structure and as a metaphor.

At the metaphorical level, the 'snap' in George's brain – when he recognises that he must kill Netta Longdon and return to the peace of Maidenhead – enacts the ambivalent drive towards catastrophe, and the simultaneous refusal to countenance it, which characterises the 'moribundian' society, of which George is product and representative. But it has a structural force, too. Throughout the novel, we move in and out of the different states of George's mind; but as it develops the 'dumb moods' occur more often, and it becomes increasingly difficult to decide which is George's 'normal' condition. In other words, as the killing (and the war) approach, there is an accelerating confusion between dream and reality:

> he was again beset by that nasty feeling of being in a dream . . . .
> Again he couldn't understand what all these people, none of them
> about to kill anybody, were up to, what they were getting at.
> They had no reality or motive. Nothing had any reality or
> meaning.[41]

The irony of this is obvious – 'all these people' *are* about to kill somebody: George's 'reality' and their lack of it are about to coincide in a full realisation of the 'dream'. The final 'crack' in his head occurs almost simultaneously with the outbreak of war, and George now remains in his trance-like state to the end. The repressed drive to destruction has become the reality – at both the private and the public levels; the forces of 'unchange', in their hatred of the post-First World War world, have identified and destroyed the enemy – Netta and Peter, representatives of modern society itself. George's myopia and self-destructive madness is that of Europe as a whole. And now the heart of the dream can be realised: the return to 'Maidenhead'. But, as we have seen, the dream *has* no heart, Maidenhead is 'no good at all', and that is the final smash. George's suicide note reads: ' "I thought I was right, but now I am wrong about Maidenhead, I may be wrong." '[42] And he kills himself. What the novel has enacted, then, is the reciprocal responsibility of George – the hangover from a moribund culture – and Peter and Netta – the symptoms of its final hectic activity – for the state of affairs which incubates the catastrophe of Europe. George pulls it all down.

Finally, and to emphasise the point, we may notice Hamilton's use of epigraphs from *Samson Agonistes* at the beginning of several of the novel's sections. This, it seems to me, is actually a redundant device in a book which realises both its specificity and its resonance so firmly within its texture. Nevertheless it is there, and it does point up Hamilton's awareness of his own strategy. It is less the gratuitous analogy of the big man destroyed by a woman that *Samson Agonistes* underlines, than the self-destruction implicit in the destruction of the overtly corrupt. George Harvey Bone pulls down the saloon-bar world with himself inside it – as he must, because he, ultimately, is one of the pillars which held it up. 'Maidenhead' is no more innocuous than Earls Court in Europe in 1939. Perhaps the final irony – within the *Samson* parallel – is that there is no sense of salvation, of purgation, of God's ways justified, here; there is no chorus to hymn George's triumphant self-immolation – just the Second World War, and one sensational headline as his epitaph. George and his society were 'wrong'.

Hamilton's post-war novels continue to dissect the persistent pervasiveness of middle-class decay. But they never again attain the control and resonance of *Hangover Square*. Here at least, Hamilton matches some other 'thirties novelists – Isherwood, Greene, Scott Fitzgerald in *Tender is the Night*, for example – who create myths of social decay out of the individual crisis. And his success – like theirs – resides in the solid credibility of the circumscribed and ostensibly insignificant world he makes.

NOTES

1 Even the 'Mr Gorse' novels of the early 'fifties – *The West Pier*, 1951, *Mr Stimpson and Mr Gorse*, 1953, *Unknown Assailant*, 1955, – are set back in the inter-war period.
2 Of his novels only *Hangover Square*, 1941 (Penguin, 1974) is generally available.
3 *Impromptu in Moribundia* (Constable, 1939), pp. 250-2.
4 *Craven House*, 1926 (Constable, 1948), p. 103.
5 *Ibid.* pp. 58-59.
6 The three novels are *The Midnight Bell*, 1929 (Bob's Story'); *The Siege of Pleasure*, 1932 (Jenny's Story'); and *The Plains of Cement*, 1934 (Ella's story'). They were published in one volume as *Twenty Thousand Streets Under the Sky* in 1935, with a Preface by J. B. Priestley.
7 *The Plains of Cement* (in the one-volume edition), p. 277.

8 *Impromptu in Moribundia,* p. 42.

9 'Ballooning' is physically depicted in the text of the novel. Unfortunately it is difficult to reproduce here – much of the effect is lost without it.

10 *Ibid.* p. 136.

11 *Ibid.* pp. 226-7.

12 *Ibid.* p. 284.

13 *Ibid.* p. 165.

14 *Ibid.* p. 144.

15 *Ibid.* p. 171.

16 The phrase is Arnold Bennett's in *Books and Persons.*

17 *Hangover Square* was written soon after war broke out and published in 1941. The edition used here is the Penguin edition, 1974.

18 *Ibid.* p. 103.

19 *Ibid.* p. 58.

20 *Ibid.* p. 101.

21 *Ibid.* p. 143.

22 *Ibid.* p. 169.

23 *Ibid.* p. 37.

24 *Ibid.* p. 104.

25 *Ibid.* p. 104.

26 *Ibid.* pp. 31-32.

27 It is the focus of the action in *The Siege of Pleasure* (Vol. II of *Twenty Thousand Streets* . . . .) and in the radio play, *To the Public Danger* (first broadcast, 12 February 1939, and published with *Money with Menaces* by Constable in 1939). Cole, the drunken driver in the radio play, is 'about 35, has the smooth, precise, off-hand, yet arrogant and beefy tones of a slightly second-rate ex-officer and public school-boy'. (p. 49).

28 *Ibid.* p. 273.

29 *Ibid.* p. 74.

30 *Ibid.* p. 50.

31 *Ibid.* p. 130.

32 *Ibid.* p. 168.

33 *Ibid.* p. 128.

34 *Ibid.* p. 129-30.

35 *Ibid.* p. 249.

36 *Ibid.* p. 280.

37 *Ibid.* p. 259.

38 *Ibid.* p. 121.

39 *Ibid.* p. 183.

40 *Ibid.* p. 279.

41 *Ibid.* p. 190.

42 *Ibid.* p. 280.

Total Attainder and the Helots

Arnold Rattenbury

Authors now sixty or more were once young for a while and remember the 1930s – oddly, it sometimes seems, often so flatly as to contradict avowals published at the time. Poets suppress or doctor early work. More oddly still, all memories agree where one might have expected the individual recollection to differ as, for example, in life. 'I will allow that a man may change his opinions', wrote Hazlitt of an earlier case of thinking back from now to then, 'but there is no need to pass an act of total attainder on one's past.' Nonetheless we are increasingly possessed of a condemning, flat, unlifelike orthodoxy about Thirties literature: ordinary humane concern at hideous inhumanities drove sentient English beings towards the revolutionary Left; that Left was in the grip of soul-sold communists; only to the extent that authors avoided, or later shrugged off, that grip could they blossom as truly creative and soulful. Political engagement was not with Reality but with Dream. In *The Thirties: A Dream Revolved*, writing about a necessarily damnable *Left Review*, Julian Symons puts it thus:

> The paper's editors—at first Montagu Slater, Amabel Williams-Ellis and Tom Wintringham, later Edgell Rickword and Randall Swingler—did not lack sensibility or talent, but they thought it right that this talent should be fitted into a Communist pattern. 'It is the strongest argument for a Writers' International', Slater remarked, 'that it can bring writers into touch with life. "Life", in this context, equals the class struggle.' They abdicated from their responsibilities as editors in the sense that their chief concern was not to raise the level of writing among their working-class contributors but to extirpate the heresies found among the bourgeois writers of talent who were sympathetic to Communism.

Only the art editor, James Boswell, escapes this blanket condemnation:

> It is much easier, no doubt it is, to be satirical about politicians than to show truthfully the wretched lives and narrow horizons

of the poor or to depict lyrically the advance of the masses, but the level at which the paper's black and white artists worked was a consistently high one.

At the end of his book Symons restates the central problem of the Thirties (if I understand him aright) as being how to be a revolutionary without being a revolutionary, smooths the blanket, tucks everyone up.

> Those who tried to solve the problem by subordinating their art entirely to political feeling became Communist Party helots, or like Edgell Rickword found themselves subdued to silence, or like Day Lewis produced inferior work.

All this deals neatly with those most deeply committed to political action: that is to say, one need not further examine what they actually wrote or drew, either inside or outside the covers of *Left Review*. (Of course it is possible to be more charitable – as was Frank Kermode, in a relatively friendly notice of the journal's reprint in the 1960s – but the essential orthodoxy remains. To represent the helots Kermode quotes a sloganising boilersuit poem by Sylvia Townsend Warner of 1936, but fails to mention the huge detachment of her troubled, unbigoted, questioning novel of that year, *Summer Will Show*.) With the politically committed thus tidied out of the way, one can proceed with those impelled towards revolution but not to the point of engagement; and in 1976 orthodoxy could offer such titles as Samuel Hynes's *The Auden Generation: Literature and Politics in the 1930's* or *Young Writers of the Thirties*, the National Portrait Gallery's photo-record of the five friends Auden, Isherwood, MacNeice, Spender and Day Lewis.

Auden's talents are undeniable – as they were indeed to the editors of *Left Review* – and he had friends: a group. But one group only a generation? And after all the pains he later took to disassociate himself from Time? Essentially these many forms of a single orthodoxy seem to me rubbish-founded and a-litter with lies – at least, let us say, with sherds not yet assembled into a pot that might conceivably hold water.

*   *   *

Left Review ceased publication in 1938 in a blaze of announcements about a new journal. Outside events, and large ones, intervened – the Russo-Finnish War, the Stalin-Hitler Pact, Munich, to communists a Just-or-Unjust War – and no such journal immediately appeared. So it was that awaiting call-up through 1940 and 1941 I found myself as teaboy among the helots – Montagu Slater, Randall Swingler, Nancy Cunard and James Boswell particularly – still attempting to found what was in the end to be *Our Time.* Later, my army service ended abruptly in an unlikely military skirmish in Trowbridge market square, I returned to the paper, to yet more helotry, at the end of 1943. The younger people – Swingler, Boswell – by then away at war, to the older Slater were added Edgell Rickword, Sylvia Townsend Warner, Jack Lindsay and others. All this seemed to me then, and does now, an enormous privilege and great good luck. Poetic and generally creative issues had been joined in the youth of all these elders of mine which are important to me – partly, no doubt, because the same conclusions came to form myself – but also, on the present occasion at least, because they have been so persistently misrepresented and consequently (if unwittingly) ignored by others. Such understanding, then, as I have of the Thirties and the degrees and kinds of political engagement of their authors is that of a tyro let loose among his heroes, particularly the avowedly communist among them: writers attempting to continue beyond that complex what they had done within it, not even remotely interested in disavowals or shrugging a grip. That is one sort of credential for writing as I shall. There is another.

In terms of the class privilege of that time the gulf that lies beween school and university is not the one now dug there. (Indeed in the years I am recalling the ground was quite unbroken between school, university, officers' mess and, should you live, commercial boardroom or university commonroom; and it is another piece, I suppose, of my great good fortune that I never got higher than a busted corporal.) So insofar as it is true that public-school intellectuals through the Thirties became politically engaged, engagement was a gradual thing – a matter with which Julian Symons deals witheringly and well. Schoolboy poetry was nationally published and not infrequently nationally reviewed. Notoriously the schoolboy Mortmere world of Isherwood, Upward, Auden was known to Oxford even before all its authors. Biographers often make it seem more precocious than it was that the excellent poet John Cornford joined the communist party at Stowe School, or that Churchill's nephew Esmond Romilly bolted from Wellington, by way of the Bomb Shop in Red Lion Square for the International Brigades. What would nowadays be called an underground journal in my own school naturally included articles by relatives fighting in Spain. One's poems, if one wrote them, went on ahead with other information; and when I eventually reached Cambridge I found myself already known there for so small an incident as having helped to distribute *Daily Workers* in a dormitory.

None of this is pleasant to contemplate, for it is part of a wholly nasty network system. But there it was. Part at least of intellectual engagement in the Thirties was boyish. In the particular place that incarcerated me the newer books I remember would-be authors among us clubbing together to buy were by Auden, Spender, MacNeice, Day Lewis, Idris Davies, Rex Warner, Hemingway, Djuna Barnes, Dorothy Richardson, Frederick Prokosch, William Faulkner, Arthur Calder Marshall, Henry Williamson, D. H. Lawrence, Henry Miller, Dos Passos, Carson McCullers, James Hanley, Nicholas Berdyaev, Katherine Mansfield, Richard Jefferies, James Joyce, (Eliot had achieved the school library). The Journals we read were the ones attending to such names and certainly included, for instance, the surrealist *Transition.* It was not unusual to see a crimson or orange Left Book Club cover sticking out of the ubiquitous black blazer. The older literary influences, like the new, were roughly those at work in the adult world if that can be distinguished. Helen Gardner's work on the Metaphysicals was new. *The Complete Poems of Wilfred Owen* was a new title. Gerard Manley Hopkins and Edward Thomas were being newly discovered, as were Elizabethan lyricists. And if you perceive some confusion in such a listing of pacifism, anglo-catholicism, American cosmopolitanism, surrealism, communism, nature-love, escape and the Left Book Club, then good. Presumably because of that footling dormitory incident I was, as an undergraduate, whisked straight into the communist party without the usual period of probation, and my head was full of that confusion. No-one there or among the helots at *Our Time* considered it odd that it should be.

To think of the Thirties as a decade during which by far the greater number of English intellectuals came to associate themselves with leftwing movements and that these were increasingly communist-led, seems to me, in the large loose way in which such whoppers ever can be, correct. But to distinguish between the large statement and the small, the leftwing and the communist, and to suppose that the latter were all one kind of individual, whatever is meant by that strange phrase 'basically political', possessed of a kind of identikit mind, moving in unison, addicted (if writers) to Proletkult – the notion that working class writing must always be simple and only needs tuition – is to be mad or, which is next to madness in my lexicon, Malcolm Muggeridge. Slater's phrase, 'Life, in this context, equals the class struggle', all communists would have accepted. But Symons's comments upon it – that they thought their talents 'should be fitted into a Communist pattern', that their chief concern should have been 'to raise the standard of writing among working-class contributors' and not, as he says it was, 'to extirpate bourgeois heresies' – bewilders me and must have made them laugh. They were of that time, as Symons was, or Auden. If most intellectuals were leftwing, some communist, then most of the people rediscovering Raleigh, the Silver Poets, the Metaphysicals, Clare, Blake, the Radicals, Hopkins, the First World War poets and, as it happens, nuclear fission, were leftwing, some communist. If the Thirties were, in the whopper sense, political, they were also a time of intense intellectual rediscovery and invention inside and outside parties. Of course Helen Gardner was knitting blankets for Spain while editing Crashaw, as she recalled in a recent newspaper interview. Communist or not, I will be damned if she ever had much of a brush with Proletkult or heresy, or that anyone tried to brush her with them.

*   *   *

> Life in the thirties was hard for the working class and soft for the *bourgeoisie,* so that every decent middle class person was haunted by guilt . . . any educated person with imagination and conscience felt unease that his comfort derived from the poverty of workers at home and the indescribable misery of a coolie Empire.

So writes John Wain, reviewing Samuel Hynes's book, and with accuracy: 'guilt' and 'unease' are the right words for describing what was rather Feeling than Thought. I wish to be exact rather than condescending in calling this response, boyish or adult and certainly at the start my own, Sentimental. The working class was poor. The poor were helpless. Whole areas of Auden's beloved midlands were literally harrowing to visit. The fact that you were harrowed did not of course make a revolutionary of you, and this particular response could come from liberal, pacifist, socialist, christian, communist and just occasionally (and quite distinctly) marxist, according to how else you viewed events. The matter spells itself out for individual cases in the *Left Review* pamphlet prepared by Nancy Cunard and others called *Writers Take Sides on the Spanish War*. Some ninety per cent of the very wide range of those approached are listed as opposed to Franco, and so can be said to be leftwing; but their individual statements cover a wide political spectrum and so are not leftwing.

As events succeeded one another through the Thirties – from the failure of Labour government and then to Macdonald's betrayal, to the growth of fascism in Germany, to the unemployed workers movement and the start of fascism here, to the war in Spain – Sentiment became more and more associated with socialist and communist programmes, less and less with the pacifism and liberalism so evident in the Peace Pledge Union and the Peace Ballot of its beginnings. This was naturally so. Revolutionaries had predicted such a sequence of events, and they were right. They had also predicted the growth of a mass movement in opposition to events; here too they were right; and it is no insult nor cynical to remark that to creative artists a mass movement means, among other things, mass audience. Feeling is up or down, sees black or white or heavens on earth, and in its polarisations at that time quite easily set against the murky inhumanities of English capitalism a Russian promised land. This was indeed a part of communism, but also not. The god-seeking Muggeridge saw things so; the right-wing A. J. Cummings volubly defended the Russian treason trials in the liberal *News Chronicle;* it was Auden, no helot, who relied on Soviet models for writing

> We made all possible preparations,
> Drew up a list of firms,
> Constantly revised our calculations
> And allotted the farms

and John Lehmann, no helot, whose fearsomely Sentimental *Letter from Tiflis* began 'Dear Bill, Did you read the new Russian Constitution?' Certainly communists too wrote such things. Also communists did not, as also others did not.

I state the thing very badly, but what I attempt to distinguish is a route by which people came to support, and with great warmth of feeling and expense of energy and knitting of blankets, policies sometimes coincident with communism without themselves being remotely communist, certainly not marxist. Sentiment needs an object to love – the poor, a promised land, sometimes a dogma – feels; wants its feelings attached; attaches itself; expresses itself in such simplifications as even the loved one cannot always recognise but does not necessarily spurn for all that. Sentiment found the dogma it sought in marxism, dogged it and uttered not the actual philosophy there but, forgive me, dog-marxism. The 'inferior work' which Symons notes of Day Lewis is of that order: brash, loverlike, heartfelt, mindless – for of course, if attachment went far enough, poets could end inside the communist party without so much as a whiff of marxism about them. Such another was Stephen Spender who described his route there as *Forward from Liberalism,* where marxism proper must surely have offered *Forward Against Liberalism.*

There was however a totally different route, for the writers at least, and one rather older – less the immediate response of Sentiment to public misery as Wain describes it than of Reason to creative work.

Towards the end of the Twenties *The Calendar of Modern Letters* under Rickword's editorship had given form and direction to a growing attempt to subject literature and the whole creative function to a Rational critique. Established reputations, like those of Galsworthy and Barrie, were meticulously analysed, not to say decimated. The traditions they represented were increasingly seen to be those of a largely moribund literature, and increasingly the issue was posed as to whether this was not because the whole of the society producing it was moribund. The final number of *The Calendar* came to the conclusion that in fact this was the case, and that the proper preoccupation of writers must now be social change. The questions had been literary, the answer political. Two points need emphasis about this decision to cease publication. First the Rationalism of *The Calendar* was a spirit far wider than itself: I. A. Richards's *Practical Criticism,* for instance, may be seen as another of its faces and the postwar nothing-on-trust and savage satires of Powys and Huxley and Sylvia Townsend Warner as yet another. Second, although on its reprint some years ago, it was the *critical* element that called forth almost universal paeans of praise, the journal essentially conglomerated *creative* talents. Stories and poems by Lawrence, Turner, Graves, Muir, Huxley, Rickword himself emphasised that the concern was always with the creative preoccupations of the time, the criticism was mostly by the creators, and when this was not the case – as, for example, with Leavis, another of *The Calendar's* discoveries – critical positions were always directed to this point. Although the decision to close may have been Rickword's, although the spirit of Richards continued to develop through Empson, although Patrick Hamilton was to extend the satirical tradition, although Leavis continued, almost without break, into his own journal, it was a decision that fitted precisely the course *The Calendar* had taken. It was in a way a representative decision.

So into the beginning of the Thirties there entered such a bunch of intellectual toughs as we have not seen since, whose espousal of political causes arose from an approximately hegelian philosophy turned marxist, in turn arising out of creative impasse. Classically, the whole and all the parts of Nature were seen as matter in conflict, changing one form of matter and proceeding to other conflicts and yet further change. In detail this could embrace internal conflicts within the poet, even the working of images within the poem, or the poem's content against its form, or the poet against society, or History against the Present, or society itself in what was now the far more publicised conflict of class with class.

Now here is a totally different route into the Thirties than that of Sentimental response to 'guilt' and 'unease'; and I think no useful understanding of what the Thirties were about is possible unless both routes be seen – for they very soon became confusingly entangled. I do not suggest that one should discern a kind of wet and dry distinction between those moved to pity by events and those impelled by a strictly reasoned anger at the impossibilities of creative nexus. Rickword, by his earliest writing a poet of the First World War, is second to none in this century in his sense of pity; and on the other course, why even a liberal can have Reason. The two streams intermingled within the individual human body like kinds of blood. Reason can be passionate, and Sentiment educate itself. But I am concerned about the use and misuse of words like communist, marxist, fellow-traveller, leftwing, stalinist – not then a word much in use and never with its hindsight meanings – sprayed as they are over

everyone from the apparently inexhaustible aerosols of remi-
niscence and so-to-say literary criticism. I think it useful therefore
to distinguish, even by exaggeration, between writers driven by
the logic of their own engagement as writers to intellectual
positions which in the end involve them in political action, and
writers whose politics had no such profound connection to those
springs of being out of which they write, but is rather an
immediate response to happenchance.

Essentially the position was that the Rational route could
march, via philosophical marxism, to communist party membership, just as the Sentimental route could maunder towards the
same point holding hands with Stephen Spender. The Rationalist
could grow mawkish, it's true, especially when and if the mind
were engaged elsewhere. The Sentimentalist could adopt a
toughish stance, could even become as exceedingly tough as Day
Lewis at least in manner. But it serves no useful purpose – for the
paint won't take on the hard wood of trying to write – to squirt
a word like helot over the lot of them, regard the job as done,
skip the War and land in the Fifties. What matters is the way
their minds were actually engaged; in terms of person, what they
were like; in terms of writing, what they wrote.

*   *   *

Randall Swingler, until his call-up after the third issue of *Our
Time*, had been editor of the *Daily Worker* book page and a
leading communist, even by way of being the party's chief cultural
spokesman. An article of his about Blake in *Left Review*, called
'The Imputation of Madness' and concentrating upon the pro-
phetic books rather than the Songs of Innocence and Experience,
had as it happens first awakened in me as a schoolboy some
inkling that communism might be more altogether than Sentimental allegiance with the working class. (By that nasty network
system – my music master was a friend of his – I had also read
two novels and much poetry by him while still at school; and it
was of course the same net that worked me towards *Our Time* in
the first place.) In that founding year I lived with him and his
family in their London flat and Essex cottage, and they did what
they could with the boy, with his black and white, his Hell and
his promised land. Married to a pianist, Randall himself had at
one time been a flautist with the LPO, and music filled both

homes. This was 1940, the *Daily Worker* considerably confused, Randall much preoccupied there with the politics of whether the War was just or not, quite apart from founding *Our Time*. And writing, perpetually writing. It was at this time of constant public debate about the defence of the Soviet Union that I first learned that neither boilersuit poems nor promised lands would do – for, inevitably, the private talk was about the writing. We don't have a barely literate working class, he'd say, we don't have a living peasant tradition, our people has a long industrial culture, theirs doesn't, we had Dickens a hundred years ago so why repeat him now? The thing to discover, boy, is where and what you are and write from there. I'd burn that lot if I were you. He himself was tussling with images of hedgerow, tree-form and seasonal change in the Essex countryside, things of which all his poetry stinks, making real in a new way and with the materials most moving to him his larger political certainties. There was no question of 'fitting into a Communist pattern', but of making a communist out of what he was, let that be what sort of a communist it may.

At this level Randall was in Auden's grip rather than Stalin's. The Sentimental boy of course thought Auden a rat for going to America. But no. Sad that may have been, but Auden was wholly admirable – for his technical abilities, yes, but chiefly for his attempt at the big inclusive myth or the big image: a mountain, a Northwest Passage, a beast with a scaly tail, the map of Spain – things fitter for the time, so Randall thought, than anything he himself could achieve being hedge-bound, tree-tied. Everyone writes from a shifting point of tension, he'd continue. Let him first find and then preserve that tension, follow it where he will, into a party, over an ocean. And so my education proceeded. I have neither the art to describe him shortly nor space to run to. For all his crowded political life we spent, it seems, an incredible amount of time afoot. He liked to act and dramatise his speech and would dart behind a hedge or a London hoarding only to dart out again as an African bishop or Marie Lloyd or holding in silent wonder some bug or bud he had discovered. He was a man of enormous zest, also a very funny man. Some helot.

Montagu Slater was another enormous man but housed, this time, in a tiny birdlike bobbing body. A perpetual pipe-smoker, one half of his stomach lately removed and his breathing curious, he had a way of snuffling through speech which made it almost impossible to distinguish laughter from conversation from the dribble in the pipestem from a possible bronchial condition, and all of this apostrophised with donkey-brays of derision. Son of a tradesman in the small mining port of Millom in Cumberland, his background was totally different to Randall's enclosing network or mine, and he was older far. Born in 1902, he rose by classics through secondary school and then, the local boy made good, by scholarship to Oxford and philosophy, then on to the *Liverpool Daily Post* and a bed in a dockside settlement, joining the communist party far earlier than most of the Thirties intellectuals. The wonder of that journey never left him: its dockside and mine enmeshed in classical myth and all the possible philosophies. Indeed in 1940 our relationship at first was clouded by the fact that, fresh from Cambridge as I was, I had paid no attention at all to Wittgenstein of whom he approved as an original. Montagu prized originality, and wanted to wonder, above all things (and Julian Symons's quotation from him in *Left Review* might have been better picked, since it is ripped from a running argument over several issues in which it is Montagu, as editor, who advocates the widest, most catholic attitudes to creative art). His gods were Brecht and André Obée and Alexander Blok from whom he was forever quoting a phrase I have never traced about the artist 'having to put up prototypes that either fly or other men shoot down'.

First a poet, last a novelist and film-writer, his abiding love was drama. Seven plays of the Thirties survive intact, with signs of perhaps five others. Two were performed, one with music by Benjamin Britten (so Britten told me shortly before his death, but his score is lost). He also wrote songs and puppet plays with Britten and enormous pageants for the Co-op movement, some-times with Britten's music – a collaboration which was to culminate in that superb dramatic poem, not much indebted to Crabbe, the eventual libretto for *Peter Grimes.* All the dramas are before their time in the sense that they experiment with song and chorus, with audience-stage relationships, and often express the action itself in verse. Talent 'fitted into a Communist pattern'? Perhaps – in Randall's sense of making whatever you can of where and what you are, but in no other sense. Poems and sketches and things called 'fragments', often opaque to my under-standing then (and now), never sectarian, always filled with dockside, mining, classical philosophic reference, were stuffed in books, fell out of files – once, I remember, out of a slipper I borrowed where it had wedged the toe – for after demobilisation I lived in Montagu's home, as before call-up I had lived in Randall's. A very different place of course. He had, for a start, a far wider reputation in areas nowhere near the communist party – the theatre, Fleet Street, the Co-op movement, the documentary film world – and people from anywhere, it seemed, might wander into the Slaters' open house on Sunday nights. The place was full of daughters and animals too: when I lived there the count was three girls, four dogs, three birds, five cats – insofar as breeding cats can ever be numbered. He loved the muddle – I think because muddle was what the mind must necessarily work on anyway – wandering about from room to room, suddenly removing the pipe from his mouth for a statement of total clarity: 'You ought to stop reading Fielding and read all Sterne, the sermons included. The view's more sensible in and out of a Pulpit than from the Bench.' Or, in the same way wandering into speech at an editorial meeting, 'We ought to do something about the Nonconformist Conscience. You can't cheat History, and the Russians have got it still to come. We ought to help.' A truly Rational man. To me quite reasonably, to orthodoxy presumably not, the one chosen as founder-editor of *Left Review*.

Nancy Cunard was never, I think, a communist in the sense of dues-paying membership. I very much doubt if she ever joined anything, but I include her here because she was there. You can neither fix her, as I have attempted to fix Randall and Montagu, among the Rational, nor hope to tame her voracious, swooping responses into Sentimentality, for all her involvements were passionate to as far as you wish to stretch that word. Rather later, discussing the chance of her getting material out of her great surrealist friend Tristan Tzara, then in the Resistance in France, she suddenly confounded me by saying, 'Dear boy, Aragon has the most beautifully shaped head. You really must feel the back of it.' But chiefly her passions were hatred of the privileged wealth into which she had been born, concern for such social outcasts as negro and homosexual, delight in the socially unacceptable, destructive arts. She wanted to tear the world apart and let what would grow through the rents, was little concerned with future worlds. She was fastidious about the way she tore, though. The oddities of her Twenties appearance (which would be fashionable now) – the finger-curls, the maquillage round her enormous eyes, cloches, scarves – were placed and presented with exacting care;

the great African bangles which encased her arms and made her habit of cuffing one painful, she polished assiduously in meetings, on bar-tops, at table; the wayward, often French-constructed English of her copy could drive you mad with its emendations of emendations seeking the only apposite word.

James Boswell would come into *Our Time* on leave in battle-dress, bearing sketchbooks – this was the Phoney War – showing great officer bulls afloat on blocks of blanco in seas of bullshit where soldiers struggled not to drown. Randall had for him that almost jealous regard he had for Auden, the big imager: aircraft for Boz were always flying dragons, beasts with scaly tails, warfare always an incontinent bull. Between these monsters, the sketch-books were filled with portraits of fellow conscripts and mud-scapes dwarfing them against hollow army nissen huts – as Boz's conversation was filled with their life histories. Big, brown, bearlike in battledress and greatcoat, his beaming countryboy grin disguised an insatiable curiosity for every conceivable human detail; and a certain glittering wickedness of eye – the usual 'twinkle' will not do for it – excited the most extraordinary degree of confidence from strangers. His company in public was a constant and quite unpredictable adventure. Our meetings moving, as they surely did, to the pub, out would come pen and sketchbook and on to the page go all the drinkers, often enough to leap back off the page and join us in the flesh. (How Julian Symons came to miss Boz's perpetual showing 'truthfully the wretched lives and narrow horizons of the poor' I shall never understand, since not infrequently such drawings – in a pub, on a street, through windows and doorways into homes, at work – had appeared in *Left Review* and constantly in lithographs issued by the AIA, a body which his book describes.)

In 1941 Boz seemed all of a piece with the times to me: the tenderness of his portrait sketches a proper complement to the savagery scored into facing and backing pages. Things were heightened now in the un-Thirties climate in which we lived, but were essentially the same things heightened. The dude bankers of his *Left Review* cartoons had become a bestiary; the crowded streets and demonstrations of the earlier drawings, a pathos of pointless isolation. As I was coming to understand them, the Thirties had driven these new friends of mine with a passionate belief in the possibility of a Revolution that would void the holocaust of world war, as it would every other social inhumanity.

The often pacifist disarming mood of their beginnings this passion subsumed rather than rejected; involvement in Spain had been an attempt to scotch the greater holocaust before it started. Now we were in a war, but without the numerous movement the Thirties had contained. Moreover this was a war that wasn't being fought. It is easy enough, these later days, to deride the confusions of communist policy about the Justice or Not of what was happening – at least I find it so myself, who was part of them – but in fact we lived through a break-up of family and all habitual community and blitz and air-battle that was also not, in the sense of purpose or total engagement, a war at all. We were in some foul parenthetical hollow of a Thirties worsened. Boz drew it with a loathing precision grown of experience, also with a fond, familiar love for its victims.

Patrick Hamilton was different again. In great pain at that time, he was usually drugged and always propped up in bed when I called on him as messenger-boy from the office. I bore at first a typescript of *Hangover Square* and, later, early drafts of *The Duke in Darkness*: in both cases there was, I think, some possibility of our publishing extracts though we never did so. And of course I only dimly knew the worth of what I bore. For Hamilton, too, something had finished and yet only a heightened expression of what had gone before was possible. In 1939 he had forsaken the exact satiric observation of that small social milieu which had characterised his earlier plays and novels and published, in *Impromptu in Moribundia*, an altogether wider-sweeping sardonic political tract. Now – being where and what he was, as Randall would have put it – he returned in *Hangover Square* to that same milieu but like a somnambulist, without satire, to write a novel heightened almost into a scream. It is, if you like, the continuing agony beneath those surfaces MacNeice had lately caught with such precision in *Autumn Journal,* and Hamilton supremely right to pick as hero a drunken besotted lover trying to escape the net – the girl in this nightmare inevitably Netta – of a love already dead. (If you want the end of the Thirties, then go to *Autumn Journal* and *Hangover Square,* for there it is entire.) By the time of *The Duke in Darkness,* more was needed; one could not only scream; scope, perspective, vision, if lost, need not be dead. So, out of that toying with levels of meaning which was the 'what' of his art, Hamilton makes a wholly unfunny, unsatiric, costume drama about an imprisoned man, imprisoned

again within his prison by a blindness either real or feigned, and
you are never to be certain which, except that behind the blindness some obstinate vision somehow persists – the 'where' of his
times. (If you want the emergence from Phoney War, then go to
The Duke in Darkness, for it stands alone, neglected by orthodoxy
left and right.) Given his condition when I saw him, and my
unimportance, he said very little I can remember – except once.
I had mumbled something about my sense of wonder at his play.
'So you noticed?' he said, straining forward from the pillows,
'There, the Duke's speech, at the top of the page – there – it's
a paraphrase of Lenin's *One Step Forward, Two Steps Back',*
and then sank down again into stupor. For one so young this was
dumbfounding, the back of Aragon's head once more. Neither then
nor later has that play borne any relation to any pamphlet.

Or there was Sylvia Townsend Warner who, from the moment
of *Our Time's* founding, began to send us those delicate prose
balloons of hers describing pretension – our own as well as those
of others – which then she pricked . . . . Or Mulk Raj Anand,
perhaps the jolliest of these people, though all were jolly in what I
was beginning to know was near despair – for he at last had
company in this paralysed time of inaction. Love of his native
India must always have made a lonely paralysis seem as
native. . . . Or, a little later, Jack Lindsay. In the somewhat
chaotic perpetual editorial meeting that was work at *Our Time,*
with people dropping in and out on leave or in transit, there had
been a constant threnody of 'where the hell is he?' about Jack.
Apparently, to me mysteriously, he would be bound to have a
poem or short story to hand, or would review this or do an article
about that or a series about those; but no-one knew where he
was. As it happens it was I who discovered him, as a fellow
signalman in the barracks at Trowbridge. He dispersed all sense
of mystery at once, for he was writing, I recall, a novel about
slavery in Elizabethan England, a book of poems, a translation
(from Catullus?), something to do with egyptology, plotting
another novel – earphones clapped to his head, scribbling away on
the backs of printed forms on which he should have been recording Morse. (There may be some conflation here, since I was later
to share digs with him; but neither then nor later did he ever have
less than five or six projects in hand at once. At this time he used
the many pockets of a battledress as a handy filing cabinet, re-
serving I think it was his field-dressing pocket for money and

another for waste paper. I have reason to remember this because on one occasion when I was broke and he was to buy the drinks, in haste and in the then prevailing blackout, he mixed the pockets up, it cost him his last ten bob note to have a shit; and we went thirsty.) . . . Helots?

I describe these people because they seemed to me, and were, a continuum from the Thirties and, though probably at their most defensive and sectarian, so various in individual response as writer, as artist; also so unled. To speak true, I do not really know how helots are supposed to behave, but assume that it must be at someone else's dictation. We had none of that. We had, most of us, communist loyalties of course, – but who is not, in the end, loyal to the dictates of an inner will? – and kept the party posted about what we intended for each month's issue. By and large if it disagreed with us we went ahead just the same, but by and large it didn't. If, on the other hand, I have made my friends seem less than pro-Soviet, that is an error to do with re-stating what pro-Sovietism meant to them. Belief in Revolution is always, surely, a response to the unacceptability of the life about you, and that life was English. In fact we spoke as little as we published about Russia, bad for Russia as those years also were, and fearful as we undoubtedly felt this to be. But this isn't a political essay, concerned with possible political gullibilities – that was an agony came later – so much as a memory of individuals as parts of actual events. Founding *Our Time* was a lonely business, particularly lonely to those from the crowded Thirties. Partly of course we were dealing with the chaos of war. People were being called-up, posted, scattered about the country and the world. But in 1940 and 1941 we were also dealing with a dispersal of mind which had been widening ever since the Spanish defeat – just as the massive movement which had supported a concentration of mind dispersed. Reason by definition can only proceed from the point that it has reached, so the Rational of my definition, however politically perplexed, were here; but Sentiment had fled. Nancy's ninety per cent of writers opposed to Franco had shrunk. If Wain's words 'guilt' and 'unease' were right for earlier, now the word should be 'fear'. Authors were often literally in hiding, more often simply burying their beliefs in anonymity if not yet in recantation. Contributors were very hard to find.

On my return to the paper in 1943 this eerie parenthesis of the

F

Phoney War was over. Sentiment, albeit the dogmas now, were those of a united war effort and a wholly apolitical russophilia, was back in flood.

*   *   *

One of the difficulties of publication from the very outset of war was that you could not simply found a journal, buy the paper and print on it. Paper was rationed and only to journals whose periodical appearance had been recent. *Left Review* had been too long dead to qualify under these terms, and *Our Time* acquired its ration by taking over a Workers' Music Association publication, *Poetry and the People*.

Politics in the Thirties bred – as periods of large movement in English labour history always have – an enormous cultural activity far wider than any attempt by professional artists to organise themselves in a *Left Review*: a whole area of increased WEA courses, Left Theatre guilds and groups, the Left Book Club, a Co-op movement mounting Montagu's pageants in Wembley Stadium, Unity Theatre, worker-writer circles everywhere. Amabel Williams-Ellis tells me that her sole and virtually full-time function as one of the founder-editors of *Left Review* was to cope by letter and meeting and monthly competition with an ocean of manuscript flooding the journal from such sources. In all this liveliness the WMA was particularly concerned with collecting and disseminating the labour movement's huge backlog of song and with the creation of new songs up to and including ballad operas. Certainly in taking over *Poetry and the People* we got the paper ration. We also got, if we did not still retain from *Left Review*, whatever worker-writer ideology the Thirties held. But what ideology, if any, was it?

A workman does not write because an intellectual tells him to do so. The liveliness I speak of was there spontaneously as part of the politics, as were professional artists also there. I think it helpful to put things this way round, though latterday orthodoxy does not. When Symons complains that *Left Review's* editors did not 'raise the level of writing among their working-class contributors' he implies a superiority not theirs, at any rate not felt by them to be theirs. The presence of untutored writing beside professional writing expressed an alliance, not a tutorial; and such alliances ran right through the cultural life of the Left.

Swingler, along with such prominent musicians as Alan Raws-
thorne, Constant Lambert, Alan Bush had been active in the
WMA, much as Slater with Benjamin Britten had written for
Co-op pageants and Left Theatre guilds. Only for those whose
political allegiance was, as I see it, wholly Sentimental, whether
Day Lewis or Spender and communist or not, did this not obtain.
For them the comparable arena of performance was the Group
Theatre – middle-class, private in reference and humour, centre
of the Auden group and consequently ascribed by orthodoxy a far
greater importance than it occupied at the time. From there,
doubtless, it appeared that the Rational should be conducting a
tutorial, perhaps to educate an audience. From where the
audiences were sufficient to fill Wembley Stadium, not so.

It is of course perfectly possible to thumb through the pages of
Left Review, count up the references to Proletkult, to writing
'from the factory bench', to national and international conferences
of working class writers, and sketch out the graph of an argument
conducted in those terms. It is equally possible, in any collection
of books by decades, to pull out of the Thirties titles by Idris
Davies, B. L. Coombes, Lewis Jones and others and start a new
(if a small) shelf of Proletarian authors. It is even possible – or so
I gather from Jürgen Enkermann's 'Annotated Bibliography of
British Working-Class Prose' in *Workers and Writers*, Birming-
ham 1975 – to fill that shelf out by adding to it books with
worker-heroes, written by persons of whatever social origin and
of pretty much any political persuasion or none.

All these seem to me the essentially dotty occupations of a
pigeonholism run mad, to lack all sense of Time as History,
merely to hugger-muggeridge that actual issue of alliance.
Certainly, given the concerns of those years, discussion of an
aesthetic of simplicity generally labelled it proletarian; but there
doesn't seem much to choose between 'the utmost simplicity and
plainness (of language), suited to every capacity' and 'This poetry
speaks in your language (for) the ordinary people in every town
and village of Great Britain.' The first is the Rev. John Wesley
puffing off his hymns in 1779, the second *Poetry and the People*
appealing for money in 1940. Moreover, even within the pages of
Left Review, few practising writers – few of the 'helot'
Rationalists who here concern me – engaged in such discussion,
and when they did it was not on the side of bigotry. Certainly, if
infrequently, working men wrote splendid books; but so they had

done, also infrequently, throughout the nineteenth century. Certainly writers from other backgrounds often enough conceived novels with worker-heroes; but that, too, was to settle to work within a now long-standing and sturdy English tradition – if sometimes a grossly Sentimental one. Most certainly of all, the climate within which all three of these things were done in the Thirties was different. By the standards of anything since the Labour landslide of 1945, that climate was one of mass movement. However profound the intention, the extrapolation of this or that theory of writing from the total environment of which it was a part can be perfect in its meaningless. I am aware, for instance, that only a few lines since I characterised the Group Theatre as 'middle class, private in reference and humour', without at the same time remarking how deeply its authors felt politically committed beyond their class, regarding themselves and themselves regarded as in political (though inactive) alliance. Even so sexually specialised and belittling a book as Isherwood's *Christopher's Friends* is clear about that – if only, it seems at times, to muddle the clarity.

As late as February 1940 Stephen Spender co-signed the *Poetry and the People* 'Appeal' quoted above: that's to say, he placed himself quite naturally in the company of worker-writers. And while it is true that the two founding hardback volumes of *New Writing* came from the communist firm of Lawrence and Wishart, where Rickword worked, it is also notable that no sense of strain marks the continuance of that same mixture of types of contributor into the *Penguin New Writings* of John Lehmann's editorship. The change in climate was to be quick – so quick indeed that within a year this series of paperbacks evidently planned by Allen Lane and Swingler as the political *Left Review*'s successor had become wholly apolitical. If pressed, yes, I think I would argue that all aesthetics of simplicity since Wordsworth's have been profoundly Sentimental – insultingly so indeed, for it is not my experience that working men and women are any less able than others to understand what they wish to understand. The change in climate was partly at least the parting of Sentiment from Reason. But before that change, and to me at least, the indisputably great poems by Auden, the good ones by Day Lewis and what is tolerable in Spender, all sprang from precisely this time of outer awareness and what I have called alliance. When, only a little later, the miner-writer B. L. Coombes honoured me

with his friendship, *of course* we spoke more about Auden than
any other living author in our hours and hours of talk.

Look at things for a moment as the helots did.

In 1936 Montagu Slater published a short book of reportage
called *Stay Down Miner*, recounting the events covered by his
play of the same name. Towards the end of it he revisits the area
of those pit-bottom sit-in strikes of 1935 and picks, as typifying
that action at its noblest, a lay-preaching miner who had led
services at the coalface. He starts to describe an evening with
him thus:

> He lives in a cottage older than most hereabouts. There is a
> huge yard beside the railway and behind the drill hall, and here,
> unexpectedly, the black soil blossoms in garden, cherry-trees and
> poultry farm. Behind the orchard are two cottages, roomy, solid
> and old.
>
> I sat by the big fire in his parlour, read part of a manuscript
> novel, some short stories, his poems, and finally an account he
> had written of the stay-down strike . . . .

The unexpectedness, it is to be noted, is reserved for the blossoming soil, not for the worker-writer, nor for the fact that Montagu,
an intellectual, should be shown the writing. The matter is not
returned to, merely mentioned casually in passing. On this, but
not on every occasion the intellectual's, not the miner's account
was published.

At about the same time Swingler wrote a very simple WMA
ballad-song called 'Sixty Cubic Feet' in which this measurement
represents the area a miner occupied in birth, at work, in death.
I can remember giving him no greater pleasure ever than when,
long after the war, I told him of hearing this song sung in the
Army by a soldier who, when I told him I knew its author, called
me a bloody liar and damned near knocked me down because, he
said, it was an old traditional Durham work-song. That figured. The
whole preoccupation with the creative nexus which characterised
the Rational could only leap in delight at such an incident. But
the situation producing it couldn't be manufactured. There had
to be a movement of which you were a part for such a coincidence
of almost metaphysical imagery with common feeling. You did
not look such a gifthorse in the mouth; but neither did you sell
off the actual function of yourself as artist merely because you
happened not to be proletarian. You no more 'wrote down' than
you expected your ally to 'write up'. You accepted yourself as

matter, and about yourself that to certain other matter – be it
Essex hedgerows or the works of Crabbe – your responses were
of a sort to make you write, and you entered that process of
creation which is largely intellectual, and which involved the
organisation of this matter into your whole conception of reality –
a reality also political. Swingler, in his 'Epilogue' to the largely
personal poems of *The Years of Anger*, put it thus:

> I do not think that poetry speaks only with this voice, nor does
> this represent all the poetry I have written during these years
> (1936-1945). Poetry can and should also sing and shout, in the
> open air, in the theatre, in the concert hall. Poetry also whispers
> and murmurs, around the fire or in the ear of a single person. It
> depends entirely upon what community the poet feels himself to
> share, and to press around him, at the time of utterance. If he
> feels himself to be alone and isolated, he will talk to himself, and
> it will probably sound like gibberish.

In 1941 at *Our Time* the community pressing around us was
small. No ocean of worker-writing flooded the office. There was
nothing, in that line, to be ideological about, and none of us had
ever been in the habit of writing hortatory verses.

Orthodoxy views things otherwise. Leafing through *Left
Review* (or even through Symons's partial quotations from it) one
notices how rarely are the fake-proletarianisms, the boilersuit, the
dropped-H syndrome, the soupy expressions of solidarity, by
helots who continued helot, how those who wrote these Sentimental things were most often to end in orthodoxy's bosom, even
if they are not chief among orthodoxy's authors. And that tendency
Symons notes 'to extirpate heresies found among the bourgeois
writers of talent who were sympathetic to Communism'? Can he
mean Rickword attacking Day Lewis for the wetness of making
floodwater proletarian in *Noah and the Waters*, or attacking
Philip Henderson for omitting Byron from progressive literature
because Byron was a Lord? But that would be to attack Reason
for being Rational! And indeed that seems to be the case, alas.
The sillinesses, the dog-marx, the simplifications to points beyond
absurdity which orthodoxy now attacks were those of Sentiment
then, and were attacked by Reason then. So it is Sentiment now
that describes the way itself behaved in the Thirties, says there
was no other behaviour than its own, ignores what doesn't fit;
and all our orthodoxy is, after all, only Sentiment appearing once
again in farce.

* * *

By 1943 *Our Time* was no longer recognisable as what the tyro's heroes had founded. None of them was left there, the pages were full of villainous poetry Sentimental beyond bearing, writing from the factory bench (all right by me) but also from private desks dressed up as factory benches (not all right). Sentiment was in full flood; the thing that mattered most was loving Russia as much here as in the *Daily Express*. It is a long story, and another, and one involving a rather tortuous form of political in-fighting; but in not too long a time we had Slater back on the board, Rickword as editor, Nancy Cunard and Sylvia Townsend Warner contributing again, Jack Lindsay in amongst us – eventually, demobilised from their hideous wars in Africa and Italy, Boz and Randall back. Certainly, and even under Edgell's remarkable editorship which marked the paper's high point, we published mawkish stuff enough – by myself, for one. (Hell, if you have understood me, we were awash with Sentiment ourselves. And who was not? Though nowhere near in communism's grip this time, even Sentiment's beloved Proletkult was back in little reviews called *Forces Writing* or *Khaki and Blue,* as well as in *Penguin New Writing,* among the more predictably intellectualising *Fulcrum* and *Kingdom Come.*) But Rationality was back. And a movement massive enough to make the Labour landslide of 1945. And as part of it again that characteristic sweep of popular cultural life. We were politically engaged and also thinking and working out of that engagement: a serious journal, taken sufficiently seriously for many issues to look remarkably like that old alliance between a vital, labour culture and a general cross-section of leftwing intellectuals, some communist, some not, Julian Symons himself among the latter. But it is not a period in time, of course, that orthodoxy cares to mention or account for, having settled as finished in the Thirties what hasn't been finished yet.

Perhaps I put things poorly, being unaccustomed to memoir and polemic both; but orthodoxy lies and someone, if only a boy at the time, must say so. That the Thirties were made of Auden and friends and such influences as reached them is as unlikely a notion as daft. That writers who follow political Feeling as far as political Thought and Action betray their writing denies half English literature. And these particular writers who have moved me? Edgell Rickword, in the far more luminous minds of Empson and Fuller, is one of the few great poets of this century, and chuckles when I see him now to be living on into recognition at last. That he was ever 'subdued to silence' by communist party membership is fatuous both because his years of publishing and editing and 'Twittingpan' and 'To the Wife of a Non-Interventionist Statesman' don't amount to silence and because, by so ridiculous a rule, Blunden must have been subdued to silence by pacifism, Empson by sinophilia or ambiguity – charges at least not so far orthodox. Montagu Slater? Three of his Thirties plays, if not others as well, are important in the sense of carrying English drama forward from Lawrence to Arden, by being here only a little less than Brecht was there, are possibly great. Randall Swingler? It's hard for me to say other than that he wrote from a centre of his times, while Auden wrote roundabout. His achievement seems to me – from what and where I was – colossal because of what he attempted; Auden's, at least until his later academic frivolities, matchless at attempting less.

'I will allow that a man may change his opinions, but . . . .' In the end the way one values an author's work depends on seeing the nature of what the author undertook. Most men – I certainly – have changed opinion; and most accept responsibility for what they did and do. The imputation of helotry in others is only a poor and a feeble and a less than Reasonable excuse for begging pardon of the past. And why? Sentiment and Reason alike combined in the Thirties in such a movement, instinct with art, as almost defeated fascism before, therefore without, a war, and even then proceeded to win that war. That Reality is no Dream. Auden's disclaimer that any Jew was saved from the gas chamber by any poem of his cheapens himself and others. Helot's a sneering, I would say also a lying word.

Poems by Randall Swingler

Randall Swingler was born in 1909, one of seven children of an Anglican Rural Dean. He was educated at Winchester and at Oxford, where he stayed only two years. On leaving, he married the concert pianist Geraldine Peppin whom he had met two years before, and they lived at first in London where Swingler earned his living as a teacher. In 1934 they moved to the country in Oxfordshire where Swingler joined the communist party, attending meetings at Banbury, its nearest branch.

In 1936 the Swinglers, now with a young daughter, returned to London and to wider political, musical and literary engagement. They were at once active in the Workers' Music Association founded that year, in the Left Book Club and the new Unity Theatre, and by 1937 Swingler had begun on a career as editor which was to continue, broken only by the war, until 1960 – on the *Daily Worker* book page, *Left Review* (of which he was the last editor), *Poetry and the People, Our Time, Arena, Circus* (the last three of which he co-founded) and *The New Reasoner* (on whose board he served). But before the war ordinary political branch life much occupied him, and he was in demand both locally and nationally as a platform speaker and poet.

His war service, from 1941 to 1945, ended in the merciless Italian campaign where he was awarded the M.M. – as a ranker, for he withstood all attempts, whether by Army or Party, to make him take a commission. After the demise of *Circus* and some years doubt he left the Communist Party in 1952, thereafter living largely by WEA and extra-mural lecturing and reviewing for the T.L.S. as well as by some hack work. He died in 1967.

*　　*　　*

Two novels, *No Escape* and *To Town*, had been published in 1935 and 1938 respectively, but he was always chiefly a poet and, except for a period of several years in the early sixties, an extremely prolific one. Nonetheless his published collections are

F*

few: *Poems* (1932) and *Reconstruction* (1933), both Shakespeare's Head Press, Oxford; *Difficult Morning* (1933), Methuen Gateway Poets; *The Years of Anger* (1946) and *The God in the Cave* (1950), both Fore Publications. The two long gaps in this sequence – 1933-1946 and 1950-1967 – included his most prolific years. In the first of them particularly he was widely published in periodicals, by no means always of the left, both here and in the States. Words he wrote for Alan Bush, Alan Rawsthorne, Benjamin Britten, Bernard Stevens and others appeared between the staves if (which was not always the case) their music was published. His wife, her sister, his son-in-law were professional musicians, he himself an accomplished flautist, and his collaboration in musical projects grew to be prodigious in both quantity and scale – including, for example, long cantatas. Much of this work was done through the Workers' Music Association in which politics and music alike involved him. Similar involvement at Unity Theatre and in the Left Book Club's short-lived theatre section drew from him rhapsodic verse declamations, sometimes for several voices. Generally speaking he did not keep copies of this kind of work for public performance, perhaps because he regarded it as published already, by no means because he despised it: 'Poetry can and should sing and shout, in the open air, in the theatre, in the concert hall', he wrote. Nonetheless, Swingler's public poetry is very dispersed and its collection, now in train, a lengthy and complicated matter.

'Poetry also whispers and murmurs, around the fire or in the ear of a single person', the passage quoted above continues. At this more personal, lyrical level, his papers relating to the Thirties include evidence of four collections never published. These are *The Risen* and *Poems from the Country* of 1936/7, *The Triple Test* of 1939/40, and *The Testing Years* which is either a wartime or an early postwar attempt to collect prewar work. There is some indication that sequences of 'Winter Soliloquies', 'Winter Sonnets' and 'Pastorals' from *The Risen* may have been considered for separate pamphlet or journal publication, and other equally early poems certainly formed parts of *The Triple Test* and *The Testing Years*. These unpublished collections were cannibalised in turn to form the first three sequences of *The Years of Anger*, the eventually published collection of 1946, which are entitled 'Premonitions 1936-38', 'The Ordeal of Love 1936-41' and 'Farewell 1937-40'. Poems removed from earlier collections to later and from later to last have clearly sometimes been reworked – slightly, as a rule – in the process of transfer to their new environment, and in many cases only exist in final form. Even where a list of contents survives, the unpublished collections are therefore almost impossible to reconstruct with anything like precision.

*   *   *

Swingler's habit of mind was always large. Poems and closely-related sequences of 300 lines or more are common from the early *Reconstruction* through to *The Map*, his last poem, of 1966. 'Testament of an Army of Fatalists' (reprinted here as it appeared in *The Years of Anger*) is by origin the last third of a poem only; 'Pastoral XII' is the shortest of a long set, all linked. The nineteen poems of *The God in the Cave* are in two sequences so close-knit as to be in effect two poems. 'Enter the City', a work of more than 4,000 lines in sixteen-line stanzas, probably of 1937, is unusual only by maintaining one verse structure throughout. More often the big pieces contain a mixture of manners on which the changes are rung to make a mounting pattern of deliberate contrasts. *The Map* – because the last, necessarily not subsequently disturbed at all – contains a sonnet and several sets of rhymed quatrains within a framework of free and sprung verse. Such a mixture of forms is always the case when, as so often, parts of earlier work are re-assembled with other work later. Perhaps this is inevitable in the case of any poet relatively little published; but there is, I suggest, another reason.

'All I *want* to do is make a huge single statement', Swingler once told me, 'All I *can* do is make notes in passing.' On another occasion he said that if you wished to climb a mountain and describe it but couldn't, the only thing to do was walk round the foothills making as many notes as possible and saying why. The largeness of his poetic vision was of this order. Although he wrote many little poems, in a sense the little poem complete in itself bored and irritated him: better the imperfect piece pointing to something beyond. But his mind had also that interior coherence which obsessive image or recurrent theme gives any poet. A sort of geography, for instance, is always there – 'acres of power within me', 'no landscape but my own being', eventually *The Map* itself, possibly the one occasion on which he did eventually describe his mountain (but in the Sixties, not the Thirties). In a similar way, the succession of images 'sudden wilting of all our nourished purposes, all those green hopes', 'words fall sighing away into the undergrowth' and 'life goes underground and does illegal work' might, in another poet, have made a poem called 'Autumn to Winter' but are in fact from three separate pieces printed here, and the actual image is little worked in any of them save the last ('Interim').

The effect of this is odd but, I think, deliberate. On the one hand an individual poem often agglomerates images and thoughts in what sometimes seems a chaotic manner and doesn't pursue them back inside its lines. On the other, one constantly picks up echoes from one piece in another apparently quite differently occasioned. This I conceive to be precisely what he was after. The real poem was always the mountainous one not written yet. He *expected* each written one to be effected by where you found it among others, and *wanted* them – at least so he almost always presented them – in groups and sequences because on their own they couldn't perform this mapping function. It is rather as if each were a bearing and needed cross-bearings to give sense – not to itself, but beyond itself. Not that the group or sequence could only be assembled in one way: the same bearing could be read as crossing others. He could, and did, pull a piece out of context and place it in a totally different context – as with 'Testament of an Army of Fatalists', the neighbouring poems to which in *The Years of Anger* bear no relation to the rest of the longer poem from which he took it. This naturally sometimes involved some minor emendation here or there, which only he could make. And it renders the business of selecting poems to represent his Thirties work, as here, peculiarly difficult. One of his favourite stories – he used to tell it with enormous glee, hamming it up all round the walls of whatever room he was in – was the one about Turner's reputed habit of pointing up parts of his canvases, and toning down neighbouring canvases, on Varnishing Day at the Royal Academy. But it is the point of the story that Turner did the 'varnishing' himself.

When Swingler himself selected his Thirties work in the first three sections of *The Years of Anger* he severely limited the kinds of poems from which he chose. (Indeed the Epilogue at the end of the book reads in part, 'I do not believe that poetry speaks only with this voice, nor does this represent all the poetry I have

written during these years', and then proceeds to the two statements about 'public' and 'private' verse already quoted.) No
'public' verse was included and very little of the freer rhapsodic
'private' verse either. The book had great stylistic coherence – a
high proportion of pieces in formal rhyme and metrical schemes,
for instance – and was chiefly composed of short poems. But in
no sense, as he said, did it 'represent' his Thirties, for it was the
essence of the man that arbitrary divisions into 'public' and
'private' were not at the same time divisions of style. He used all
manners variously. Free verse could be either personal or for the
hustings; traditional forms could be for confidential, almost
metaphysical argument or for singing on the march. Of poems
printed here the formality of 'Sixty Cubic Feet' was all along
intended for public performance, that of 'Goaded beyond All
Patience' clearly for shouting aloud, while the similar formalities
of 'Acres of Power' or 'Rigid within Me' were nearer his
'whispers and murmurs . . . in the ear of a single person'. As it
happens, I find *The Years of Anger* magnificent, but it also
limits him.

Albeit very long poems cannot be included, the present selection, on the contrary, does try to 'represent' his Thirties – in a
way that perhaps he never would have done himself, at least not
without a good deal of Turneresque 'varnishing'. The only rule
of selection has been to choose 'private' and 'public' poems about
equally, and formal and free of both kinds; the only rule of
arrangement, to place them in their probable order of writing
between 1934 and 1940 – again, precisely *not* the arrangement
adopted by himself in *The Years of Anger*, with its overlapping
1936-38, 1936-41 and 1937-40 and even then no date-order
within each sequence. Such an attempt is bound to botch him:
what is wanted now (and it is in preparation) is a big fat book
with all his 'notes in passing' assembled and his mountains
evident, the complete atlas. Nonetheless the attempt has seemed
worth making. First, it hints at his many-sidedness as poet.
Second, it asserts what remembering the Thirties truthfully must
assert: that the enormous public political certainties of that time
rested, for those who held them and as such certainties always
will, on the resolution of personal doubt and troubled sense. There
is a sort of cartoon communist central to later writing about those
years – strident, propagandist, cocksure, silly, dummy to some
ventriloquist, dictatee, un-English, inhuman. If there ever were

such people, this poet, even at times this hectoring poet, was never one of them. He may, later, have changed his opinion, but the Epilogue to *The Years of Anger* ends by describing a quite different Thirties kind:

> I think it is important to add that these are the poems of a Communist, because it is often supposed that considerations of personal and poetic development are sacrificed as soon as the freely consented discipline of that party is undertaken, whereas I believe that Communism is the only fully creative attitude to life in our day, the only fully poetical attitude to life. They represent the efforts of one individual creatively to cope with the huge and brutal circumstances of history, to "subject the inner forces to his own control", and to achieve that personal freedom which is the recognition, and understanding, of necessity.

A.R.

PASTORAL XII

Especially when I take pen in hand
And watch the white chaos of paper
And rivers, contours, grow more complex and
Finer than spider's navel-spinning.
Especially as the world grows under
My fingers, its limit always known,
This page's edge, but growing, then I brood
Upon mountains throwing off into easy valleys
The condensations from the sky of my
Imagination, upon the white ridges
Like a serpent's wrinkled back, upon the snow
Reserved and still proud, dazzling all climbers
With remote beauty. And upon the lakes
Where birds rest and call and make
Their inspired and rhythmic flights. I look down
Upon a powerful veined land, upon
Flesh where the power is drawn up, gathered
Under the skin, knotted in knolls
And curling muscles of hills. I see evening
And morning visit, I see the abrupt silence
Of the moon. I see movement and waiting.
I am the creator. My power is here.
I look upon no landscape but my own being.

DIALOGUE

Ego

How shall we live through this time?
Shrieked at from hoardings, from screen and amplifiers
By the evidence of our coming defeat, how
Shall we be able to endure the sublime
Forever inaccessible dream
Of what so easily might have been ours?

Well for us to point the obvious way,
To explain exactly the resources and the means
The gradual unfolding, the initial procedure.
That is all very well. And yet to watch each day
The yawning spread of weakness, boys
Desperate for a last violent joy
Choosing the loudest death for leader.

To know that our words reach only those ears
Already opened to them. To know
We speak what only act makes true
And no man can refute but Fear
Of the first step, making the whole review
A mirage, stopping the finger on the gears.

Friends, is this a fine life, while our standing ground
Is daily narrowing, and the whole earth
Taunts and incenses us with its easy rondure
Of beauty's ebb and flush? Our birth
Was nothing but a drop in a cascade, the founding
Of our features only an aggregate
Of small defeats; our dreams reflecting
The sensible contraction of our power.

We were born of a dying tree,
Wrinkled fruit and to fall. It is a ghostly
Sap still passes with detached failing rhythm
The vertical memory of tallest growth and lost
Resilience in the branches, leaves loveliest
That sprang in ardour, hating nothing. These
Are the images of our sleep. For waking
Batters too hard on believing eyes the ceaseless
Barrage of factual decay.

Alter

Wait brother, was there no voice
Before the last complete eclipse: pictures of a tower
Vertical in rain, the trees lashed nude
On a comfortless coast: in the city
A tree stood in the courtyard wrapping the lamplight
In its new twigs, like a boy catching a moth,
And the light crept out softly
This way and that; the walking women
Stopped suddenly to look, something was touched
In them that lived; and they hurried away
Frightened. Do you suppose
These were chance things, or their collocation
A chance? In a high room
You had suddenly dared to tell the appalling secret.
The gate lifted: the force suddenly stronger
Than you, or you suddenly stronger
Than the prisoning force, knew perfect intimacy
Of understanding in simple shape and the gift
Transmitted with no tariff from port to port.
And then, you worked together, the hopeless task
Against time. One had failed formerly. It depended
Upon your group whether the gap be redeemed
Or the whole structure collapse, the key-link lacking.
You can never escape that moment, all of you
Linked in the compact of its power, the work
Fulfilling peace. Did earth taunt then?
On that hillside heaving girders, was the wind
Derisive? He carried your shouts, your ringing laughter,
The breath of your zeal like the pulse
Of a renewing strength. He shouted your will
Abroad like a stag's trumpet, and the curves
Of the hills leaped and the light coursed along them
Lifting and falling with the staves of your strength
And at day's end lapsing, dark into valleys, level
On roads and over water, inexplicably serene
With your exhaustion, your desire's complete respite.
No, the land opened about you then, a large
Projection of your labour. Pain's resistance
Sharpened your will to joy, as the dead air

Shapes the swallow. Was it so hard
To live through those times? Was there ever an era
Lifted men like an air-liner over the seas
Gusting their souls unasked with valour? Yet
You remember always the loss. Listen, do you know that day
Was yesterday? Do you know this morning
The silk of tentative vigour suffused your body
Like an April bud and the sun opening the curtains
Of your power? You were ready in that tomb
For easter rising. Then you were not the unfortunate,
But now, while you withhold yourself,
While you believe your words fall sighing
Away into the undergrowth like straying bullets; while
Your heart checks and doubts and the power stops
That should be charging the arm
To fill the hungering furnaces.

SIXTY CUBIC FEET

He was the fourth his mother bore
 The room was ten by twelve
His share was sixty cubic feet
 In which to build himself.

He sat and learned his letters
 With forty in a room
And sixty cubic feet of draught
 The Council lent to him.

At fourteen he must earn a wage
 He went to pit from school
In sixty feet of dust and gas
 He lay and hacked the coal.

At twenty-two they told him
 His freedom was at stake
He left his sixty cubic feet
 A soldier for to make.

He slept with seven others
 The tent was pitched on clay
The rain ran down the hillside
 And drenched them night and day.

He lay and coughed his heart out
  In sixty feet of damp
At last when he could hardly stand
  They marched him out of camp.

They brought him from hospital
  They brought him home alone
In sixty cubic feet of deal
  That he could call his own.

They buried him with honour
  The bugler blew Retreat
And now he claims of English earth
  Some sixty cubic feet.

INVITATION TO SOCIETY

1

Come, friend, slip away from your anxious evasive talking,
The crowds and the wall where the camera-men are always lurking;
Circumvent the main entrance to avoid questions,
And take this secret path, yourself at last.
You are getting no further, veering to each new demand,
Trying to mend your taint with already infected hands.
Think you, no trick can save us, no change of air,
Torchlit elation of masses and rape of power.
No, we are still alone and the time grows hot.
Hope is wilting in the catacombs of your crusted thought.
It cannot be done in a day or a night, the driving
Of stunted roots down and blocked shoots out into difficult air.
Nothing can change our world but a new daring
Of an old death, and lonely a new-born way of living.

2

Stop and consider. It is time to admit what well you know.
That the winter of your prestige is upon you already. The growing
Mistrust in the little houses of your compromise
Is frosty in these jubilant boughs. The ruse
Has been perceived by the men going home in buses,
By the men who sway and shake with the motion of the train.
Come down then, in the humility of reason, to meet the changer.
Come down to meet him, before he can overtake you,

Before he can take you by the shoulder suddenly to break you,
Suddenly to reveal you a hollow reed in the face of the crowd.
For you can delude no man of them, ever again.

3

Now you will have to admit the moment
When the finish came, when clearly, though you would hide it,
You no longer believed in your own pride,
No longer admired this one to whom they gave the honour;
But rather, could you confess it and confess the years
Of waste and easy surrender there implied,
Might have thrown away your cheque-book to grasp a stone
Learning its stillness and its instance and its simple demeanour
Washed by that watery passage it no longer fears.

4

It is time to acknowledge the end of one
Who existed only in a thousand fragments of broken glass.
It is time to make the admission, to go down
Unfaltering, unlistening to jeer
Or challenge; and to go down into death,
Who separates the motive from the act, who passes
His hand between the knowledge and the token
Between the desire and the will: who can
From the smoke-thickened lungs redeem pellucid breath
And by his wind of winnowing beat up the fire
And shape the rock with his denuding deluge.

5

The age we passed here, dodging to avoid him,
Now like sleepwalker pauses on the stair
Trembling at wakefulness while the leaves whirl up outside
Against the pane. But does not wake.
But returns
Groping through shreds of dark dreams, traps of secret desire
Threaded across his passage, that he may learn
In the morning of some intrusion nor ever be sure from whom,
And twist and torture himself through roomy
Nights in that intangible disquiet.

6

For the fact of age has descended from his always imminence
To settle upon your roof-trees and croak. And the sole sense
Of his mechanical boast is this: the owners have left
The house and ghosts live there aping their ancient habit,
And nothing is changed and nothing moves, but a dangerous
draught
Breaks in, and time lies heavy on the idle beams. The air
Gnaws away the untrodden carpets, and the stairs
Sag: the whole dead house rots and the rats will have it.

7

And you, growing old, can only confide
In the massed inertia of your years
And certain ribbons of experience
Preserved in drawers, memoirs of a brilliant day,
The dust fallen from action. But the stars have wheeled away
While you were posing, out of your hemisphere.
Yes, and the fire has sprinted across the convex heath and here
You stand petrified, where the ground is black and brown
Stubble. Those are ashes that your living leaves were.
The kite's croak the only sound and the old beams groaning.

8

Come then, this is the season for pruning. It is none too soon.
For this is the time when the nightjars throb from the telegraph
wires,
When memory slides her moons
So subtle and wistful out of the blurred raincloud,
Recalling the old ambitions, the figure they all expected,
The moods that somebody adored, the neglected
And no longer actual friends: a thousand silver illusions
Comforting sorrow with vanity's soft confusion
Of the image with the water and the well with the bounds of time.

9

Now is the season, before the rains reduce
All vigour to rejection; before the desires pass moaning
Outward on a mad rhetorical gale, and the warm juice
Withers in distraught and drooping limbs.
To cut away ruthlessly the dried and involuted plumage,
Age like a uniform, the cage of your possessions.

For the sun is choked in you, driving outward no rays
Till you have livened that centre with a real wound.

10

Tender from that death, from the ashes and the littered bones,
Invisibly the will tightened, will bud a perennial
Response, whose willing grace, with a stone's
Stillness, rounded by friction of spate and storm,
Gives back love's face, denying no roots of birth, prehensile
In earth, but unfelt, and in other hearts retentive.
Or else, locked in its form, exhaustive, motion of sleep,
Be hacked away, and from the raked pile
Again the smoke ascend, and air take remnants of that funeral.

11

What ghost abides to question this tree's rigidity
Erect in singleness as man and woman entwining
Their strength and softness, their giving and acceptance,
Their attack and repose? And the years that lie
Between their locked loins in sap, will unfold with the leopard's
Luxury and facile confidence:
And the foliage of their skin be shining
With issue of light, the full revolutions of love
And wisdom over their ocean of power, interminably moving.

ACRES OF POWER

Acres of power within me lie,
Charted fields of wheat and rye
And behind them, charted too,
Brooding woods of beech and yew.
Beyond them stretch, uncharted yet,
Marsh and mountain, dark and wet,
Whence sometimes in my dreams and ease
Strange birds appear among the trees.

The fields of corn are action's fruit,
Gripping the earth with puny root,
Their surface pattern neatly planned
Upon the chaos of my land.
Against the ruminating wood
They set a fence, but to no good;

The shadow and the sap of mind
Still weighs the harvest of my hand.

And the wild marches and the hills
Shut out by the imposing will
Yet hurl their livid storms across
To smash the fence and flood the fosse
And all his dictates and his laws
Cannot restrain that surging force,
For the whole land is my power still,
Divided, fenced, but no less real.

And one man only mourning goes
By day through the stiff planted rows
By night through the tangled wood, to gaze
On the vast savage wilderness.
The born surveyor, he that would
Turn the whole acreage to good,
Subject to one coherent plan
Dispensing the whole power of man.

But he between the fences dour,
This organizer of my power,
By rigid areas is confined
That sever impulse, hand and mind.
For he is only paid to see
That the fields grow obediently
And that the woods do not encroach
Nor the trees part to show the marsh.

For if the power that lavish there
Breaks into a sterile air,
Were planned and planted, fibre and juice,
And all my earth enlaced with use,
Then evil for his ruler's case
Whom to maintain in idleness
My fields of power are bought and sold
And all their goodness changed for gold.

Thus the land that is my life
Divided, ruled, and held in fief,
All the power it could produce
He cannot sell, but I could use.
And my surveyor, grim and harsh,

In secret now reclaims the marsh
That cultivated acres there
May bear a fruit for all to share.

INTERIM

The corn will shade again and the blown grass
Be nuptial in my sight: the hidden hills
Suddenly look out along divided country
And all the equipment of a lover's summer
Will storm the ready sky to capture nothing.
This will come again I know, though now
The acquiescent forces lie in mud
Gambling among themselves, smoking away
The thin end of the days, almost forgetting
That anything is meant to happen. Life
Goes underground and does illegal work
For whose effect but history has an eye.

IT IS NOT THE SORROW ONLY

It is not the sorrow only of men dying
Nor the dark cone of apprehension that draws up
All aspiration into its hood. It is not
The anxiety that makes the hand brittle as snow
And the heart ephemeral.

What is the main tragedy of this autumn
Is the common mind bent to the will of destruction.
Terrible for the time and despair to see
The sudden wilting of all our nourished purpose
All those green hopes of building, growing and making.

RIGID WITHIN ME

Rigid within me locked
The struggle of love and lies
Only its torture shows
Between my hooded eyes

My face is grooved with pride
My mouth is twisted too
With the defeated smile
That would both speak and hide

Now that I am all but dumb
Finding upon my throat
Falsehood's invisible thumb
Squeezing the thin truth out.

But love is breathing yet
Though worsted for the time
And there's a chance to get
Strength to avert the crime.

Love sees at last the trick,
By which its power was turned
To following images
Like visions of the sick.

It is enough to know
That love is fighting back
And the flat face of pride
Begins to crack.

And shall I find the honesty
To do the violence I must
And rescue from the sumptuous lie
The simple answers of the just?

The honour of many and the love
Of some, I must repudiate.
From their delightful purlieus move
To a small room and a cold grate.

Wary to spot the quick disguise
The quiet guardians keep their beat
To hunt out the persistent spies
Who fret the frontiers of defeat.

My will so easily deceived
Would yet be ready, for the song,
To condone those it once received
Willingly my loves among:

Apparent courage, flattering
Responsibility, and posts
Of negligible work that bring
Abrupt respect at little cost.

Oh think how lean my life, that I
Should chase the streets a nightmare's length
To bargain for respect and buy
A reputation with my strength!

At this tribunal where I sit
In judgement on a life's pretence
Though many fed the mouth that bit
And plead my friendship in defence—

Yet Mercy would be false to Love,
Pity a weakness that deceives,
One verdict and one sentence proves
Love that is free and Truth that lives.

NOW GOADED PAST ALL PATIENCE

Now goaded past all patience let us sing a song of hate
For all the wrongs of government we cannot tolerate.
For fiercely as we love the life for which we fight and long,
We hate with equal fierceness every lie that does it wrong.

We hate you first, our governors, for every promise made
To peoples like ourselves whom you have shamelessly betrayed.
We hate the slimy words of peace that dribble from your tongue
While to the rabid dogs of war our children's food is flung.

We hate your cynic speeches for the saving of your face,
While mothers starve and prices rise (and profits pile a-pace).
What do you care if workmen die and cities gasp for air,
While with the open plunderers you bargain for a share?

You have betrayed our friends, our peace, our freedom and our
trust,
And made our name through all the world a symbol of disgust.
Your smooth conciliations and your gentlemanly pacts
Conceal the plots of murderers and further their attacks.

Therefore our hatred and our wrath grows like a forest flame
And from the seats of government will drive you forth in shame
Who, zealous in the service of no interest but yours
Were cunning in avoiding truth as in fomenting wars.

Be realistic now, and go, you masters of deceit,
Our blood is up, our flames of wrath are snapping round your feet.
The truth breaks on us like a sun, and dark against it stands
Your own hypocrisy revealed, with blood upon its hands.

To keep your friends in power you have sold what was not yours
Mortgaged the lives of millions upon Munich's deed of war
You dare to say you brought us peace indifferent to the tread
Of the feet of thousands fleeing from the terror you have spread.

MARCH 1939

Man's joy is simple as the sun,
His misery tangled like decay.
For all that grows, is making one,
And all that dies, falling away.

And now this complicated doom
Only the simplest needs deny
Like sunlight in the morning room
Or spring or love or the March sky.

The weakling may be torn apart
By the fish-mouths of sickly hope
That somewhere from the ground will start
An unsuspected philanthrope—

These are the escapades of death,
The rumours of a change of heart,
A new world order built on faith
In all that has betrayed the past.

Still there remain the simple facts
Of war and hunger: and the power
Which greed in fewer hands contracts
Breeds pestilence and waste and fear.

Let spring and March speak in our ear.
Our need is simple: what we lacked
Was not the light to see it clear,
But courage and the will to act.

THE BEGINNING OF WAR

At the door of the world the thought of happiness
Looks back and leaves without another word:
A woman aged, who has made her last appeal
And failed.
        Now whirled in by a wind of horror

The dusk hangs over every house and the threat
Of plague with corpses and cordite in its breath.
Virtue is everywhere to be iron and man
Is admired for feeling nothing.
                              Oh if within
This rock there is still running the lightest vein
Of water from the spring—oh if there is still a time
When the eyes can soften and the heart float
Like the sun in restful cloud—and oh if the skin
Still gives with an unsureness, not of fear
But of expectation—then there is yet again
The chance of youth, the lips adroitly parted
To utter hope like happy rain.

TESTAMENT OF AN ARMY OF FATALISTS

In London's quivering darkness
    A million of us lie
And feel the houses shudder
    And the trains grumble by.
Our morning's expectation
    Sinks like a sleeper's sigh
For while the year is waking
    We are about to die.

We who have watched it coming
    But hid it with a lie,
The hope that none believed in,
    The fear we daren't defy,
Now feel the nets about us
    Enclosing swift and sly.
We turned our face from living.
    We are about to die.

We heard but never listened.
    We sold to them that buy
Our senses with our labour:
    Then watched them fill the sky
With broods of death and darkness
    And never asked them why.
Now we have got our answer
    We are about to die.

They minted mind and vigour:
   They drained our bodies dry:
They trapped us in the marshes
   Of workless lethargy.
They blocked all roads to living
   And scotched the will to try.
Now as our final service
   We are about to die.

You who are coming after
   To whose unblunted eye
The sun showers down a future
   And the summer signals fly,
You shall not have to name us
   Either with sneer or sigh
For not in the war they wanted
   Are we about to die!

Massed in our veins the anger
   They could not mortify
Will to their final order
   Make this our last reply:
Though it is late for learning
   And death's what we learn it by,
Fighting our own cause only
   Are we prepared to die.

THE DISPOSSESSED

We are the men no force can further maim.
Familiar every insult, every hurt.
Greater and darker we know is the shadow of fear
Than pain's more actual fire.

We are the men with no pride and no shame.
How should we envy? Do we covet the dirt
That clogs your pores, the stones that weight your shoes?
We are the victors, who have nothing to lose.

You cannot know the fulness of our silence.
We are at rest, for the worst that you could do
Was to strip off the fears that gave us pause
And leave us clean to act our cause.

You time-bound men, the agony is yours.
Yearning to stop and forget, passing your hand
Over aching eyes,—oh to be utterly blind—
To those who cannot act, it is torture to see.

Desperate sight, never unanxious love,
Distorted gesture of the body, strangled desire,
To own is to be owned: and he that wears
The prison keys is prisoner to his fears.

But we are patient, for history is our setting.
Life strikes up from the root to build its pattern
Working its way in us, moving our blood,
Never stopping, never forgetting.

'Acres of Power', 'March 1939', 'The Beginning of War' and
'Testament of an Army of fatalists', were first published in *Years
of Anger*.

Poems and a Play by Montagu Slater

Montagu Slater was born in 1902 in the small Cumberland mining port of Millom which faces North Lancashire across the estuary of Duddon Sands. His father Seth Slater, a strict lay-preaching Wesleyan, was the town tailor whose shop was also Millom's only post office. Unusually for such a time and background Slater won a scholarship to Oxford from the local secondary school and graduated in 1924, going straight from university to Liverpool as a reporter on the *Post*. While there he worked with, and lived in the open dormitory of, a dock settlement, becoming increasingly involved in local Wobbly, Co-op and Labour politics. It is possible that he joined the newly-formed communist party as early as 1927, but only certain that he was in it by 1930 and remained a life-long member. He left Liverpool in 1928 to join first the *Observer*, later the *Daily Telegraph*, in London, having returned to Liverpool to marry in 1929. Although they retained strong ties with the North, the Slaters' various homes from this time on were always in or within commuting reach of London. They had three daughters.

At Millom and Liverpool Slater had written much verse, mostly in round-rhyming heroic couplets, relating northern port-life to images of classical legend and philosophical debate. He always prized this work and a great deal of it survives. The move from Liverpool was initially however a shift to prose. In 1931 appeared his first novel, in 1934 his second; but by that time had begun his love affair with Drama in all her forms. In the decade from 1933 came a torrent of plays, seven of which survive, two of which were performed; a series of Pageants for the Co-op movement, only hints at which have I been able to discover though all were produced; the beginnings of a long career as film-scripter; and the association with Benjamin Britten which was to culminate in their opera, *Peter Grimes*. Britten, incidentally, asserted that his *Young Person's Guide to the Orchestra* would never have come into being without Slater's first setting the project up and then, in the face of grant-aid troubles, totally rescripting it.

This intense activity is inseparable from his commitment as a communist. His regular journalism for the national press ended in 1934 when he became editor-in-chief in the founding team of *Left Review*. He largely fixed its tone, and continued as a regular contributor under the subsequent editorships of Edgell Rickword and Randall Swingler. As well as those signed Montagu Slater, contributions by Ajax, C. M. Slater (his true initials), C. Slater and variously-initialled Charleses (Charles was his first name) are also by him. As a natural corollary he was politically active in writers' organisations, in the NUJ, in that plethora of small left-wing theatre groups which preceded and continued after the foundation of Unity Theatre and around the Group Theatre, in the Workers' Music Association; but he himself regarded as crucial his ordinary communist branch membership and activity and, especially, his continuing work in the Co-op movement among people with whom his background made him most at ease.

As Head of Scripts in the Film Division of the MOI during the war his creative energies turned largely to scriptwork. Nonetheless he became theatre critic of the Co-op *Reynolds News,* was among the founders of *Our Time* in 1940 and formally joined its board in 1944, later (in 1947) founding the quarterly *Theatre Today* from that base – the same political commitments continuing in the same wide way.

The *Peter Grimes* libretto of 1945, a big dramatic poem in its own right (indebted to Crabbe for only its opening and closing choruses), stems directly from the part-verse plays of the Thirties and the earlier work with Britten. Subsequent librettos of 1950 and 1956 are less poetic though they use song interpolatively – for the decade from 1944 is marked again by a switch to prose. Eight novels survive, six of which were published – *The Inhabitants* (1948) is of particular interest since it fictionalises much of his Millom/Liverpool background – and two other considerable published prose books. Slater had great hopes of Theatre '46, the trades union sponsored season of plays at the Scala Theatre which produced his *Century for George*; but in fact the recession of Labour fervour under Labour governments must have seemed total, the work within the professional theatre his old friends Devine and St Denis were to initiate too far ahead to see, and the informalities of an 'alternative theatre' of the kind he had himself implied in his thirties work even further. I can find only one later play, fragments of two, perhaps three others, and a translation.

There is plenty of activity of course. (Slater is not possible to remember without it.) I find thirty-three film or television projects in various states from treatment through to shooting script among his postwar papers, and these quite apart from the ones which actually proceeded; but they wear the air of writing to order, and Mrs Slater confirms that his income largely derived from film commissions which only rarely engaged his passions. (In only two cases out of the thirty-three, is his belief palpable.)

Indeed I read the documentary novel, *Englishmen with Swords* of 1949, in which a secretary to the Army Council relives and then inters his passionate engagement in the English Civil Wars, as to some extent Prospero renouncing magic. Be that as it may, Mrs Slater tells of an enormous bonfire of manuscript and typescript in 1950. This seems to have been a decision to proceed as lyric, not as dramatic poet. Into four folders kept in his desk go the early poems of Millom and Liverpool, ideas for poems, new poems, and pages – usually containing songs or verse exchanges between characters – ripped from plays of which no other sign remains. For the rest, novels, librettos, filmwork and some, at least, of the early plays go higgledy-piggledy into a great chest along one wall of his study.

The only serious attention paid Montagu Slater since his death in 1956 was in *The New Reasoner*, Vol. 1 No. 4 of 1958. This took the form of poems 'selected by Edgell Rickword' and a memorial piece by J. R. St John. The poems are an odd lot, often not in their final (sometimes previously published) versions, and mix the 1930s confusingly with the 1950s. Rickword tells me they were virtually all he was shown by St John, to whom all the papers had been made available by the family. The memorial too, though loving enough, is inaccurate.

*   *   *

Dating undated, unpublished and largely typewritten work is a hazardous business; and all that can be said for the supposed chronological order in which the poems are printed here is that it makes sense of family memory, the memory of friends and colleagues like myself and Rickword, occasional internal references to outer events, the occurrence of slang or fashionable words, addresses where the work in question was submitted and an address given, changes in handwriting, discoloration of paper, the styles of binding used by literary and copying agencies where one in a series can be dated for other reasons: above all, changes in style. These last are of two chief sorts.

Very broadly, the poetry moves from heroic couplets (Millom and Liverpool) to a four-stress line and half-rhymes (the early plays) and, if in lyric, four-line stanzas, to quirky irregular verse-forms and varying line-lengths which characterise the final poems. Blank verse is usually early, other unrhymed verse late; half-rhyme generally an indication that the source of a piece is a play or libretto. Equally broadly, though stated in scenes and Acts, the early plays were written with little chance of conventional commercial production, perhaps with none intended, and are structurally more adventurous – for the date, sometimes astonishingly so – than the late.

Peter Grimes and Other Poems (1946) is Slater's only published book of poetry. The verse parts of that curious mixture of prose, verse and playlet, 'The Figure of a Nobody', which concludes the volume all date back to his Millom/Liverpool beginnings. Nonetheless the folders of poetry he left indicate that he was continuing to prepare a book of that earliest verse under the title *The Venereal Hypothesis* and a general collection of his later poems. There is a handlist for this last which suggests an approximate order of writing. Where other things agree (or all else fails) I have made use of it in dating.

The poems printed here are in a sequence running from 1931 to 1940. Most have not been printed before, though 'The Fear' appeared in *The New Reasoner* group and 'Mother Comfort' is available with its published setting by Benjamin Britten. Unfortunately lines from the superb and unknown verse play *Out of Liverpool* proved inextricable from action and narrative so the chorus from *Easter 1916*, in the same manner and close in time (1935), takes their place – although it appeared in *Peter Grimes and other Poems*. It should be noted that Slater's Choruses from plays are impersonal, not usually in the mouths of dramatis personae, while songs are for characters whose natures they partly express. The Ballad from *Domesday*, for example, is sung by a confused romantic fumbling back towards an older tradition.

Finally, for anyone under the glowering lea of modern orthodoxy about communism in the Thirties, I should make the point that this selection specifically does not exclude russophile or rabble-rousing or pamphleteering or way-hay-the-revolution

G

verses. Simply, Slater never wrote them – though non-communist Auden, for instance, did. That orthodoxy, at least, is a hulk awash on myth.

A.R.

LOVE, WE CAN LIE BACK

Love, we can lie back and laugh or cry now,
Having killed our demon like Tobit with his fish.
Love, we have finished with hopes and guesses.
The past is accomplished and we ignore the future.
And you may live on, but I — I may as well depart now.

Love, it is begotten or it is not begotten.
Your flower-like flesh accepts the ambiguity,
Your nakedness native to earth as any plant,
And the trees welcome your essence to their company.
So you may live on but I — I may as well depart now.

And if it is a male child, pricked with this self-same lack
That shuts him from the idleness of trees and animals
(For even a dog in rut has no place in the sun
But grey activity bare and unmetaphored)
Live on Lillith and do not be too sorry when he also departs.

AN ELEGY

written in the shadow of a mountain in a northern mining port
which, established in the 19th century, proved superfluous to the
needs of the 20th—1931.

When the last candle of the day gives over
its conflagration of the quivering air
And riven curtains of the west discover
endless tranquility projected there:

and the sun drowns in continents of wests,
earth, redolent of shadow, never free
from sun's corrosion, till his lusty breasts
touch the horizon of a menstrual sea —

Mountain, whose rondure is determinate
by riches of your still unshafted mines,

chambers and galleries and caves intestate,
a various hoard which every twig divines:

the glimmering presence of your urgent Jove
your shoulder hummocking above the screes
where smoky clouds bend daylight as it moves
to closure in imperfect cadences

tells how an earthquake had once split the rock
and giant sparks leaping the centuries
found the dead shafts and mines of human thought
and legends of imaginary countries.

                    *   *   *

Our little lives, our chapels and our hymns,
mining and fishing — apostolic round —
a tidal river governed with its whims
neap tides renew but spring tides leap the bounds.

Once, annually, our men forsook their trade,
Hired wagonettes to where the rocks begin
climbed through the night to ambuscade
the earliest secret of the rising sun;

to see the inhuman world open its eyes,
screes at their feet and laminated shale,
on the north-west the Cumbrian mountains rise
and to the south the glimmering peaks of Wales.

And then returning to their normal lives
found that their minds were overshadowed by
a memory of the mountain, and their wives
discovered in them puzzling sympathy.

Now solemn the precedent shadow fails,
like disintoxication, like dismay
of clocks set going after drinking brawls
with unrelenting news of yesterday

and down the dream-choked gullet of the street
crab-like on an ambiguous journey led
we read in all the faces that we meet
stale news, a preterite of the nearer dead.

And being mindful of the twilight mood
and the grave charm of the alternate note
the lyric burden of this solitude,
satyricon for any golden throat;

we hold the drowsy magic of the form
till the full cycle of the song disposes
that voices rhythm-cheated of the norm
in the old dark repeat the older closes.

And touch, which is the lover's sense, implies
a membrane's pleasure when a last bird sings
of night's scarce-scented guesses, and the eyes
give up the kingdom of all visible things.

COCK CROW

The cock crows twice. I turn and toss
Dreaming the honeysuckle is so sweet
I can imagine it in sleep.
But when the cock crows I am lost.

I dread the meaning of his trumpet
From my high-gardened sleep and grieve
That coming of the day should heave
Away the contemplative blanket.

Here is another day to dress
The ruffled feathers, the brown egg
In clucking wonder to be laid.
Energy is unhappiness

Unhappiness but homing here,
Here in the garden, here the bee
Homes to the honeysuckle tree.
But the cock crows a thought too near.

The world turns . . . . . am I afraid?
I can feel conscience multiplied
By chiding voices millionfold
Cock-crowing now, 'Have you betrayed?'

The cock crew twice, crew twice. I know
One more summons is permitted
By tradition of the city.
Cock crow cock crow cock crow cock crow.

THE EBB AND FLOW OF THE MOON

The ebb and flow of the moon is now
A shuttle that imprisons you
Setting your being to a tune
Governed by ebb and flow of the moon.

The crescent moon, a pallid ghost
Stares bleakly on a naked coast
Sets in the twilit afternoon
Rises laboriously at dawn.

Third quarter is the false attempt;
For truth is great but it was meant
To prevail only when the mind
Swims like a cork on the spring tide.

Fourth quarter, hush, the night is long
The hushed sea whispers to the moon
That leans on a reflective breast.
Sing lullaby the flooded coast.

THE FEAR

Labourers and tradesmen are
The population of this star
And the solar system turns
On labouring and trading terms.

Gravitation's mystic bonds
May be measured in foot-pounds
And fixed stars raise from ancient graves
Old light like capital reserves.

Attraction — ah! the lover's debt —
Centrifugal curves offset,
And the old dissatisfaction
Is moon-hidden by rotation.

Nebulae and Milky Way —
In between them wise men say,
In blank spaces of the sky
Lurks the fear of bankruptcy.

BALLAD

Listen to the mournful drums of a strange funeral,
Listen to the story of a strange American funeral.

In Braddock, Pennsylvania
Where the steel mills flare
The spring came in like a frightened child
In an ogre's lair.

Jan Clepak a Bohemian
Going to work at five
Sees grass on the hills across the river
Plum blossoms all alive.

He sweats at his puddling trough
Half naked like a fiend
And the blossoming memories soften his heart
Make his thoughts mild

He thinks of cows and sheep
In sunny Bohemia
And his baby's little laughters and the way men sing
When they're happy and drunk.

Listen to the mournful drums of a strange funeral,
Listen to the story of a strange American funeral.

Wake up brother Clepak, wake up
Wake up, it's ten o'clock
The furnaces roar and the mad flowing steel
Pours into your puddling trough.

Wake up, the lever's cracked
The steel is running through
Wake up! Oh, the dream is ended, the steel has got you.
John Clepak's napoo.

Three tons of hardened steel
Hold at their heart and bones
The nerves, the muscle of John Clepak
And his dreams of home.

The steel mill directors
A coffin of steel will give
To the widow and family of the late John Clepak
To go in a giant grave.

His widow and two friends
Ride in a carriage behind
The truck with the three ton block of steel
With John Clepak inside.

Listen to the mournful drums of a strange funeral,
Listen to the story of a strange American funeral.

By the grave one thinks to himself
'I shall not get drunk from now on
Nor ever get married for life is a dirty
Joke like Jan's funeral'.

'I'll wash clothes, scrub floors,
I'll be a fifty cent tart
But my kids won't work in the steel mill'
Says his wife in her heart.

'I'll make myself hard as steel, harder,
Like bullets from Jan's corpse',
The other friend's thinking, listening,
What to? Drums of course.

from *Domesday*, a 3-act play, 1933, much indebted to Jack
London's *Iron Heel*.

INCITEMENT TO DISAFFECTION: A FRAGMENT

Forming up in the street
As if apologising for being there, soldiers
Very bright-eyed, Ben going up to a double file remembering the
next door banjo when Deacon's soldier son strummed all day
long, only 17 then, at Frances and Day stuff
Pompapom pompapom pimpapombimbam

> Khaki's a nice quiet colour
> Tin hats don't shine
> Sombre as a Humphrey Davy
> In a fire-damp mine.

> Soldiers, who form in double file
> With a grave space between
> Your gantry wants its cross shorings
> With bayonets in.

Death in the spirit-level
Governs your double line
Khaki's a nice quiet colour
Tin hats don't shine . . . . .

Ben saying: 'Come boys — what's the odds, your khaki against my dungarees', but they knocked him off before he got any farther.

SPEECH FOR A FASCIST

Men, comrades, now that you are going to enter
A night of fear and a winter of war
Does it seem good that we should go over
What is our cause, what our convictions are?

You know, most of you, how the Marxists
Sprinkle desire with a dry sand,
Till women's beauty and man's physical courage
Are sick with self-distrust and undermined.

You know, most of you, how the Jew in business
Has turned virtue into advertisement,
Buying and selling love; and that the Freemasons
Have made kingliness into a cheap scent.

You know we promise no millennium.
Whatever reward there is, is in the fight.
We warn you that it may not prove possible
To set mankind's twisted reactions right.

We offer you, simply the opportunity
To free your daydreams from the mirror's ghost
And free your hate — for when hate is secreted
Man's blood is poisoned and his seed is lost.

Beware of him who has no vices
There are less innocent forms of power.
We hail the dignity of laying down
Our old self-worship in our country's hour.

We shall not hide war and its bitterness.
We tell this lost battalion that its weird
Is air attack and treacherous poison warfare.
This, our Golgotha, is to free the world.

And lead mankind into a sunlight fighting,
Corpuscles flushed and lungs full of fresh air
And clean quarrels and new adventures —
Life as it was before the Jew was there!

*   *   *

You know that death and torture are our weapons
Sup full of horrors. When you feel
The steel whip on your hide, then you know our lessons
Are rudimentary but they are not dull.

Spoken by 'Leader', a figure in the hero's dream, *Cock Robin,*
1934. The fourth verse, with the last verse added, occur as a
reprise.

CHORUS (from a Pageant?)

O in this spring-tide you would say the sun
Had been drowned also, and that one by one
The waves wash over it, and the waves shout
With the diffused glory that they toss about.

Turn from the tide, the tide that overflows
Wind-laden, for its murmuring power will blow
Tonight into a storm that calendars
Will boast and marvel at in coming years.

CHORUS FROM 'EASTER 1916'

Woman Is Pity abhorrent?

Man Is pity a tyrant
When bombs, explosions
Mark her decisions?

Woman Sure bullets quiver
And shriek whenever
The warm flesh stops them.

Man Our sandbags trap them.

Woman Your thoughts are bullets
And hearts their targets.

G*

Man	Your pity's a tremor Soldiers allow for In every manoeuvre.
Woman	Until they meet Their own death in the street And swift bereavement On the white pavement.
Man	Your pity weakens Hope when it quickens.
Woman	Hope's no more needed We'll sacrifice it; But leave us the lovers For whom we prize it. Leave shillings to spend And pennies to keep And the warm featherbed Of sleep.
Man	Sleep is a death that Waking to combat Thrusts a cold nozzle Into the snuggle.
Woman	Your thoughts are bullets.
Man	And men their targets.
Woman	What wrong have they done you?
Man	Their minds are without hope.

MOTHER COMFORT

a song for two female voices

A	Dear, shall we talk or will that cloud the sky?
Both	Will you be Mother Comfort or shall I?
B	If I should love him where would our lives be?
A	And if you turn him out at last, then friendship pity me.
Both	My longing like my heart, beats to and fro Oh that a single life could be both Yes and No.

Will you be Mother Comfort or shall I?

B   Ashamed to grant and frightened to refuse
        Pity has chosen, Power has still to choose.

A   But darling, when that stretched out will is tired
        Surely your timid prettiness longs to be over-power'd?

Both   Sure gossips have this sweet facility
        To tell transparent lies and, without pain, to cry.
        Will you be Mother Comfort or shall I?

The first of *Two Ballads for two voices and pianoforte* by Benjamin Britten, 1937. The second ballad is Auden's 'Underneath the Abject Willow'.

WOMEN'S CHORUS

We are women. Is to weep
The last privilege we keep?
We are women and we bore
All the fighters in your war

Men you mustered into hell
While our daughters filled the shells
That scattered villages in dust,
And rags and sticks and flesh that rots.

We are women; and the curse
Of plague is given us to nurse.
We are women. Shall we keep
Woman's custom still, and weep?

We whose sons and lovers were
Charred and maimed, disfigured there;
We whose lives of empty waiting
Losing hope are soured with hatred —

Shall we forgive with cheeks aglow
Hearing a mournful bugle blow?
Shall a leader terrorise
Us to see through coward's eyes?

We are women and we know
Flushed cheek and fever glow,

And the music crying glory,
And the ancient lying story.

We are women and we know
How much fighting is to do;
How much blood to make a dawn;
With what pangs a man is born.

We are women, and we know
Knives are wanted to cut free.
If a priest leads to the grave
Women still lead back to life.

We are women, shall we keep
Woman's custom still, and weep?
Or take life and love in hand
Love for this or any land

For the children gazing now
Into vistas of dismay
For the gardens that will gape
Into shelter pits and graves

Women who have suffered long
Stand unarmed against the strong
Know the enemy is down
When his heart is turned to stone

Our bare hands against this terror;
Our clear truth against this error,
Against his bowing down to death
The burning of our flame of life.

Now proclaim this day to gather
All the friends of life together
Siege the monster in his lair
Suffocate the god of war.

We are women and proclaim
This is the accepted time.
Nations, peoples, men and women
Children in the glow of morning

Make a ring round the aggressor
Dispossess the dispossessor
Build the warm alliances
Of humanity for peace.

from *Towards Tomorrow,* a pageant of co-operation, performed
Wembley Stadium, July 2, 1938

THE HUNTER AND THE HUNTED

I was a Stoic philosopher
In the lonely days of youth
I studied every day and night
They told me I'd find truth
If only I worked hard enough
And goodness absolute.

I met a Cynic on the way
Who played the Socrates.
'In what way is the end you seek
Different from happiness?'
He asked. It seemed as if I looked
Over a precipice.

I told him my professors sought
The Stoics' final goal
Where having lost fear and desire
Anger they never feel.
At last — and I recall his smile —
Why, sir, they hardly feel at all.

And yet now I am older I
Regret those happy days
When not to seek was one way of
Discovering happiness.
Now she hunts me, and therefore I
Understand tragedies.

CHORUS

. . . . . Civilisation, as they said,
Is either living or is dead
And the past mastery survives
As retranslated in our lives.

Behind success in battle lies
Eagerness searching in the skies
Exploring in the stratosphere
The long watch through the Polar Year
Devising aeroplanes on skis
To land on airfields made of ice
Wresting the secrets Nature hugs
And fights over like tiger cubs.
That is the cost. Experiment
Ever watchful where it went,
Aware if Nature shows no quarter
The human foe's an uglier master.

1940 or 1941,

subsequently used in *An Agreement of the People*, Empress
Stadium, June 1942 (in which Philosopher was played by Professor C. E. M. Joad who wrote his own words).

BIBLIOGRAPHY OF MONTAGU SLATER'S WRITINGS
UP TO 1940

Published/Performed		*Unpublished/Unperformed*
	1929	THE VENEREAL HYPO-THESIS, the title under which early verse was later collected
	1930	ST. JAMES'S PARK, a long poem in the same heroic couplet style
SECOND CITY, a novel about Liverpool, *Wishart*	1931	
	1933	DOMESDAY, 3-Act prose play about the victory of fascism in England, 'indebted to London's *Iron Heel*'
HAUNTING EUROPE, a novel about the defeat of fascism by revolution, *Wishart*	1934	
	1934	COCK ROBIN, 2-Act prose-and-verse play in which the hero relives the struggle against (English) fascism while under anaesthesia. May have been performed as Part II of a Review by Left Theatre
EASTER 1916, a play with verse choruses about the Irish Rebellion. Various South London *Town Halls* and *Phoenix Theatre*, pub. *Wishart*	1935	
STAY DOWN MINER, a play with verse choruses about the 1935 pit-bottom sit-ins in South Wales. *Westminster Theatre*, pub. Williams	1936	

and Norgate as A NEW
WAY TO WIN

STAY DOWN MINER, a re-   1936
portage account of the same
sit-ins. *Wishart*

Published/Performed		Unpublished/Unperformed
	1937	OUT OF LIVERPOOL, largely verse play, 3 Acts, about a voyage to the Ballarat Gold Rush. Later (1949?) circulated as No. 15 of *New Theatre's* Play Series
'Mother Comfort' the first of TWO BALLADS FOR TWO VOICES AND PIANO, Benjamin Britten, *Boosey & Hawkes*. The other was by Auden	1937	
CO-OP PAGEANT, title unknown, for which Benjamin Britten recalls writing music now lost	1937	
TOWARDS TOMORROW, a Co-op Pageant, now lost, *Wembley Stadium*, July 2	1938	
THE SEVEN AGES OF MAN and OLD SPAIN, puppet plays with music by Benjamin Britten. The Binyon Puppets *Mercury Theatre*	1938	
CO-OP PAGEANT, title unknown	1939	
	1939	I WANT A HERO, 3-Act prose play about Byron with the International Brigades at Missolinghi
	1940	THE GOOD SOLDIER, a free version of the Hasek novel, 3-Act prose play

STAY DOWN MINER

A Play in Three Acts by Montagu Slater

Produced twice in 1936, first at the Westminster Theatre, then again for tour through various public halls, *Stay Down Miner* was published in 1937 as *A New Way to Win*. This change was largely due to the fact that Slater had also used the original title for a short reportage account of the actual events in South Wales on which the play is based. Since all contemporary references are to the play and not to that book, now long out of print and likely to remain so, and since Slater himself preferred the original title, it is here restored. The text, the only one we have been able to discover, is the slightly revised one of the published edition.

Author's Note

In the first version of the play there was a song which has disappeared from the present text. The song might well be used still during a scene-change, or at the beginning. It has been set for male voices by Benjamin Britten. The words are as follows:

These foothills which we speak of as a mountain
Are crossed by long-legged sheep and telpher span.
Mountains are formed by turmoil in earth's crust;
The minerals bear their backs and miners must.

If any peak, however weather-worn
Feels dental-drillings, then a town is born:
Sometimes unsheltered, where the bracken grew
And sometimes pouched as by a kangaroo.

The foothills splayed like fingers on a hand
Shelter the southern ports and fatter land;
Oh! climb still northward where the wrist joins on
To the Black Mountains and the hills of Brecon.

Oh! climb still northward and against the wind
Into a world of mineral-bearing ground.
Mountains are formed by turmoil in earth's crust;
The minerals bear their backs and miners must.

M.S.

CHARACTERS

(In order of appearance)

RHYS	Colliery Manager.	
WILL LEWIS . . .	Miner.	
DAI ROBERTS . . .	His nephew.	
HOWEL	Miner and local preacher.	
BRONWEN	His sister.	
BOXER JONES . . .	A local boxer.	
LLIO JONES . . .	His wife.	
GWEVRIL	Howel's daughter.	

MAGISTRATE (may double with RHYS)
POLICE INSPECTOR AND CONSTABLES

The action of *ACT I* takes place at:

The pit-head	.	. *Scene I.*
The pit-head	.	. „ *II.*
Colliery office	.	. „ *III.*
The pit-head	.	. „ *IV.*

The action of *ACT II* takes place at:

Howel's house	.	. *Scene I.*
Near pit-head	.	. „ *II.*
Llio's house	.	. „ *III.*
Near pit-head	.	. „ *IV.*
Railway line	.	. „ *V.*

The action of *ACT III* takes place at:

Pit-bottom .	.	. *Scene I.*
The pit-head	.	. „ *II.*
Pit-bottom .	.	. „ *III.*
Pit-head .	.	. „ *IV.*
A Court Room	.	. „ *V.*

ACT I—Scene I

Near the pit-head at Cwmllynfach. Down stage right the entrance to the colliery offices. Down stage left is a seat in the angle of a stone wall. Here Will Lewis, an old miner, sits smoking his clay pipe.

Rhys, the colliery manager, passes. He is a quiet, heavy man, Victorian in his outlook and in his appearance.

RHYS: Good morning, Lewis.

WILL LEWIS: Humph!

RHYS: Seeing life from your beloved corner?

WILL LEWIS: No, Mr Rhys manager. It is not my blo— beloved corner. It is free to the town.

RHYS: You don't call Cwmllynfach a town, do you?

WILL LEWIS: My father did and while he has been rotting Cwm has been rising. There are 858 people in Cwmllynfach now.

RHYS: I've noticed that Cwmllynfach people become self-centred.

(*He passes. Exit R.*)

WILL LEWIS: Do you live in Cwmllynfach yourself then? Oh no.

(*Dai Roberts comes on L., a youth about 19, Will Lewis's nephew.*)

DAI: He's but a stranger here, heaven is his home.

WILL LEWIS: Where are you going, Dai?

DAI: To see where my feet will carry me, uncle.

WILL LEWIS: Come here, Dai.

DAI: You sound like a curtain lecture.

WILL LEWIS: I am.

(*Dai comes back and waits. Will Lewis puffs at his pipe and grunts.*)

DAI: When does the lecture begin, Will Lewis uncle? Do I have to have tickets?

WILL LEWIS (*clears his throat*): Dai——

DAI: I'm waiting.

WILL LEWIS (*clears his throat*): I've something to say to you.

DAI: So you were saying—(*Will Lewis clears his throat*)—but what?

WILL LEWIS: Dai . . . Dai . . . you've been going with a woman.

DAI: No, I should not do that, man.

WILL LEWIS: What is Gwevril Williams then?

DAI: Gwevril is not a woman for three years, until she gets on speaking terms with herself, man.

WILL LEWIS: Dai, I am talking to you like an uncle, and that is difficult for an uncle has not the practice of a father. But, Dai nephew, if for a moment of quietness we can compose ourselves . . . (*he dwells on the last syllable of 'compose'*) . . . How far has it gone?

DAI (*shifting quickly to the defensive*): Uncle Will Lewis you are getting narrow-minded.

WILL LEWIS: Are you going to get married?

DAI: We have not thought of it. Why should we?

WILL LEWIS: People say——

DAI: People say—and what the deowl has it to do with them and their tongues, putting their dirty ideas into our heads!

WILL LEWIS (*solemnly*): Dai nephew——

DAI: Well.

WILL LEWIS: I do not wish to take any credit, but have I done a good job since your father came up that shaft feet foremost?

DAI: In Cwm they say you've been very generous.

WILL LEWIS: You have been to the mining college. You could be an official if there were any jobs in South Wales.

DAI: It's not my fault I have no job. It's all South Wales.

WILL LEWIS: It's all the world. . . . Do we understand each other, Dai nephew? While things are as they are, no women for you, not even Gwevril.

DAI: I've got to live, man.

WILL LEWIS: Dai nephew, you're a very young fellow.

DAI: If you'd got my blood——

WILL LEWIS: Your blood and my blood, Dai nephew, is the same colour.

DAI: It's not the colour of it, Will Lewis. You are the oldest bachelor in Cwmllynfach, while I—I—I—am like a magnet.

WILL LEWIS: Where are you going to land us, Dai Roberts? Can't you control yourself?

DAI: You can think coolly, man, because you do not know what you are thinking about.

WILL LEWIS: If you had known me in my youth, man——

DAI: That was in Queen Victoria's reign: Will Lewis was the loudest singer in the local choir.

WILL LEWIS: Dai Roberts, you shared my pay with your mother while she lived. In two days there is the end of that story.

DAI: You know where to put it then.

WILL LEWIS: Ay.

(*Dai goes; then turns back.*)

DAI: I apologise, but you started it, Will Lewis uncle.

WILL LEWIS: Ay—and you'd like me to go on feeding you and educating you. Ay. . . . You misunderstood what I was saying.

DAI: It was the usual end of a curtain lecture. I was angry and misunderstood purposely.

WILL LEWIS: No. You were merely misunderstanding. I meant that after to-morrow, Will Lewis's ordinary occupation is the late lamented.

DAI: You're not that old.

WILL LEWIS: No?

DAI: They can't sack you yet, man.

WILL LEWIS: Can't they? It is not age that is influencing. I am not the only sufferer. I have been told that they are starting the Rock Vein on Monday and all the local miners will be replaced by men from Merthyr and other parts.

DAI: They can't sack all Cwmllynfach.

WILL LEWIS: Perhaps they will try, Dai nephew.

DAI: All Cwm?

WILL LEWIS: It may come to that, man.

DAI: But it is our own mine.

WILL LEWIS: Tell that to Mr Rhys, will you?

DAI: What shall we do?

WILL LEWIS: We can take home our picks and shovels for our back gardens, and if you have youthful blood, Dai nephew, you shall use it with circumspection.

DAI: It's hard luck, isn't it?

WILL LEWIS: We are used to it.

DAI: You may be, man. I am not.

WILL LEWIS: You have lived in South Wales all your life, you should be.

DAI: It wasn't so hard in your day, uncle, you had not the same ideas.

WILL LEWIS: When we were young our heads seemed to be busy—except that afterwards we found that what was busy was not our heads.

DAI: You were all chapel-goers. There were no dances, no pictures.

WILL LEWIS: The two sexes were different, even twenty years ago.

DAI: Yes, the women sat on one side of the chapel and the men on the other: so you went—to chapel, you went to chapel, you went to chapel.

HOWEL (*who has just entered*): Some of us still do, Dai Roberts.

(*Howel is a miner and a local preacher, about 35, tall, dominating, a leader.*)

WILL LEWIS: Keep your voice down, Dai nephew, or you will be shocking the town. You have shocked Howel preacher, look, already.

HOWEL: You ought to talk to that nephew of yours, Will Lewis.

WILL LEWIS: Have you heard the news, Howel?

HOWEL: What news?

WILL LEWIS: Rock Vein opening on Monday.

HOWEL: Praises be!

WILL LEWIS: But opening without us. They're bringing a mine-full of men from Merthyr.

HOWEL: Have you been listening to public-house gossip, Will Lewis? Who says so?

WILL LEWIS: It is all about the town.

HOWEL: Idle chatter.

WILL LEWIS: You do not believe Mr Rhys, your fellow deacon, would be capable of it.

HOWEL: I believe no man would. It is a panic of the public bar.

WILL LEWIS: If he is trying to sack all Cwmllynfach we shall hear panic in other places.

HOWEL: To take a town that is living on the one colliery and remove its source of livelihood is impossible. It would be like old Hannibal starving out a place.

WILL LEWIS: Howel preacher, you know that the mine has gone into the combine. You know what these devils want. 'We want men we can trust,' they say. Yes, man, blacklegs.

HOWEL: They will not find any in Cwmllynfach.

WILL LEWIS: They say, 'If we have none in stock we will order them for you.' There is always the train, Howel.

HOWEL: I don't think that of Rhys.

WILL LEWIS: Rhys is a kind man, yes, with the voice of a harmonium. But there is figures behind him, Howel preacher, and bankers behind wire netting, smooth as Judases, and London behind them all, to which Mr Rhys is saying 'Yes, sir. You appreciate Mr Managing Director that this will mean the extinction of Cwmllynfach? Ah! you have never heard of Cwmllynfach? Then it is as well it should be extinct. Yes, Mr Managing Director, I will get in touch with the organiser of the blacklegs and of the Company Union. He will provide me with a gang. I am at your service. We will get rid of Cwmllynfach now. These people are too independent, too stiff-necked as trade unionists. We will get men more pliable. Then we can rationalise heartily.'

HOWEL: Who told you about the Rock Vein?

WILL LEWIS: I heard the telegraph poles singing it to the wires.

HOWEL: If I thought it was true—you don't trust the roof not to fall in, or the endless rope not to break, or the shot not to fire back, or the cage not to fall—but you do trust . . . people . . . somewhere to have limits.

WILL LEWIS: You get less trusty once you leave chapel. Ask Bronwen your sister. It is thirty years since she darkened a chapel. She has monopolised your family wisdom.

HOWEL: You've got to trust that in the long run men see and think fairly.

BRONWEN (*entering*): What is the use, Howel? You are only preaching again.

Bronwen, Howel's sister, is a woman of about 60.

BRONWEN: Move out of the way, that is the young man I want to see. You had better not try shuffling off, Dai Roberts.

WILL LEWIS: That is not what we are discussing, Bronwen.

BRONWEN: Yes, Will Lewis, shelter him. Why was he sheltering behind my back door last night long after nine o'clock, and where were your eyes Howel, not to see him?

WILL LEWIS: We are discussing the situation caused by Howel's friend Mr Rhys, Bronwen. He is staffing the Rock Vein with foreigners.

BRONWEN: I care very little what you are discussing, Will Lewis. I am busy preventing that young official from disorganising the morals of the village.

WILL LEWIS: Forget him, Bronwen. He was listening to the late news on your wireless. But Taffy's job will be going if our news is true.

BRONWEN: Taffy's job? He is working at this moment!

WILL LEWIS: What will he be doing in a fortnight, then?

HOWEL: You said the Rock Vein.

WILL LEWIS: The West Pit follows if he gets away with it.

BRONWEN: Taffy's job is all right, but like nephew like uncle, it is a tongue with no sincerity. Get out of the way, man, and let me get hold of Dai there.

WILL LEWIS: Howel's job is gone. Mine is gone. Taffy's will go.

HOWEL: If it is true.

BRONWEN: If it is true? If what is true? Howel's job's gone?

WILL LEWIS: They are opening the Rock Vein on Monday and staffing it with a mine-full of miners from Merthyr.

BRONWEN: Strangers—coming here?

WILL LEWIS: First they appointed a new manager—now new miners.

BRONWEN: Well, you know what to do.

WILL LEWIS: We don't. You had best tell us.

BRONWEN: Does anyone need to be told in Cwmllynfach? Doesn't Cwm lead South Wales—

HOWEL: If Will Lewis is right, we will have a meeting at the pit-head on Monday and get a vote for a lightning strike.

WILL LEWIS: Strike, eh? We've been sacked so we come on strike? I don't see as we need to.

(*They look at each other, puzzled.*)

HOWEL: This is a new situation.

WILL LEWIS: A new heaven and a new earth preacher—Here's one who will tell us. (*Calling off.*) Boxer Jones!

(*Boxer Jones comes on L.*)

BOXER: What is it? I'm in a hurry, man.

WILL LEWIS: In a hurry to get to work, Boxer? Are you one of those with jobs in the Rock Vein?

BOXER: Are you telling me about a job, man? I've been looking for one ten years.

BRONWEN: Tell us what you know, Boxer.

BOXER: Sure—it's Ma Bronwen I've got some news for. Your old man's down the pit. You needn't keep his dinner ready.

BRONWEN: It's in the oven waiting for him.

BOXER: It needn't wait. That's all. He's staying down.

BRONWEN: Staying down, of course, till the end of the shift.

BOXER: Staying down for good.

(*Bronwen goes pale and sets off towards the pit-head.*)

BOXER: Where are you going, Bronwen?

BRONWEN: (*trembling*): I am going to the pit-head now.

BOXER: It is not an accident.

BRONWEN: (*turning*): You say he is staying down. Tell me what has happened. I can stand it.

BOXER: He is staying down on strike with the rest of the shift. They refuse to come up though the cage is waiting.

BRONWEN: On strike is it? At pit bottom?

WILL LEWIS: That's it. That's it. They have hit on it, Howel.

BRONWEN: My man is sixty-four and this is winter. If he stays at pit bottom there in a wet singlet—

DAI (*pointing to Bronwen*): Get hold of her arm, Will.

WILL LEWIS: I'm here, Bronwen.

HOWEL (*to Boxer*): Come y'ere, scab.

BOXER: Who are you calling scab, preacher? I have not worked in your mine.

HOWEL: There may be dead men in the pit before this is over. If ever you dare scab . . .(*They glare at each other. Howel turns and speaks over his shoulder.*) Get your men posted, Will Lewis. Stand by the pit-head. Dai, telephone the miners' agent.

BRONWEN: Will, I am too old to understand. Are they staying down the pit for long?

HOWEL: Go to the pit-head, Will Lewis.

BRONWEN: Taffy is sixty-four. He is exhausted at the end of a shift. He cannot stay longer and without his dinner. Nobody knows what will happen.

DAI (*soothingly*): Nothing can happen, Bronwen.

BRONWEN: Nothing can happen? Have you ever been down a pit?

WILL LEWIS: Come and sit down home, Bronwen.

BRONWEN: Will Lewis miner, I've been a miner's wife through twenty strikes and lock-outs, and I've never sat down home.

WILL LEWIS: Let me take your arm.

BRONWEN (*shakes herself free*): No . . . Nobody's arm . . . I'm going. (*With an effort she gets control and strides off slowly.*) I'm going to the pit-head.

(*Will Lewis follows, and then Dai.*)

BOXER (*to Howel, who has turned away*): You called me a scab—you dared to call me—me—

(*Howel does not hear him. He is thinking aloud.*)

HOWEL: Lead us not into temptation but deliver us from evil. Though I should walk through the valley—(*Pause, then louder*)—Though *we* should walk through the valley of the shadow of death we will fear no evil.

VOICE (*Off*): Howel! Howel! (*Pause. Then Howel goes. Mr Rhys enters R.*)

RHYS: What's to do, Boxer?

BOXER: You will learn in the office soon enough.

RHYS: Has something happened?

BOXER: Yes. (*Muttering.*) Lead us not into temptation but deliver us from evil.

RHYS: What's that?

BOXER: It was the text now of one of their preachers. You are the temptation. I am the evil.

RHYS: Boxer—have you been drinking ? (*Exit.*)

BOXER (*to himself*): Deliver us from evil? (*Laughs.*) That's me!

CURTAIN

ACT I—Scene II

Same scene. Some hours later. Evening. It gets darker through the scene.

Boxer shadow boxing. His wife, Llio Jones, on the seat watching him. Dai is on sentry-go at the door of the colliery office.

LLIO: You're a miner now. You won't want that stuff.

BOXER: I'm going back to the gym tomorrow.

LLIO: Excuse me, you're going down the pit.

BOXER: You've heard what's happened. They're staying down on strike.

LLIO: That is in the West Pit. It doesn't affect you.

BOXER (*almost out of breath—still boxing*): Yes, but—

LLIO: Are you becoming a philanthropist?

BOXER: I have an idea I shall be able to get another fight.

LLIO: You got beaten up enough last time.

BOXER: Ay, and you got beaten in the Eisteddfod.

LLIO: That was because the judges had been bought.

BOXER: Bought, eh?

LLIO: Bought, and paid for, by that frog-voiced harpy.

BOXER: The more you sang the more they hated it.

LLIO: They didn't listen, I tell you, they didn't listen. Eh— you're not going to get out of it by starting a quarrel now. You're going to be a miner from to-morrow.

BOXER: You seem to think you've got the right to plan my life for me. Even if your father did keep a grocer's shop, mine kept a sweet shop. It was a smaller turn-over, but a bigger profit.

LLIO: Oh yeah—then show us some.

BOXER: You're very determined, woman, for *my* job.

LLIO: You're afraid.

BOXER: I'm afraid.

LLIO: Not even ashamed to admit it.

BOXER: I'm not a coward. That's why.

LLIO: You're not a coward. Only frightened.

BOXER: That's all. I'm just thinking. . . . Things are different now with this stay-down invention. Maybe we can go on without a job. We are used to it. These lot take it so hard. They say it's *their* job—stolen.

LLIO: Not stolen. Mr Rhys gave it to us properly.

BOXER: You and your Mr Rhys.

LLIO (*in a flat voice*): Let it be then. We've not had a job as long as it takes to lose interest. Let it be. Let the others have it.

BOXER: That's what I was thinking. (*Pause.*) Hi! You weren't saying it in the same way as I was . . . Llio, you are not going to get like that, are you?

LLIO: Like what?

BOXER: You are enough to give a man the creeps with your moodiness.

LLIO: I shall be moody enough if you leave me starving.

BOXER: You will sing better for it.

LLIO: Come here. (*She begins to straighten him up.*) Put your scarf straight. Now pull your cap off your eye. Now you are going to take a walk because you are not going to see the sun to-morrow. You are going down, d'you hear?

BOXER: It is too much to ask in these circumstances. We shall be too unpopular.

LLIO: We've always been that. The common people have been jealous from the beginning.

BOXER: Of your singing?

LLIO: Or of your boxing when you came home in an ambulance? . . . They'll want a man like you if there's going to be trouble.

BOXER: And yet you grumble when I do a bit of shadow.

LLIO: You make me feel a fool. Do it round the corner, man.

BOXER: It's getting darker. Nobody will notice.

LLIO: Do it round the corner.

BOXER (*going*): Good-bye, sweet singer—(*mocking*)—sweet— sweet—sweet.

(*Pause. Llio is knitting. Boxer out of sight, Dai on sentry-go. A low whistle. Dai stops and whistles a reply. Then in a whisper:*)

DAI: Gwevril!

GWEVRIL (*still out of sight and whispering*): Dai—is it all right?

DAI: People are all over the place. But it is getting dark now. We'll risk it.

(*Enter Gwevril. Dark, good-looking, 18.*)

DAI: I am on watch here.

GWEVRIL: Is there anybody in the office?

DAI: Yes. Come round the corner.

GWEVRIL: What was the row about this morning?

DAI: Us.

GWEVRIL: Aunt Bronwen was after you?

DAI: She would have been, but then news came of the strike.

GWEVRIL: Dai—what is going to happen? Will any of them die?

DAI: Why should they?

GWEVRIL: It is very cold.

DAI: We are going to send them food.

GWEVRIL: How?

DAI: I am going down myself.

GWEVRIL: Dai—be careful.

DAI: They will need me down there. I am trained and have all the first-aid certificates.

GWEVRIL: Yes. You'll be able to see how they're getting on.

DAI: I shall stay.

GWEVRIL: If there are any first-aid cases?

DAI: I shall stay down.

GWEVRIL: Dai, you might get cold.

DAI: It is a risk, certainly.

GWEVRIL: When shall I see you again?

DAI: I don't know.

GWEVRIL: Dai—it is dangerous.

DAI: Maybe.

GWEVRIL: But Dai, you needn't do it.

DAI: I am going to stay down.

GWEVRIL: You say it as if you never meant to come up again.

DAI: Maybe.

GWEVRIL: Maybe, maybe, always maybe!

DAI: Nobody understands this sort of business, Gwevril. It's new to us.

GWEVRIL: Dai, come nearer.

DAI: What's the matter with you?

GWEVRIL: When the soldiers went to France in the war, very often their girls had an omen they would not see them again.

DAI: Don't be gloomy, Gwev. (*Puts an arm round her.*)

GWEVRIL: I was trying to think of a way of not being gloomy.

DAI (*suddenly ardent*): I can think of one.

GWEVRIL (*breaking away*): Is this your way of watching?

DAI: It is my way of saying good-bye.

GWEVRIL: They used to think in the war it was a good enough excuse.

DAI: Yes. Yes.

GWEVRIL: It wasn't, it wasn't. (*She breaks away.*)

DAI: Gwev, Gwev, don't leave me.

GWEVRIL: I've got to, Dai . . . Things are upside down. Everything's upside down.

DAI: Gwev, I don't understand.

GWEVRIL: If you did you wouldn't be trying to commit suicide in Rock Vein Corner.

DAI: (*catching her*): What does it matter, Gwev? What does anything matter?

GWEVRIL: Dai, Dai, I am proud because you love me. Dai. . . . What is it? Where are you going?

DAI (*thrusting her away*): You had better keep watch for me.

GWEVRIL: Don't go, Dai.

DAI: I am going to find Howel.

GWEVRIL: Dai, stay, I shall try to be calmer. . . . Dai.

(*Dai goes.*)

LLIO (*who has come up behind her*): Excuse me, Miss Gwevril, but you did not see I was here. I have been wanting to talk to you for a long time.

GWEVRIL (*turning, startled*): Oh, it's Mrs Jones.

LLIO: Does that make any difference?

GWEVRIL: Well . . . no.

LLIO: I've been wanting to talk to you, because you look young and intelligent and not like the rest of them here. . . . Why don't you two run away?

GWEVRIL: Run away?

LLIO: You can see why. There's no life here for you either as lovers or married people.

GWEVRIL: That is our business, Mrs Jones.

LLIO: Yes. I'm only giving advice. You won't get it from the others. Go to London. There are jobs to be had there.

GWEVRIL: What sort of jobs? Dai would become a barman and I should have to be a skivvy.

LLIO: Well, if you are so stuck up, you mining people . . . yes, you would both lose your characters and it would do you both good.

(*Enter Bronwen.*)

BRONWEN: Gwevril, come over here. I know why you are hanging round the doorway.

GWEVRIL: I was just speaking to Mrs. Jones.

BRONWEN (*sharply*): Come here when I tell you.

LLIO: You are not very polite to me, Bronwen.

BRONWEN: Gwevril!

GWEVRIL: Mrs Llio Jones—how would you set about getting to London if you were Dai and me?

BRONWEN: Do you hear what I say, Gwevril?

GWEVRIL: I'm going to walk part of the way with Mrs Jones.

BRONWEN: Be careful, girl, or you'll be finding my door shut on you. (*To Will Lewis, who enters.*) Where is Howel?

WILL LEWIS: He is coming up now. He has been leading a deputation to the shops and public-houses for them to close early as a mark of respect for the strikers.

BRONWEN: Will they shut?

WILL LEWIS: I think so.

BRONWEN: He'd better come back. We shall want a man to manage these young ones.

HOWEL (*entering*): What is it you want, Bronwen?

BRONWEN: Gwevril making a friendship with Mrs Jones blackleg.

HOWEL: Never mind that. I shall want you for something else, Bronwen. We have got ham and loaves. We have milk, we have tea. The shop people are sending them to the Federation hut. We shall get permission to feed the men down below and I shall want you to take charge of it.

BRONWEN: I am old. I can organise nothing.

WILL LEWIS: You ought to consider as you said yourself, that Taffy could not live down there in the cold without his meals.

BRONWEN (*wearily*): I am past bothering.

HOWEL (*sitting down heavily*): Think about it, Bronwen. We shall not want you for a little time.

WILL LEWIS: I have been thinking: supposing Taffy went to sleep down there and woke up to find he was in the world no longer. He would be saying to himself, 'I thought it would be hotter.'

HOWEL: Bronwen, our men have to hold that pit against the blacklegs. They can't do that on wind.

BRONWEN: There are plenty of other women.

HOWEL: There's only one Bronwen.

WILL LEWIS: I was thinking that there must be some pleasure for Taffy in being down there for the sake of not working. Howel, have you heard about the new agreement?

HOWEL: What's that?

WILL LEWIS: A new agreement for all the miners of Rock Vein Corner. Fifteen bob a week, live in.

HOWEL: Bronwen, I'm asking you for the last time. We have to organise sandwiches and tea for sixty men, to be prepared at the Federation hut and sent down, as soon as we can find Rhys to arrange it. I am asking you to be our Food Captain.

WILL LEWIS: It's a job for you, Bronwen.

BRONWEN: Tell Will Lewis to stop talking.

> (*Dai has come back and is at the office door again. Llio and Gwevril walk by the pit-head. Llio, breaking in:*)

LLIO: I'd go home, Bronwen.

BRONWEN: Go home? Who said that?

LLIO: I did. And it's sense.

BRONWEN: I shall be here, Howel. It doesn't matter if they want breakfast, dinner, tea and supper for three months. I shall do it for them. Why are we waiting?

WILL LEWIS: Till Mr Rhys comes.

DAI: He'll be here presently. They're waiting inside for him.

WILL LEWIS: He may come by the other door.

DAI: I'll tell you.

(*They walk up and down in little groups. It gets darker.*)

HOWEL: Why doesn't somebody sing?

(*Llio, on the far side of the stage, begins to sing 'All through the Night.' Gwevril has gone to Dai again. Bronwen talks through the singing.*)

LLIO (*sings*): Love fear not if sad thy dreaming.

BRONWEN: It's dreaming she wants to be, not living.

LLIO (*sings*): All through the night.
          Though o'ercast bright stars are gleaming.

BRONWEN: She'll be seeing stars, her and her husband, before this is over.

LLIO (*sings*): All through the night.
          Joy will come to thee at morning
          Life with sunny hope adorning
          Though sad dreams may give dark warning

BRONWEN: Warning—she says—warning! Then let her look out to-morrow.

LLIO: All through the night.

DAI (*at the office door*): Mr Rhys is coming in now, Howel.

HOWEL: Ask him to receive a deputation.

(*Dai goes in. Pause. Dai returns.*)

DAI: He says he will only receive a deputation of one.

HOWEL: Who is it to be?

WILL LEWIS: Go on, Howel.

DAI (*speaking into the door*): Brother Howel is coming to you now.

(*Howel slowly goes out. Llio begins to sing the verse again. Stage darkens.*)

CURTAIN

H

ACT I—Scene III

(Colliery office, Rock Vein Corner. Rhys and Howel.)

RHYS: Howel, this is very serious.

HOWEL: Too serious for us two to discuss alone, Brother Rhys.

RHYS: Then why are you here?

HOWEL: I have come to ask—to demand—to use the telephone to speak to our brothers in the pit.

RHYS: What do you want to speak to them about, Howel?

HOWEL: First to put them in touch with the Miners' Lodge. We shall need to arrange things.

RHYS: Arrange?

HOWEL: We shall want to establish a first-aid station here for the Federation.

RHYS: You will provide your own man?

HOWEL: We shall provide a rota, a first-aid man will represent us here night and day.

RHYS: Here?

HOWEL: Here in this office—at the pit telephone. Then we shall need to arrange to send them food.

RHYS: I thought they were on hunger strike.

HOWEL: They have been hungry long enough. If they are going to stay we shall need to send them food regularly, four or five times in the twenty-four hours.

RHYS: You'd like to do that through the office, too?

HOWEL: We shall provide the food and the organisation. You will arrange about sending it down.

RHYS (*changing his tone*): Howel—why do you stand away? Are you afraid that if you came any nearer you'd become reasonable?

HOWEL: I've said what I've got to say.

RHYS: Well, now tell me what you think yourself.

HOWEL: What I think I have said.

RHYS: Translate it from official language. After all, we are deacons of the same chapel—and friends.

HOWEL (*slightly relaxing*): It's time you did some talking. I have had my turn.

RHYS: Very well. Another manager might describe your demands as outrageous. I won't. I'm going to meet you on all the points you've mentioned.

HOWEL: I can speak to them on the telephone then?

RHYS: In a moment. There are one or two other things.

HOWEL: What are they?

RHYS: We were going to have three pits working from Monday on full time till further notice.

HOWEL: I heard so much.

RHYS: There's one pit out of action for the moment. Leave that aside. Howel—you work in the Rock Vein, don't you?

HOWEL: Well?

RHYS: I am asking you to start work first shift to-morrow.

HOWEL: Do you want my answer now?

RHYS: Yes. And I want you to promise to take the rest of the shift with you.

HOWEL: What about the East Pit?

RHYS: The West Pit is out of action till the stay-down strike is over.

HOWEL: I said the East Pit.

RHYS: The East Pit—it is not decided. Tell me, why did the stay-down strike start?

HOWEL: Because of a rumour that the Rock Vein was to be staffed to-morrow by blacklegs.

RHYS: Well, now you know what the truth is. I'm asking you to take the full shift to work with you in the Rock Vein.

HOWEL: What about the East Pit?

RHYS: Who said anything about the East Pit? The East Pit is closed and it is for me to decide when to open it.

HOWEL: And with what staff?

RHYS: Howel, why have you become so suspicious of me?

HOWEL: What did the company have in mind when they sent you as a new manager? New manager, new policy?

RHYS: We've been on very friendly terms till now. I've been one of your admirers ever since I came here.

HOWEL: Humph!

RHYS: I remember—always shall—one of your sermons. It was the one about Ruskin—Unto This Last. I never remember a sermon full of more social zeal and progressive thinking.

HOWEL: Humph!

RHYS: You remember the text of it? 'They likewise received every man a penny. And when they had received it they murmured against the goodman of the house. . . .'

HOWEL: Saying, 'These last have wrought but one hour and thou hast made them equal unto us which have borne the burden and the heat of the day.'

RHYS: Now we come to the operative bit. 'But he answered one of them and said, "Friend, I do thee no wrong. Didst thou not agree with me for a penny? Take that is thine and go thy way. I will give unto this last even as unto thee. *Is it not lawful for me to do what I will with mine own?*" ' . . . You called the sermon 'Unto This Last,' after Ruskin.

(*Pause.*)

HOWEL (*brusquely*): On consideration, Mr Rhys, I am accepting your offer.

RHYS: Offer?

HOWEL: I shall go to work to-morrow. The shift will probably come with me.

RHYS (*hesitantly*): That sounds all right.

HOWEL: What are you suspicious of?

RHYS: I don't like things that happen suddenly.

HOWEL: Can I go to the pit telephone?

> (*Howel goes out. We hear a bell ringing. Mr Rhys looks round the office and grunts once or twice. We hear Howel's voice off.*)

HOWEL (*off*): Taffy, Taffy – is that you, Taffy?

> (*Mr Rhys tiptoes towards the office telephone.*)

RHYS: Get me the Cardiff police, please. . . .

CURTAIN

ACT I – Scene IV

> (*Pit-head, dark. Bronwen walking up and down alone. Murmur of voices off. Enter Gwevril.*)

GWEVRIL: Aren't you coming home, Bronwen?

BRONWEN: No.

GWEVRIL: Howel has gone.

BRONWEN: He is going down the pit to-morrow at six.

GWEVRIL: He's got to get some sleep he says. It is two o'clock, aren't you coming?

BRONWEN: No.

GWEVRIL: Will Lewis has gone too.

BRONWEN: Will Lewis is going down pit to-morrow?

GWEVRIL: Yes.

BRONWEN: I shall watch here.

GWEVRIL: What good is it? You are not helping them.

BRONWEN: I can argue with myself whether I am helping them.

GWEVRIL: There are other people about if anything should happen.

BRONWEN: Will you go home, girl?

GWEVRIL: I think I ought to stay with you.

BRONWEN: Gwevril—

GWEVRIL: All right, Aunt—if you feel strongly about it.

BRONWEN: Good night.

GWEVRIL: Good night, but—

BRONWEN: We shall all meet here at six o'clock.

GWEVRIL: You won't be staying here till then?

(*Singing off*): Love fear not if sad thy dreaming
              All through the night.
           Though o'ercast the stars are gleaming
              All through the night.

GWEVRIL: You won't be staying all night?

BRONWEN: I shall be here. Good night.

GWEVRIL (*going hesitantly*): Good night.

    (*Exit.*)

BRONWEN: Though o'ercast the stars are gleaming, is it? With a thousand foot of rock and solid earth o'ercasting them for Taffy. (*Grimly*) Maybe he knows they're there by implication.

    (*She paces up and down wearily. The song goes on.*)

CURTAIN

ACT II – Scene I

(Howel's house, the kitchen. Gwevril at door, calling upstairs. 5a.m., dark still.)

GWEVRIL: Howel. . . . Father. . . . It is time.

> *(There is no answer. Gwevril busies herself laying breakfast. Presently Howel comes in with a candle.)*

Have you been to sleep?

HOWEL: Yes. Where is Bronwen?

GWEVRIL: She has not come home.

HOWEL: Still at the pit-head?

GWEVRIL: I didn't want to leave her, Father, but you know what she is like.

HOWEL: There are women of the working class whose lives are compelled to become such an outpouring of energy that their strength becomes intolerable.

GWEVRIL: No sermonising, Father. Remember, she's your sister. Did you sleep yourself?

HOWEL: Did you?

GWEVRIL: Sure.

HOWEL: *Are* you sure now?

GWEVRIL: Of course I'm sure. . . . Mrs Williams's light has been on all night, look.

HOWEL (*at window*): There is a light on in every house in the village. Yet they are not all on morning shift. They have been burning all night it looks as if.

GWEVRIL: Yes, they have.

HOWEL: They have even a light in Llewellyn's shop window, look.

GWEVRIL: They got frightened of the dark with thinking of Taffy and his mates in it. Your breakfast is ready, Father.

HOWEL (*still at window*): There is something very new in this. Do you feel that it is modern?

GWEVRIL: I don't know what is modern. Your breakfast is ready, Father.

HOWEL: You ought to know. You are modern yourself.

GWEVRIL: Why am I?

HOWEL: The generations are a puzzle to each other. On such occasions as this I wish you could tell me what it feels like.

GWEVRIL: Father, get on with your breakfast.

HOWEL (*coming back reflectively*): First there was pneumatic drills, then main haulage was electric lighted, then there was conveyors, then machine cutters and a mine became noisier than an ironworks. The old miner with his pick and Davy lamp was a gravedigger and solemn accordingly. The new one spends his life dodging machinery, and he ought to be a jazz man. I could not see any hope in it at all except the scrap heap for most of us until this staying down—with all the lights of the village the whole night burning—showed that we have an answer. Old Taffy is sixty-four, but he has an answer. We are feeling what it is like to have the veins of a young one.

GWEVRIL: Father, you have not eaten any breakfast.

HOWEL: Evidently I have not scored with my audience.

GWEVRIL: It is a new sermon with you, is it?

HOWEL: I am preaching at Blackrock on Sunday week, and giving an address the following Thursday at Crumlin. Give me more help, will you?

GWEVRIL: I am not interested in sermons. I want to get to the pit-head.

HOWEL: It is the tragedy of life that when a man is in a moment of illumination, a woman's thoughts become practical.

GWEVRIL: At such a time I cannot keep my mind on what you are saying.

HOWEL: At such a time you do not share what is going on in my mind.

GWEVRIL: What is the use of it going on in your mind when all you can do is to obey Mr Rhys's orders and go to work tamely?

HOWEL: Gwevril!

GWEVRIL: Oh, I know that it cannot be helped and that a strike would be useless.

HOWEL: Gwevril, are you so blind that you cannot see what is preparing? (*Suddenly changes.*) Gwevril, when you were at the secondary school you were good at mathematics?

GWEVRIL: Why? Father, we have to get to the pit-head.

HOWEL: I have never been able to master the calculus. It seems to me that it is the key to the modern world and I cannot master it. I have tried. I have not the background. It seems to me that the modern generation is in an aeroplane and I am on the ground and Cwmllynfach is no airport.

GWEVRIL: The calculus on a morning like this!

HOWEL: It is natural when a man is going on a journey he should take stock of his previous failures.

GWEVRIL: Here is your dudley. It is time to be going.

HOWEL: Gwevril, run quickly and get me a double ration.

GWEVRIL: Double ration, what for?

HOWEL: Do as I tell you.

GWEVRIL: Howel—you are not planning?—

HOWEL: Do as I tell you. Don't look so gloomy now. This is what I should call a cheerful crisis.

(*Gwevril goes out. Howel shouts to her in the next room.*)

HOWEL: Whenever I see an aeroplane I envy the pilot his knowledge of the art of navigation. That is another thing.

GWEVRIL (*off*): They can't all navigate.

HOWEL: Gwevril, before I go down the pit there is another thing I want to mention. Be careful what risks you are taking with your life.

GWEVRIL (*coming back hurriedly*): It is the worst of being a preacher, Father. You always shout the most intimate things.

HOWEL: If you had stayed there it would have been easier to say it. It is that boy. That Dai Roberts—

GWEVRIL: What about him?

HOWEL: I am an old pick and shovel miner and you are the generation of aeroplanes. I do not like to say anything. . . . Only remember as you have just said they do not all know the science of navigation.

GWEVRIL: What about Dai and me? What do you mean about us?

HOWEL (*turning away*): I have said what I wanted to say.

GWEVRIL: But if I didn't understand, it is no use for you to have said it.

HOWEL: It is a pity that I can only speak in parables, and all women dislike parables.

GWEVRIL: You know what Bronwen says, Howel—if you were an auctioneer you would not like to bring the hammer down —and the first lot would still be standing.

(*Enter Bronwen.*)

BRONWEN: Howel, you will be late.

(*Howel bustles. Collects his things.*)

GWEVRIL: He is ready, Aunt Bronwen. You go to bed.

BRONWEN: No, I am all right.

GWEVRIL: Has anything happened down yonder?

BRONWEN: I walked up and down till daylight. There are police sleeping in the offices.

GWEVRIL: Hurry up, Howel.

HOWEL: Was anybody with you, Bronwen?

BRONWEN: There were other women.

GWEVRIL: Hurry up, Howel.

BRONWEN: Howel, it seems wrong for you to be going to work. Can you not go on strike after all? Never mind tactics. It would relieve our feelings.

(*Howel pauses and looks at her quizzically.*)

HOWEL: Is that what you say, Bronwen? You are behind the times.

BRONWEN: If the times are for defeatism, I do well to be behind them.

HOWEL: I am going to descend the mine. I am going now to the pit-head.

BRONWEN: Wait. I am coming.

HOWEL: But you have just come away, Bronwen.

GWEVRIL (*at window*): Who is that shouting? Is there a fight there?

GWEVRIL (*at window*): Listen! There is Dai Roberts and Will Lewis.

BRONWEN: While Taffy stays down my place is at the pit-head.

GWEVRIL (*at window*): And there is Boxer Jones too.

(*Shouting off.*)

HOWEL: What is this?

GWEVRIL: There is a fight here. Quickly.

(*Gwevril runs out the door.*)

HOWEL: Are you coming then, Bronwen? . . . It is beginning.

(*Howel goes. Bronwen follows.*)

CURTAIN

H*

ACT II – Scene II

(Near the pit-head. Boxer Jones enters backwards, facing the advancing forces.)

A shout off: Boxer Jones blacklegging.

BOXER: Come on, then. Only I am warning you what will happen.

WILL LEWIS: The job you have taken belongs to another.

(Will Lewis comes on, followed by Dai.)

BOXER: I will take you on one at a time or all at once, if necessary. And when I have finished there is a special train-load of men coming from Merthyr who will pick up the pieces.

DAI: I'll stop your boasting, Boxer.

BOXER: There are a hundred police, too, and when I have finished with you it will not be me Black Maria is taking.

DAI: Come on then.

WILL LEWIS: Look out for yourself, Dai. He is a professional.

BOXER: Wait young fellow. You know who I am.

DAI: A played-out boxing champion, a has-been.

BOXER: All right. Do you know how to hold your hands up?

DAI: I'm going to teach you, champ, what a real fight's like.

BOXER: All right. Stick 'em up. Are you ready? All right. Leave 'em there. No, that's not right. Put your right hand higher. A coupla inches. *(Dai hits.)*

(Dai makes a rush. Boxer parries easily.)

BOXER: No, no. Lead with your left. *(Dai hits.)* Take your time now. Judge your distance. That to steady you *(a blow in the face)*. Try again. *(Dai swings.)* . . . No. . . . No. . . . That makes you look silly. Like this. Come on. Come on. *(Two swings from Dai.)*

BOXER: You'll tire yourself, Dai. Try it this way.

DAI: Don't call me Dai.

BOXER: All right, Dustbin, official, bright boy, sewer grating. Come on. Take it.

DAI: To hell with fighting pretty.

(Dai rushes in and kicks.)

BOXER: Kicking, is it? Right. Take it proper then.

(Dai is knocked out. As he falls Llio enters.)

LLIO (*to Boxer*): You fool. What have you been doing? making it worse?

BOXER: Ask him.

LLIO (*leaning over Dai, who still seems unconscious*): Are you much hurt?

(*Enter Bronwen and Gwevril.*)

BRONWEN: Get back, Mrs Jones. We want to keep you clean for the Eisteddfod.

GWEVRIL: Dai, Dai.

BOXER: That is your Dai, is it? He brought it on himself. He will come to in a moment and we will repeat the mixture.

WILL LEWIS: You, Boxer Jones, you are going to pay for this.

BOXER: You want some too, do you?

(*Enter Howel.*)

HOWEL: Step back, Will Lewis.

DAI: Let me get at him again.

GWEVRIL: Are you hurt, Dai? Your eye is cut. Look! And your mouth is twisted.

HOWEL (*to Boxer*): You are proud of your strength. You have had your demonstration. Now go.

BOXER: He is as strong as I am.

HOWEL: Your skill then. We approve of it. Only for this morning take yourself out of the village.

BOXER: You think you own the earth, preacher, but you have been organised out of your job now. You and your Federation thought yourselves the masters' masters, but now it is your turn to be on the scrap heap. There is to be a new order of things in Rock Vein Corner and you are superannuated. A mechanised pit wants young men, not preachers, disciplined men, quick movers, not trade unionists, talkers.

HOWEL: Boxer Jones, I have no wish to talk to you. We will deprive ourselves of your company.

BOXER: I have not finished yet. Your face, Howel preacher, is no prettier than Dai Roberts's. It needs my beauty treatment.

HOWEL: Here I am then. Will you do your bashing or are you going?

BOXER: Put your hands up.

HOWEL: I am not entering into your brawling.

BOXER: Put your hands up and I'll knock you down.

HOWEL (*folding his hands*): I am waiting.

(*Boxer makes as if to hit Howel; then:*)

BOXER: I've had enough of this prayer meeting.

(*Boxer goes.*)

BRONWEN: Moral strength, Howel, is all very pretty, but you have
let him go holding his tea-can. Go and rob him of his tea-can,
somebody, and kick him while you're doing it. Spoil his tea on
his first shift. At least we can do that for him.

WILL LEWIS (*shouting off*): Stop Boxer Jones there. Push him
into the overflow.

VOICE (*off*): Come and do it yourself.

LLIO (*looking into the audience*): I've never seen a passenger train
coming up the valley. Where is it going to? That is only a line
for coal trucks.

BRONWEN: Are you going to get his tea-can, Will Lewis?

WILL LEWIS: What is the use of getting his tea-can? Push him
into the overflow.

BRONWEN: Go and—

VOICE (*off*): Do it yourself.

BRONWEN: He said it.

GWEVRIL (*still kneeling*): There is a passenger train stopping by
the gate in the valley.

WILL LEWIS (*shouting off*): Stop Boxer Jones there. He is scabbing.

(*Boxer Jones up behind him.*)

BOXER: Well?

WILL LEWIS: Well? (*He retreats.*)

BOXER: Well?

(*Howel goes up to them.*)

HOWEL: Give up this idea of taking the jobs of our men, Boxer.
In the long run you cannot get away with it. You will be
punished.

GWEVRIL (*shouting towards the audience*): Look about you, a
train of blacklegs has come into the valley.

BRONWEN: The ghost train has come to Cwmllynfach now.

GWEVRIL: The ghost train!

BRONWEN: The doors are opening now, every carriage packed
with men, pouring out, running. They are coming over the
coal-tip.

(*A siren goes.*)

BOXER: What did I tell you now? We've got your bloody jobs.

GWEVRIL: They are coming over the top now. Who is going to stop them?

BRONWEN (*facing the audience*): Two, four, six, eight, ten.

GWEVRIL (*facing the audience*): You, you, you, marching on our mine, invaders. You're not even Welshmen. You've got English faces.

BRONWEN: Twelve, fourteen, sixteen, eighteen, twenty.

(*Boxer puts on a tin helmet and picks up a miner's lamp.*)

HOWEL: Where did you get that lamp, Boxer?

BOXER: We've got your jobs, comrades. We've got your blasted jobs.

(*Boxer goes out.*)

WILL LEWIS: Get hold of him, quick. Come on, Howel.

HOWEL (*holding him back*): Quietly, Will Lewis, we are going down quietly now, quickly. Follow me, Dai. We are going down.

BRONWEN: Twelve, fourteen, sixteen, eighteen, twenty.

GWEVRIL (*facing the audience*): You look mean as if you've been robbing the poor box. Only this isn't a church you'll find. You're the kind to take a blind man's collecting tin, but we're not blind men. You're robbing our jobs. D'you hear? You're robbing our jobs.

BRONWEN: Twenty-two, twenty-four, twenty-six, twenty-eight, thirty.

GWEVRIL: You know what it feels like to be a thief now. It feels cheaper still with the cops on your side, doesn't it? You haven't got a conscience, but there's a scab where it used to be. If you scratch it, it smells. If you've got a wife or a girl she won't be able to kiss you now, for scabs are catching.

BRONWEN: Thirty-two, thirty-four, thirty-six, thirty-eight, forty. Are there more or is that enough of you?

GWEVRIL: You don't look like miners. You're not miners. You can't bear being looked at. Ay, swear, but you're frightened when you're swearing. You'll be dizzy going down the pit-shaft. Your stomachs will be staying up here with us, and you down at pit bottom .

BRONWEN: Forty-four, forty-eight, fifty-two, fifty-six, sixty.

GWEVRIL: There's blood on the coal, they say, but it won't notice now. It's black.

(*Howel, Dai and Will Lewis return, carrying miners' lamps.*)

HOWEL: Keep together.

WILL LEWIS: Keep behind me, Dai, and the overseer will not see you.

BRONWEN (*still facing audience*): Sixty-four, sixty-eight, seventy-two, seventy-six, eighty.

(*Howel and Will Lewis go out. Dai lingers.*)

GWEVRIL: Maybe if you'd stop and talk things over it would help. Maybe you let them bamboozle you into thinking the jobs were vacant.

DAI: Good-bye, Gwev.

(*Gwevril does not hear.*)

GWEVRIL: They belong to our miners. Once you know that you try and keep them. Better pinch anything than another man's job.

DAI: Good-bye, Gwev.

(*Gwevril does not hear.*)

GWEVRIL: It's all his life. It's the food for his wife and children, and his house and his bed and his clothes in winter.

(*Dai has gone.*)

BRONWEN: All the blacklegs in the world have come to Cwmllyn-fach now.

LLIO: Dai has gone down the pit, Gwevril. He was saying good-bye to you.

GWEVRIL (*turning*): Dai has gone down?

BRONWEN: Praise God, Howel! You have taken the pit over. You have conquered the Rock Vein.

GWEVRIL: Dai has gone down? But he has no proper clothes.

BRONWEN: He will not be working.

GWEVRIL: But he will be cold—and he was hurt.

BRONWEN: He has plenty of company.

GWEVRIL: He is not used to it.

BRONWEN: The experience will be useful to him in his profession, if he ever begins his profession.

GWEVRIL: What has it to do with Dai? He is not even a worker at the mine. What does he want putting his nose in? (*Making as if to run after him.*) Dai! Dai!

BRONWEN: Stay, fool. He has his chances.

LLIO: We will call Mr Rhys. There is no need for him to go down. Look, there he is passing. Mr Rhys! Mr Rhys!

(*Enter Rhys.*)

RHYS: Who was calling?

LLIO: I was, Mr Rhys. There is a boy there who has gone down Rock Vein who has no right, because he does not work there. He has a black eye and he will take cold yonder.

RHYS: What do you expect me to do? Run down and fetch him?

LLIO: Get him to come up and there is one thing saved in all this confusion. These two children have no need to be drawn into the business.

RHYS: Who gave him his black eye? Your husband?

LLIO: Yes, but that is not it. These two children who are in love with each other have no need to be in it.

(*Gwevril comes in between them.*)

GWEVRIL: Llio Jones, will you take your mischievous tongue out of it. Rather than bring him up now I would marry one of those blacklegs.

LLIO: I was trying to help you. I seem to have got it wrong again.

GWEVRIL: You have.

(*Gwevril strikes Llio across the cheek twice.*)

CURTAIN

ACT II – Scene III

(*Llio's house. She is listening to a song (from Madame Butterfly) on the gramophone, beating time, sometimes joining in, sometimes stopping the record and going back a few bars. A voice outside near the window is heard. Llio stops the record.*)

VOICE (*off*): Comrades. There is only one blackleg in Islwyn Street. Lives at Number 16. Name Jones, the ex-boxer and

Llio Jones his wife, the singer. The house is to be avoided by all except the pickets who will watch the door. (*Shouts.*)

> (*Llio starts the record again, as if to drown the voice. She begins to sing, but her voice quavers. Again she stops the record.*)

VOICE (*off*): On behalf of the Cwmllynfach stay-down strikers I ask you to keep away from Number 16. On behalf of the Rock Vein Corner stay-down strikers I ask shop-keepers, milkmen and hawkers to refuse to serve Llio Jones or Boxer Jones now scabbing at Rock Vein Corner, Cwmllynfach. Breadmen and travelling butchers and greengrocers should avoid the door. We ask all their neighbours in the street to assist in the boycott. Bus drivers and conductors should refuse to carry them as passengers. (*Shouts.*) If they belong to any choral or dramatic society they should be requested to resign. The same with the sports club. Any institutions belonging to churches or chapels which Llio or Boxer Jones are connected with should operate the boycott.

> (*Confused voices.*)

VOICE: Steady, comrades. We are doing nothing unlawful. I can see that the police are gathering in a bunch and it is no use comrades tweaking my legs. I have finished now and we are going on to the next blackleg street. Islwyn Street, remember Number 16, Blackleg Jones, Llio Jones the singer. Isolate them.

> (*A shriek. Voice:* Look out, look out!)

VOICE (*speaker*): Keep your heads, comrades. No panicking.
WOMAN'S VOICE: Cossacks! Cossacks!

> (*Police whistles. Shrieking. Rushing feet. Confused noise. In the midst of it the door opens and closes quickly. Gwevril has come in to avoid the police charge. She crouches near the door.*)

LLIO: You?
GWEVRIL: Yes, me.
LLIO: Get out of here.
GWEVRIL: When the police go.
LLIO: In the morning you can smack my face. In the afternoon make use of my sitting-room! It's a burglarious entry.
GWEVRIL: I came in till the police had finished charging.

LLIO: Afraid—frightened—as soon as a policeman comes round the corner.

GWEVRIL: My head is more useful thinking than broken.

LLIO: Are you alone?

GWEVRIL: Come and see.

LLIO: Come farther away from the door.

(*Gwevril takes a step or two.*)

LLIO: Farther still.

(*Gwevril complies. Llio goes behind her and locks the door.*)

GWEVRIL: Are you going to call the police or what?

LLIO: I am going to leave you for Boxer.

GWEVRIL: O.K. by me. You think because you can't think of anything to do he can?

LLIO: He will be able to think of something. He is a boxing champion.

GWEVRIL: I don't generally think so badly of people. Boxer's keen and quick and strong. That's why he's been a champ. Now he's forced to be a worker. He comes at it backside forwards, but he comes at it. In himself he's all right. It's Mr Rhys and the system puts him wrong. I'm not afraid. I'll wait for your boxer.

LLIO: If you knew him as I did, you'd be afraid.

GWEVRIL: Lucky you married him first.

LLIO: What are you trying out, girl?

GWEVRIL: I don't believe even you would get in wrong with us, left to yourself, Llio.

LLIO: That's enough. We've talked before, haven't we? Last night first and then this morning.

GWEVRIL: Yes.

LLIO: Well then—

GWEVRIL: Well then what?

LLIO: Hold your tongue.

GWEVRIL: This stuff doesn't get me, Llio. Fundamentally you must be human, or you wouldn't sing so well.

(*Without answering, Llio slowly takes the key from her pocket, unlocks the door. Gwevril has scored a bull's eye. After a pause*)

LLIO: You'd better go.

GWEVRIL: No, I want to see Boxer while I'm here.

LLIO (*breaking out*): You don't think it's *nice* for us, do you, with that shouted at the door? 'Butcher, baker, boycott Boxer Jones and Llio Jones the singer!'

GWEVRIL: It's not meant to be nice.

LLIO: What do we get out of it? We've got to work for our living.

GWEVRIL: All right, but not at our expense.

LLIO: At *your* expense.

(*Confused noises off. Boxer's voice.*)

BOXER: All right, Inspector. I shan't want you to-morrow.

INSPECTOR'S VOICE: We shall come with a bodyguard twice as big, regardless what you say, sir.

BOXER: I don't want you, I tell you.

INSPECTOR: All right.

BOXER: I don't want you.

(*Boxer comes in, dejectedly. Drops on to a chair.*)

BOXER: Shut the door, lass.

LLIO: Can't you shut your own door?

BOXER: I'm through. I've finished.

LLIO: You're soon tired with a single day's working.

BOXER: It's not that. And that's bad enough.

LLIO: Get yourself washed.

BOXER: I don't mind if I can find a man to hit now. But this staring and staring. . . . Who is this? Gwevril Williams? One of them here now? (*On his feet, threatening.*)

GWEVRIL: I ran in here when the cops were baton charging. They have gone now, and I will.

BOXER: Tell me—you're on the other side and you ought to know. What is the game in this staring?

GWEVRIL: Do we scare a champ by looking at him?

BOXER: This staring. Ten police brought me home, alone in the middle, a hundred round about, staring, followed me all the way, two or three at the door even now, staring: at the station, in the shops. I wanted a packet of fags now. I was shy about asking the Inspector to halt—and there at the door Joe Lewis tobacconist, staring. If there were something I could meet with my fist. . . .

GWEVRIL: Here am I from the other side. Try me then.

BOXER (*sitting heavily*): I have given in. You can have your jobs back. They are more important to you than to me.

LLIO: Not important? And can we be starving?

BOXER: I do not mind that. I have done it a dozen times in train-
ing. So long as they do not stare—

GWEVRIL: I am the first one that's speaking to you again, Boxer
Jones, after you have made your statement. First, if you will
stop scabbing and make your statement in public, things will
be different for you.

BOXER: I'll tell them—I'll tell them. But how can I do it? I cannot get near them.

GWEVRIL: You can write in the local paper.

BOXER: Will you write it for me?

GWEVRIL: Yes. I will write that Boxer Jones renounces Company
Unionism and renounces scabbing. You will have to sign it.

LLIO: Boxer—think of Mr Rhys.

BOXER: I'm not frightened of him. He's only one.

LLIO: He's everybody that matters.

BOXER: Maybe they matter in London and other places. Not in
Cwm.

GWEVRIL: It is not easy to become a miner when you come of
shop-keeping people and have never worked ordinarily. You
are learning one of the first things. You are learning about trade
unionism.

(*A knock.*)

BOXER: Who is that?

(*Knock repeated several times.*)

BOXER (*shouting*): Who is it?

GWEVRIL (*going towards the door*): Shall I open it for you?

BOXER: Come away.

(*Enter Mr Rhys.*)

RHYS: Sorry to push in. I didn't want to be seen at your door,
Jones. I can't stand on ceremony. I hope I haven't interrupted
you.

BOXER: What do you want, sir?

RHYS: You can do a little job for me. I want you to get two
or three of your friends to go about bars and places—you'll
know what to do.

BOXER: My friends? That's good.

RHYS: It's a serious point, Jones. Listen to what I'm saying. I've
been hearing one or two stories about an attempt to dynamite
the train to-morrow. I want your friends—and you if you get

a chance—to check up on it. We shall need to take precautions.

GWEVRIL (*coming forward*): Dynamiting the train?

RHYS: Yes. Who is this? I seem to have seen you.

BOXER: She is Howel's daughter.

RHYS: Is this some monkey-business, Boxer? Why didn't you tell me she was here?

BOXER: You didn't give me time. And anyway, I'm out of this. I've pitched my towel in. You can keep your job and your pit.

RHYS: Boxer Jones, I'm playing fair in this. I haven't asked you to go to work without telling you. I shan't ask the others to travel in the train if there's any real danger. I've helped you. Now I'm asking you to help me.

BOXER: Dynamite or no dynamite, spying or no spying, train or no train, I'm through with your job and you can give it back to the man that owns it.

RHYS: This after a single shift, Jones? One day?

BOXER: Yes, one day, Mr Rhys, one quarter hour, one walk from the pit-head to the house, one look at the pickets in this street.

RHYS: The police cleared the street once to-day. We'll have them do it again.

LLIO (*hysterical, but quiet*): I can see that train and the dynamite sticks under the line and the engine getting nearer and nearer and nearer.

BOXER: Be quiet woman.

LLIO: I can see the engine rolling over in the black smoke and hear the screams and the groans. My God, I can see it.

GWEVRIL: Rhys is a liar. There is no question of dynamite. He has been listening to his own palpitations.

LLIO: You will have to stop it, Mr Rhys. Stop it before it gets there.

RHYS: If you think I'm going to call it off because of your squealing, woman, you've misjudged me. The train will run, but we'll find the dynamite first.

LLIO: What if you can't? What if you can't find it?

RHYS: Better attend to your wife, Jones. She's hysterical.

GWEVRIL: You'd better get home, man.

LLIO: I'm going to stop the train. I'm going to stop it.

BOXER: You?

LLIO: The miners will if I call to them. Why should the others go to work if you can't? Why should they be blown into eternity?

(*Llio is putting her hat and coat on.*)

RHYS: How are you going to stop it, Mrs Jones?
LLIO (*at door*): That is for the engine-driver to discover.
RHYS: Here, wait a minute there.

(*Llio has gone.*)

RHYS (*to Boxer*): You'd better go after her and see what she's up to.
BOXER: Not me. Not out of that door there.
GWEVRIL: We cannot have train wrecking, can we? This will ruin everything, the strike and everything.
BOXER: She's going to stop the train-wrecking.
GWEVRIL: Is she? ... I shall have to run.
BOXER: Where are you running to? You're going to write my letter to the paper.
GWEVRIL: I'll have to go and tell Bronwen.
RHYS: Who is Bronwen?
GWEVRIL: Bronwen is the only woman who can handle this.

(*Exit Gwevril.*)

RHYS: You'd better follow your wife, Jones. Find out what's on and report to me quickly.
BOXER: Not me. Not out of that door. D'you hear. (*Gets Rhys by the arm.*) D'you see that photograph? Gunner Blick the human tornado. When he'd finished with me I couldn't see for three days and my hands were hurt with hitting. I couldn't eat because my mouth was twisted, I couldn't quench my thirst. I couldn't sleep. I'll fight Gunner Blick again—but I'm not going out into Cwmllynfach. D'you hear?
RHYS: I'm ashamed of you, Boxer.

(*Rhys goes out. Boxer pulls the blind, lights the lamp, turns it out again and, as he does so*),

BOXER: Now they can't stare.

(*Exit.*)

CURTAIN

ACT II – Scene IV

(Near the pit-head. Night. Bronwen; she walks to and fro across the stage throughout scene. Gwevril (off) calls after her.)

GWEVRIL: Bronwen, Bronwen, I have been looking for you all night.

(Enter Gwevril. They walk together.)

BRONWEN: I have been to Mergoed.

GWEVRIL: Mergoed?

BRONWEN: To get hold of the branch of the Railwaymen's Union. They ought to stop the ghost train from coming here.

GWEVRIL: Is it all right, then? Have they stopped it?

BRONWEN: No.

GWEVRIL: The train is coming then?

BRONWEN: Yes.

GWEVRIL: Oh—Bronwen—

BRONWEN: They couldn't get the branch together to-night, they said. We got some of the women from the guild. They think they can stop it by Wednesday.

GWEVRIL: Bronwen.

BRONWEN: I wish you would not talk like a female evangelist.

GWEVRIL: Wednesday may be too late.

BRONWEN: Too late? What for?

GWEVRIL: There's a story they're going to dynamite the train this morning.

BRONWEN: Who is going to dynamite the train?

GWEVRIL: The ghost train.

BRONWEN: You have been standing at street corners and listening to idle boasters.

GWEVRIL: I think it is the truth, Aunt Bronwen.

BRONWEN: You think it is the truth, do you? Who else does?

GWEVRIL: Well—

BRONWEN: If you can't tell me that, tell me where did you hear it.

GWEVRIL: Well—

BRONWEN: What have you been up to, girl?

GWEVRIL: In Llio Jones's house.

(Bronwen stops in her walk.)

BRONWEN: Llio Jones again? What game are you playing?

GWEVRIL: I was in Islwyn Street with the boycott party when the police charged us. I dodged into the door. Boxer Jones has given up scabbing.

BRONWEN: I'll believe that when I see it.

GWEVRIL: Aunt Bronwen—do you mind if I ask you to come for a walk down the railway track just in case?

BRONWEN: 'In case' is a hysterical way of talking. I will walk down no line.

GWEVRIL: We've got to get somebody there with a sense of responsibility. We ought to have stopped the train at Mergoed. It ought not to come to Cwmllynfach a second morning.

BRONWEN: If Howel were here that would have been done already. We women have tried and failed for the moment. It is too late to prevent it now—and there is no Howel.

GWEVRIL: It is getting light. If we are going to walk back on the line we shall have to move quickly.

BRONWEN: I am not going.

GWEVRIL: I hoped you could save the situation.

BRONWEN: If Howel were here he could have. I am an old woman and there is no power left in me.

GWEVRIL: Bronwen you're as good as Howel is.

BRONWEN: As good as Howel?

GWEVRIL: Yes, as good as Howel.

BRONWEN: It would be a good thing if that were true, for we women seem to be in charge now and we seem in danger of making a mess of it.

GWEVRIL: Walk down the line and see what happens.

BRONWEN: We shall be walking for miles.

GWEVRIL: Never mind.

BRONWEN: You may not mind. I have been to Mergoed. I have been standing at the pit-head for two days without ceasing.

GWEVRIL: I know you're tired.

BRONWEN: I am not tired. But I cannot see to everything.

GWEVRIL: It was old Rhys's story. He came in while I was hiding to ask Boxer to scout round—

BRONWEN: Rhys's story?

GWEVRIL: Yes.

(Bronwen has turned round and is walking in the opposite direction.)

BRONWEN: I am going back down the line. If any boss's rumour is going to be an excuse for incitement it will be an end to industrial action. Come along with you, quickly.

GWEVRIL: We shall reach the line in twenty minutes.

BRONWEN: When Benjamin, our youngest, married and went out of the front door Taffy said, 'We'll have a decent few years of resting.' And now Taffy is finding his own resting-place at pit-bottom and mine—mine seems to consist of walking.

(*Exeunt slowly*).

ACT II – Scene V

(*Scene, the railway line. Night. Lanterns moving about. Broken songs.*)

VOICE (*singing*): Nearer my God to Thee, nearer to Thee.

ANOTHER VOICE: Put a sock in it.

VOICE (*singing*): The people's flag is deepest red,
                It shrouded oft our martyred dead.
                We'll keep the red flag flying high,
                Beneath its shade to do or die . . .

FIRST VOICE: Stuff that one, too.

VOICE: They're staying down at Cwmparc somebody said.

ANOTHER: That's nothing. They're fighting at pit-bottom at Taff-Merthyr.

VOICE: There wouldn't have been anything without the Rock Vein Corner men.

FIRST VOICE: It's terrible—it's terrible. (*Sings again*). 'Nearer my God to Thee, nearer to Thee.'

SECOND VOICE: It isn't nearer to their God they are at pit-bottom, boy.

FIRST VOICE: And one day you will know the pit that has no bottom.

THIRD VOICE: That's one of these modern pits.

VOICE: They've come out at Blaengarw to-night.

VOICE: They've been out at Cross Keys since yesterday.

VOICE: And they damn well ought to be. Nobody ought to be working.

(*Llio comes in.*)

LLIO: Listen! There is a heap of stones by the roadside at Hafod, and at the bridge over Gaergwaun Hollow a loose coping-stone over the track. If we stone the train at Hafod, smash every window of the ghost train at Hafod, and if some of us shout to the driver, 'Take care, there is a stone on the line at Gaergwaun Hollow,' maybe that will be a way to beat the ghost train. The coping-stone on the bridge at Gaergwaun is very easily pushed over. It would fall on the line and break it. We should hurt nobody, we should give plenty of warning.

> (*Voices on the stage, in the orchestra pit, in the auditorium repeat:*)
> Stop the ghost train, stop the ghost train, stop the ghost train.

LLIO: Do we want blacklegs invading Cwmllynfach? Do we want invaders? This is not Abyssinia.

VOICES: Stop the ghost train, stop the ghost train.

LLIO: I will tell you where the loose stone is, if you listen.

VOICES: There are stones at Hafod.

VOICE: This is not Abyssinia.

VOICE: Yes, Abyssinia has come to South Wales.

VOICE: There is a loose coping-stone on the bridge at Gaergwaun.

LLIO: It is big enough to break the line. Not a man need be injured. Only stone the train first at Hafod. Warn the engine-driver against passing Gaergwaun Hollow.

VOICE: There is a loose coping-stone on the bridge at Hafod.

VOICE: No, at Gaergwaun.

VOICE: I said Gaergwaun.

VOICE: You said Hafod.

(*Bronwen and Gwevril enter.*)

BRONWEN: Listen, men. You are trade unionists, or if you are not you ought to be. You may think that what you are indulging in is direct action. It is nothing of the kind. Direct action is action to some purpose, action that will gain an end even at the loss maybe of a man or two in gaol. This is not the case with what you are doing.

VOICES: Stop the ghost train, stop the ghost train.

BRONWEN: Ay, you may shout 'Stop the ghost train' till you are

black in the face, but that does not alter the truth that by de-
railing it you will be playing into the hands of the police your
enemies. I have nothing to say to the police. They are a mercenary army, and we are an army of volunteers good enough
to defeat them.

VOICES (*louder*): Stop the ghost train, stop the ghost train.

BRONWEN: All you are doing is running yourselves into difficulties.
Do not go in for casual violence. Trade unionists must go into
fighting with organisation, and with leadership.

VOICE: Come on, mother. Pick your stones up!

BRONWEN: I am not coming. I am staying here.

VOICE: You're speaking for the blacklegs.

BRONWEN: I am advising you not to try beating the police in the
wrong way. You are bringing the scabs into the shelter of men's
pity.

VOICE: Come on with us, mother. We can't be bothered. Pick up
your stones!

    (*Voices receding* – Stop the ghost train – *they fade out
    gradually.*)

BRONWEN: It is not much good waiting here.

GWEVRIL: You've done your best, Aunt Bronwen.

BRONWEN: My best is not as good as a meat tea—(*then shouting
loud*)—Throw your stones straight then. Make a good job of it.

VOICES (*very distant*): Stop the ghost train, stop the ghost train.

VOICES (*loud*): Pick up your stones!

    (*Exeunt.*)

SLOW CURTAIN

ACT III – Scene I

(*The stage darkens. A metronome set at* largo *is in the orchestra
pit. A drum takes up the rhythm, various percussions die away into
the sound of the metronome again. This continues through the
scene. A miner's lamp.*)

WILL LEWIS: Dai, look, how long have we been here?

DAI: I don't know. Three days.

WILL LEWIS: Days? What are days? The little hand of my watch goes round twice and I have never seen it move so slowly. Do you call that a day?

DAI: What time is it now?

WILL LEWIS: Twelve twenty-five.

DAI: Which?

WILL: Which what?

DAI: Day or night?

WILL: You knew where you were at breakfast this morning. You will have to be more careful to keep count.

DAI: Tell me which it is yourself then.

WILL: I—I'm not quite sure.

DAI: We have been here too long. We have been here till we are beaten. How much longer? How much longer?

WILL: You are constipated with too many sandwiches.

DAI: How much longer?

WILL: You should be more careful. This is not a Christmas treat.

DAI: This noise is beating us. This noise.

WILL: Which noise?

DAI: This noise.

WILL: Oh! This? I am so used to it I never hear it. It is an air-lock in the pipes. At least it tells you that the pumps are working.

DAI (*breathless*): Will Lewis miner.

WILL: What is it?

DAI: Suppose they let the pumps stop?

WILL: It is our mates working them.

DAI: But if Rhys were to break them down?

WILL: He is not so careful of us, maybe, but do not worry, they are all very careful of their mine.

DAI: *Let* them stop their blasted pumps. What do I care when the noise is beating us?

WILL: What you need is some recreation. Come over here where it is lighter.

> (*Will and Dai move across the stage. Bluish light slowly reveals them.*)

WILL: Have you the pack?

DAI: Where shall we play?

WILL: Here. Sit on the ground then. (*He lowers himself.*) Did you hear me creaking? The pit-bottom or my own is worn. I do not know which is which at this stage of proceedings.

DAI: You will take cold. Better squat on your heels.

WILL: It is not necessary now I am acclimatised. And there is another reason.

DAI: For an old man –

WILL: For a what?

DAI: For an elderly miner, sitting on the ground is dangerous.

WILL: To squat would be dangerous in another way.

DAI: Why?

WILL: I am like Mr Rhys's mine.

DAI: You are like Mr Rhys's mine?

WILL: I am nearly through my seams.

(*Dai has been dealing. They take up their hands.*)

WILL: You are a poor dealer.

DAI: I go nap.

WILL: A very poor dealer.

(*Will and Dai play it out.*)

DAI: I get it.

WILL: What did I say we were playing for?

DAI: The same as last time.

WILL: I said nothing of the kind.

DAI: Since you said nothing, we assume it.

WILL: You have won six and sixpence to-day already.

DAI: And this is another sixpence.

WILL (*groaning*): Give me sixpence. That was my last shilling.

DAI: You had three and sixpence.

WILL: It was still my last shilling. The other is half a crown. I am going to deal carefully. Everything depends on my winning back.

DAI: You don't want money here.

WILL: What about when we go upstairs again, Mr Mines Inspector?

DAI: We might go up on a Friday.

WILL: And we might go up on a Monday, with five days to live on three shillings. . . . Will you pay me for my next week's wages, if necessary?

DAI: You might never have a next week's wages.

WILL: I can give you an I.O.U.

DAI: We have no pencil here, nor paper.
WILL: We will ask Howel.

(*Enter Howel.*)

HOWEL: What is it you were going to ask?
WILL (*hurriedly*): Nothing, Howel. (*He snatches up the cards, dropping one.*)
HOWEL: Have you been playing again for money?
WILL: There is so much time, Howel, we must do something to pass it.
HOWEL: Is it wise to teach this boy to gamble, Will Lewis?
WILL (*indignantly*): *Teach* him! I do not teach the Knave of Spades to play cards.
HOWEL: It is time for your watch. Are you ready?
WILL (*putting up a coat collar*): I am not ready. It is too cold out there.
HOWEL (*kindly*): I know, but the two hours soon pass. We can arrange shorter shifts if you like.
WILL: Is it necessary to watch at all? Dai, look, is shivering.
HOWEL: Let me look at you, Dai. Do you feel cold?
DAI: Coldish. It is nothing.
HOWEL: Come here. Give me your hand. You were feverish after fighting Boxer. That is when the cold gets you. (*Feels his pulse, puts a hand to his forehead.*) Go on watch for the moment, Dai. I will get you relieved as soon as I can find a substitute.
DAI: No, I'll stick it, Howel.
HOWEL: Better to take the precaution. To be over-plucky in a small thing robs you of the chance of a big one.
WILL: I move, Howel Chairman, that we abolish watching.
HOWEL: Why Will?
WILL: This is not a ship. We are not sailors.
HOWEL: No, but we are miners on a stay-down strike. Are you honestly tired of watching, Will Lewis, or is it a joke, or have you Dai's cold?
WILL: I have been thinking it over. I do not think it is necessary to keep watches.
HOWEL: I don't understand your attitude. If we are not to know who comes down, if we are not to hold the pit as we said we would, we might as well be pit-props, or go now to the surface.
WILL: All right, Howel, if you are going to start preaching.
HOWEL: That was not called for, Will Lewis.

WILL: It was not meant to be insulting.

HOWEL: I know. I am a bit puzzled.

WILL: What about?

HOWEL: I do not understand your point of view.

WILL: I do not know that I do, either.

HOWEL: I do not understand how you are able to get rid of seriousness. Here where we live day and night in the face of eternity, you get rid of seriousness.

(*Will Lewis has tiptoed away. He beckons as he goes out.*)

WILL: Come on, Dai.

(*Dai follows him. They have dropped one of their cards. Howel picks it up, looks at it closely, holding his lamp to it.*)

HOWEL: They told us as children that there was sinfulness in the very colour of this king here. I wonder if they were right?

WILL LEWIS (*off*): Howel!

HOWEL: What is it?

WILL LEWIS: There is Mr Rhys here has, come down in the cage. Do we let him through?

HOWEL: Bring him.

(*Enter Mr Rhys between Dai and Will Lewis.*)

MR RHYS: All right down below?

HOWEL: Everything is all right.

MR RHYS (*pointing to Dai*): He looks sick, doesn't he?

HOWEL: We will look after him.

MR RHYS: Well, Howel—I can't understand you. Frankly I can't.

HOWEL: We will be able to talk better when it is all over.

MR RHYS (*to Dai*): You'd better come up with me, young fellow.

HOWEL: Do you want to?

DAI: I'll die down here if I'm going to.

HOWEL: It is not going to be a question of dying. We shall ask you to go up if your cold develops. We have agreed on the principle.

MR RHYS: Well, I suppose that's all we can do. I brought a batch of sandwich boxes.

HOWEL: We will ring on the pit telephone if the boy's cold develops.

MR RHYS (*turns to go, shuffles back*): There's been trouble up there to-day. It'll end by putting paid to all your accounts if I'm not mistaken.

HOWEL: Trouble?

MR RHYS: Some of your friends pushed a coping-stone on the Company Union train at Gaergwaun Hollow, where the line goes under the bridge. It tore a hole in the guard's van. They say nobody's killed, but you never know what to believe in these days.

HOWEL: Has the ghost train stopped?

MR RHYS: The Railwaymen's Union has banned it; but we shall attempt to run it.

HOWEL: You have brought us good news then.

MR RHYS: Good news? Good news with red riot and a train half destroyed?

HOWEL: If it means we are winning.

MR RHYS: Have I gone mad or am I talking to a Methodist local preacher?

HOWEL: You have not gone mad.

MR RHYS (*goes off muttering*): I'm lost in all this. Everything is upside down!

(*Exit.*)

HOWEL: Dai—you are shivering. Put my coat on.

DAI: No. Keep it on yourself, man.

(*Howel takes off his coat and puts it over Dai's shoulders.*)

HOWEL: Let me find a corner for you in the stable. Keep an eye open, Will Lewis.

WILL: Ay, ay, Howel. (*Exit.*)

HOWEL (*shouts after him*): Will Lewis!

(*Will returns.*)

HOWEL: Will, look, you dropped your King of Spades. (*Gives him the card.*) Come Dai. (*Exeunt Dai and Howel.*)

WILL LEWIS (*looking at the card*): I should have thought he would impound it. Howel preacher, have you been converted?

(*Music. The lights go up very slowly to simulate coming to the surface. Possibly a song.*)

CURTAIN

ACT III – Scene II

(The pit-head. Enter Police Inspector.)

INSPECTOR: Sergeant! *(Sergeant enters.)* Take your place there.
INSPECTOR: 159! *(159 enters.)* Take your place there.
INSPECTOR: 273! *(273 enters.)* You there.

(They are at the four corners of the stage.)

INSPECTOR: The first one is coming now. Arrest her when she has passed me.

(Llio, singing off, the song approaching. Llio enters towards the end of the song. She walks past the Inspector. The Sergeant stretches out his arm and stops her.)

INSPECTOR: Yes, that one.
SERGEANT: You're to come to the police station with us, missus.
LLIO: What for?
SERGEANT: You know very well.
LLIO: What did I do?
SERGEANT: Are you coming quietly? 159, handcuffs!
LLIO: Handcuffs? I cannot go through the street chained to a policeman. Do you know who I am?
SERGEANT: We shall soon find out, anyway. Handcuff her.

(Sergeant hands Llio over to 159, who takes her out, returning himself in a moment.)

SERGEANT: Any more, sir?
INSPECTOR: Yes, stand by. There's another on the hill now. Keep quiet. . . . Now!

(Gwevril crosses the stage. 159 touches her on the shoulder. She turns quickly.)

GWEVRIL: What is it?
159: We have to ask you to come to the station, missie.
GWEVRIL: Has anything happened? Is it Dai?
159: Who is Dai?
GWEVRIL: Dai Roberts—stay-down striker.
159: No, nothing to do wi' i'm. Come this way.
SERGEANT: Put bracelets on her.
159: Need I, Sergeant?

INSPECTOR: Obey your orders.

159: Come on, missie. He's losing his temper.

(*159 marches Gwevril off.*)

INSPECTOR: Here is the last now. Go and get her. Quick!

(*273 and the Sergeant exeunt quickly and return with Bronwen.*)

273: This the one, sir?

INSPECTOR: Course it's the one.

BRONWEN: Why are you pulling me like that, man?

273: You'll know soon enough.

BRONWEN: You're not trying to arrest me, young man?

273: We have done, missus. (*Snaps the handcuffs.*)

(*159 returns.*)

BRONWEN: What is the charge?

INSPECTOR: We'll tell you that at the station.

BRONWEN: You'll tell me now.

INSPECTOR: You are charged with inciting to riot. If you have anything to say it will be taken down in writing and used as evidence against you.

BRONWEN: I've got a good deal to say.

(*159 takes out his note-book.*)

INSPECTOR: Are you going to say it here or at the station?

BRONWEN: I'm going to say it at both places, and all the time and everywhere. You—you're a Liverpool bobby, aren't you?

INSPECTOR: It has nothing to do with you where I come from.

BRONWEN: Yes, you're a Liverpool bobby—and that one over there's from Bristol. And I charge you with inciting to hatred and ruin—and anything you may say will be remembered and remembered against you.

159: Not so fast, please, missus. I'm not getting it all down.

(*Police take Bronwen off.*)

CURTAIN

ACT III – Scene III

(In the pit. Howel bending over Dai who is covered with coats and sacks.)

HOWEL: It is all right, Dai. It is all right. Your head is not as hot as it was. It will be passing. You are going up in a minute.

DAI *(shouting)*: I am not going to go up. I am not going to go up.

HOWEL: All right, Dai. All right. You'll be famous on the pit-top when you get there. It isn't everybody who would stay down with us out of sympathy. Not many lads of your age.

DAI *(through his teeth)*: I'm going to stick it out, Howel. D'you know why?

HOWEL: You are going to stick it out, of course.

DAI: Because I came down here not for trade-union principles, but for notoriety.

HOWEL: You are hot-headed, Dai. Keep quiet.

DAI: I came down here because I wanted to impress Gwevril. I came down here for the wrong reasons.

HOWEL: You came down here like the rest of us, to hold the pit against the scabs.

DAI: But you'll promise not to send me up, Howel. You can't send me up with things like they are. I want to hide . . . some of the truth . . . from everybody.

(Enter Will Lewis.)

HOWEL: Did you get him?

WILL LEWIS: I telephoned. It was Will Saunders.

HOWEL: He'll fix it.

DAI: You're not getting me sent up, are you?

HOWEL: Will Lewis. *(He beckons. They change places. Will Lewis puts his arm under Dai. Squats down and puts the boy's head on his lap. Howel is going.)*

WILL LEWIS: Before you go, Howel—I have made jokes because you are a local preacher. I want to say that there are times when some of your thoughts are soothing.

HOWEL: I don't want to be apologised to, Will Lewis—not here.

WILL LEWIS: I think it would be a good occasion for—for reading the lesson, Howel.

HOWEL: Do you mean that sincerely, Will Lewis, or is it part of your apology?

WILL LEWIS: That psalm of yours has good words.

HOWEL: 'Though we should walk through the valley . . .

WILL LEWIS: 'Though we should walk through the valley of the shadow of death, we will fear no evil.'

HOWEL: 'Thy rod and Thy staff shall comfort us, Thou preparest a table for us in the presence of our enemies. Our cup runneth over. Surely goodness and mercy shall follow us all the days of our life, and we shall dwell in the house of the Lord for ever.'

WILL LEWIS: Howel?

HOWEL (*with unction*): Yes?

WILL LEWIS: Does that mean that we shall get our two bob in the long run?

HOWEL: I don't know.

(*Howel goes out hurriedly.*)

DAI: You spoiled your apology, Will Lewis.

WILL LEWIS: In apologising, Dai, a man so often goes too far.

DAI: What was that you were telephoning to the pit-head about?

WILL LEWIS: That is all right. You have to keep quiet now. You are in a convalescent home. . . . Are you asleep?

(*Dai is asleep. Will Lewis sits motionless with the boy's head on his knees. On each side of the stage stands a dimly-lighted figure, a man and a woman. They recite the following chorus.*)

MAN: Time, in the shape of a mine, time, in that shape
Has the same backward progress underground,
And past explosions are now lighted roads.
Then turn away from lights and trams and whitewash
Into the critical *Present* where workings narrow:
Bend double at coal-face, bend double and approach
The blank wall of the future.

WOMAN: Pit-prop carefully behind you,
Pit-prop and scatter stonedust.

MAN: Time in the shape of a mine –

WOMAN: Can you go on now?

MAN: Whether with pneumatic drill shattering eardrums
Or whether the mechanical cutter hauls
Its great bulk into the underface like a tank,
Or whether, after your drilling, the charge of dynamite
Implies 'stand back' and the fireman's signal

And thunder blasting unknown addition to
Time, in the shape of a mine, stretching back. . . .
WOMAN: Stretching back, maybe, this time, with
A fallen rock between you and the world
(Two or three cut off) and a rescue party
Tapping at the other end of the solid.
MAN: Sound travels. You can hear through solidity.
WOMAN: And die in the dark hearing. Then it is finished
Miner's knowledge and his skull cracked
Instantaneously. . . . Time in the shape of a miner
Left for dead in the workings.
MAN: Another time, along main haulage roads
Past the conveyors, trams, electric lights,
Comes fire, flood, chaos and general death.
One thrust at the future brought that mighty death.
WOMAN: Time in the shape of a mine is three dead every day.
It is a shape of time, one thousand and seventy-three in a year.
MAN: We have our roundabout apart from yours,
Twenty-four hours divided into shifts.
Your marriages, your pregnancies and deliveries
By district nurses hurrying on bicycles
Your shops, your credits, have no obvious harmony
With this dark round of ours, this onward march
Of Time along with death and fire and flood
And speed against time weighing coal we get;
This nice precision of the hewer's path,
This separate world; this pit; this underground,
Time, caring little for the upper crust.
WOMAN: Have you got new men (otherwise we are lost)
Have you got new men, themselves shaping
Time in the shape of their knowledge of necessity, shaping
Time according to the seam, according to geology
Time for man, not man for Time,
Time for man! Time for man!
Have you got new men? (Otherwise we are lost!)
And mines will feed on men as wars do.
Have you got new men to fight this other time?
New men, new men to overcome it, till
Time, in the shape of a mine, is the equation
Of an enriching life!
MAN: Yes. We have new men.

The new man, here, now, braving novel death,
Stands upright in the mine, and in that posture
Shakes more than pit-props.

(*Howel enters on tiptoes.*)

WILL LEWIS: Hush! He is sleeping.

HOWEL: Something is happening up there. I do not know what.

WILL LEWIS: What makes you think so?

HOWEL: Listen.

WILL LEWIS: I can hear nothing.

HOWEL: Listen again. There is singing.

WILL LEWIS: I cannot hear it.

HOWEL: Now.

(*The singing is quite near. 'Cwm Rhondda'*)

WILL LEWIS: They are in the shaft, man.

HOWEL: They are going up in the cage.

WILL LEWIS: It is the men from the West Pit.

HOWEL: They are going up.

WILL LEWIS: Singing.

DAI (*waking up*): What is that noise, uncle?

WILL LEWIS: Get to the pit telephone.

HOWEL: They must have won, brother.

DAI: We've won? We've won?

(*Howel goes out. We can hear his voice off.*)

HOWEL: What is it, Will Saunders? We can hear the men in the shaft from West Pit singing!

(*Singing louder.*)

CURTAIN

ACT III – Scene IV

(*Pit-head. Three women.*)

FIST WOMAN: Two or three have fainted.

(*Enter a fourth.*)

SECOND WOMAN: They are falling down like flies in the baths.

THIRD WOMAN: How many have fainted?

SECOND WOMAN: Thirty or forty.

FIRST WOMAN: We ought to go and help.

THIRD WOMAN: There are plenty of first-aid men.

FIRST WOMAN: Another cage is coming up now.

(First woman goes to back and comes in holding Dai's arm.)

DAI: I can't see anything.

FIRST WOMAN: That is nothing. You are dazzled.

DAI: Where is Gwevril?

(The women look at each other.)

DAI: She must be here. Gwevril!

FIRST WOMAN: You will be seeing her later.

SECOND WOMAN: Yes, later.

DAI: She ought to be here now.

FIRST WOMAN: Come to the baths, Dai. You will—

DAI: Who are you? I cannot see you.

FIRST WOMAN: A neighbour.

(They lead him off. Third woman brings in Howel.)

SECOND WOMAN: Can you see, Howel?

HOWEL *(hand in front of his eyes)*: Not yet. I am covering my eyes to get used to it gradually. Where is Bronwen?

SECOND WOMAN: Not here.

HOWEL: Nonsense, she must be.

(They go out. Third Woman (Bronwen masked) brings in Will Lewis.)

WILL LEWIS: My eyes are old ones. They can take the transition.

THIRD WOMAN: Who am I, then?

WILL LEWIS: One woman is the same as another. Who *are* you?

THIRD WOMAN: Aren't you expecting anybody to meet you?

WILL LEWIS: Not a woman in the world, thank God. I am a miner married to the workings.

THIRD WOMAN: That's not very nice to me for helping you.

WILL LEWIS: By the look of your face you are kind-hearted.

THIRD WOMAN: Can you see it?

(Will Lewis pauses.)

WILL LEWIS: It looks very like a face now.

THIRD WOMAN: Whose is it? Can you see?

WILL LEWIS: Of course I can see. It is a face, but it is not yours, is it?

(*Exeunt.*)

CURTAIN

ACT III – Scene V

(*Scene—Court Room. Magistrate sitting at table, L. A. Clerk of the Court sits near him—canopied seat. Prisoners in roped-off space right stage facing audience. They are Howel, Will Lewis, Dai, Bronwen, Gwevril, Llio. Witness-box C.*)

CLERK: Silence in Court.

MAGISTRATE: Prisoner Howel. You are now on oath. Be careful how you answer my questions. At six o'clock on the morning of November the eleventh, did you present yourself for work at Rock Vein Corner?

HOWEL: Yes.

MAGISTRATE: Was this by instruction from the Company?

HOWEL: Yes.

MAGISTRATE: Did you draw your lamp from the lamp room?

HOWEL: In the ordinary way.

MAGISTRATE: It has been stated that you gave another lamp to the prisoner Dai Roberts.

HOWEL: That is true.

MAGISTRATE: Was that irregular?

HOWEL: I smuggled it.

MAGISTRATE: How long have you been a miner?

HOWEL: Fourteen years.

MAGISTRATE: Therefore you were aware of the serious nature of that action?

HOWEL: I was.

MAGISTRATE: And of its possible consequences?

HOWEL: Yes.

MAGISTRATE: You then proceeded to the pit-head of the Rock Vein?

HOWEL: I did something before that.

MAGISTRATE: Is it relevant to the issue?

HOWEL: I would like it to be in the deposition.

MAGISTRATE: Well?

HOWEL: I saw some other workmen proceeding in the direction of the East Pit. They were not the usual employees of the Rock Vein Colliery.

MAGISTRATE: Is it any affair of yours whether they were or not?

HOWEL: It is my affair as a trade unionist.

MAGISTRATE: And what did you do when you saw these men?

HOWEL: I consulted the others.

MAGISTRATE: What did you decide?

HOWEL: To stay down the pit.

MAGISTRATE: Without working?

HOWEL: Yes.

MAGISTRATE: What was the object of this extraordinary procedure?

HOWEL: We decided to stay down till the blacklegs were dismissed and our own men given their rightful jobs again.

MAGISTRATE: 'Blacklegs' is not a word you may use in this Court.

HOWEL: I do not know a better name for them.

MAGISTRATE: Listen to me, Howel—We are not here to examine your political philosophy or your motives or those of anyone else. What I have to decide is whether there is a prima facie case against you. You know what that is?

HOWEL: Yes.

MAGISTRATE: What is it?

HOWEL: You have to decide whether you dare send us for trial.

MAGISTRATE: Say 'Your Worship' when you are addressing the Court.

HOWEL: I was addressing you.

MAGISTRATE (*hurrying on*): Did you descend the pit-shaft?

HOWEL: Yes.

MAGISTRATE: Called the men together at pit-bottom and decided on a stay-down strike, warning the officials accordingly by pit telephone?

HOWEL: Yes.

MAGISTRATE: You agree that you were in technical possession of the pit without lawful right or authority?

HOWEL: I agree.

MAGISTRATE: Your presence prevented the Rock Vein Colliery who are the rightful owners of the pit, from working the same according to their normal usage?

HOWEL: Yes. We kept the blacklegs out of the Rock Vein pit.

MAGISTRATE: Have you anything more to add?

HOWEL: Yes.

MAGISTRATE: I must tell you for your own good that you would be better advised to reserve any defence you may have till your case is heard by a judge and jury at the Assizes.

HOWEL: I have something to say.

MAGISTRATE: Well, what is it?

HOWEL: I want to say a few words.

MAGISTRATE: You won't do yourself any good by making speeches.

HOWEL: That is for me to judge.

MAGISTRATE: I warn you—and I ought not to do this but I am doing it out of kindheartedness—that there is every likelihood of my deciding that a prima facie case has been established—by your own evidence if nothing else; and this means that I shall have to commit you to the Assizes at Newport. Anything else you say now will be taken down in writing and may be used against you in that trial.

HOWEL: I am here now among my own people. Newport is miles away and they will not hear what I have to say there. It is here, in Cwmllynfach, I must be speaking.

MAGISTRATE: If you try to use this Court as a propaganda platform, I shall have you sent out.

HOWEL: Your Worship, I have given to the best of my ability a truthful testimony. In this business, I was not through any virtue of my own, but through circumstances, a leader. I do not deny we seized the pit and held it as strongly as we could against all comers. Although it was not lawfully ours, we took it. And I am not prepared to cover the hard meaning of that statement. Your Worship, I'm a Christian.

MAGISTRATE: You are making it worse for yourself, Howel.

LLIO: Let him go on.

HOWEL: I am a Christian, and many will be wondering why it should happen that I would commit, knowingly, an unlawful act.

MAGISTRATE: You're getting yourself in deeper. Let me advise you.

K

HOWEL: There arc many ways of reading the New Testament, but there is only one true way, which is to accept the logic of it and not mind where it leads you. I think that the money-changers in the Temple at Jerusalem were carrying on their business according to their custom. I think, too, it was lawful and they were in their rightful places. Yet they were turned out and beaten with whips by a man who symbolises the pressure of the times. It was his teaching that law and custom harden till they have to be broken. It was his teaching that systems break and stunt the growing thing until they have to be broken, because they are a denial of life.

MAGISTRATE: Your Christianity leads you into acts of violence.

HOWEL: My Christianity leads me into the belief that every man has the right to live decently and peacefully among his fellows. My Christianity leads me into the belief that men have a right to work, and on the other side that no man has a right to be idle. My Christianity leads me into a belief in the right of people to have food—(*pause*)—and clothing and the benefits of education.

MAGISTRATE: Your Christianity sounds suspiciously like Social-ism, Howel.

HOWEL: My Christianity is not that of the coal-owners.

MAGISTRATE: Is that all you have to say?

HOWEL: That is all.

CLERK: Stand up.

MAGISTRATE (*standing*): Benjamin David Howel, I commit you to be tried before a judge and jury at the Assizes at Newport, on the twentieth proximo at ten o'clock in the forenoon. I charge the police to be responsible for producing your person at the Court at the aforesaid date and time.

MAGISTRATE (*continuing*): Will you step down please. And now the ladies. Who is first? Bronwen Matilda Jones and Llio Jones. Are they here?

BRONWEN: We are here.

MAGISTRATE: You are sisters?

BRONWEN (*indignantly*): No.

MAGISTRATE: We shall take you in alphabetical order. Bronwen Matilda first.

BRONWEN: Here I am.

MAGISTRATE: Have you anything to say before you are commit-ted to trial before a judge and jury at the Assizes?

BRONWEN: Yes.

MAGISTRATE: This is your chance.

BRONWEN: Everybody here knows—

MAGISTRATE: Address the Court, please.

BRONWEN: Everybody here knows that it is against my principles to have anything to do with rioting. I am a Labour woman.

MAGISTRATE: We have nothing to do with your principles, we are concerned with facts.

WILL LEWIS (*shouting*): Go on, Bronwen.

MAGISTRATE: Will you please keep quiet.

WILL LEWIS: Give her a chance then.

MAGISTRATE: Go on, please.

BRONWEN: I am a Labour woman.

MAGISTRATE: Please address your remarks to me. I don't want to know anything about your politics.

BRONWEN: I do not believe in playing into the hands of Courts like these and of men like you.

WILL LEWIS: Stick it, Bronwen.

MAGISTRATE: Quiet, please.

BRONWEN: But if it must be it must be and, being in, I will fight you.

DAI AND GWEVRIL: Go on, Bronwen.

BRONWEN: I was against this action. Action ought to have been taken by the trade union branch at Mergoed, to prevent the ghost train getting as far as Hafod.

WILL LEWIS: So it ought.

BRONWEN: But once it got to Hafod I would not answer for the consequences. If I am to answer for them in this dock, a great many other people ought to be here too.

VOICES (*from behind*): We all ought to be there.

VOICE: Take us and we'll surrender.

VOICE: We'll come into the dock with them.

(*There is an uproar.*)

HOWEL (*sternly*): Silence! Listen to Bronwen.

BRONWEN: I am not a believer in riots, nor in throwing stones even at trains full of blacklegs but if there is no other way to stop a scab train than by throwing stones, then I say throw them straight. I say smash the bloody train to smithereens if you're going to.

(*Cheers from behind.*)

MAGISTRATE: Bronwen Matilda Jones—this is a Police Court.

BRONWEN: I've said all I've got to say, mister. I'll add one for you specially. You—and your kind—are against people breathing, and you only show your own cleverness when you complain we become violent. These people in Cwmllynfach are very peaceable, which is the reverse of you and your policemen. They let themselves be scared by hobgoblins and by your long charges with your judges and their paraphernalia. But I am old, I, Bronwen Matilda Jones, as you call it, I do not care for you and your prisons. I am old and I have never been able to rest for one moment. I do not care if you give me twelve months. Inside it will be quieter—and I hope not so hard on the feet. That is all.

MAGISTRATE: Llio Jones, it is your turn. I hope you will be briefer. (*Looking at his papers.*) Ah—this is different. You are the wife of the boxer. Your husband had the good sense to go on working during these disturbances till he was terrorised into staying at home.

LLIO: You are putting it unfairly.

MAGISTRATE: We will talk about that later. Meanwhile, if you can give the Court an adequate explanation of what brought you to Hafod and to Gaergwaun Hollow on the morning in question, you may perhaps avoid the terrors of the Assizes.

LLIO: What do I have to do?

WILL LEWIS: Give her hell, man.

DAI: She's the scab's wife.

MAGISTRATE: Quietly—I have warned you already.

WILL LEWIS: She is the only one who oughtn't to be here.

MAGISTRATE: That is what we are inquiring into. Mrs Jones, will you tell the Court what brought you to Gaergwaun Hollow?

LLIO: I had a good reason.

MAGISTRATE: I'm sure you had. But we must know what it was.

LLIO: Do I have to tell you everything?

MAGISTRATE: It's for your own good.

WILL LEWIS: She came to look for her old man.

MAGISTRATE: Never mind intimidation. We will protect you. Please speak freely.

LLIO: I heard that the train was going to be wrecked.

MAGISTRATE: Who told you?

GWEVRIL: You aren't allowed to ask that.

DAI: You're out of order, man.

WILL LEWIS: Let him ask her. That's what we want to know.

MAGISTRATE: I have warned you once already.

BRONWEN: Let her speak. Let her tell what she knows.

MAGISTRATE: Go on with what you were saying.

LLIO: I was told the train was going to be wrecked.

MAGISTRATE: Yes, yes. You said so.

LLIO: I knew that there was a pile of stones at Hafod, because I had been past on the road two days before. It is a very lonely road and not many people would have known about them.

MAGISTRATE: What has this got to do with it?

LLIO: I knew that there was a loose coping-stone on the bridge at Gaergwaun Hollow. I had been past there too. I often notice that kind of thing.

MAGISTRATE: Very observant, Mrs Jones. But what is this leading to?

LLIO: It is all relevant.

MAGISTRATE: Yes, yes, but to what.

LLIO: I thought the others might not know about these things.

MAGISTRATE: But you were afraid some of the wilder spirits might find out.

LLIO: I was afraid they mightn't.

MAGISTRATE: I beg your pardon, Mrs Jones. I didn't catch what you said.

LLIO: I was afraid they mightn't know about the heap of stones at Hafod and the loose coping-stone on the bridge at Gaergwaun Hollow.

MAGISTRATE: You're putting it the wrong way round, aren't you?

LLIO: No.

MAGISTRATE: But in that case I can't understand.

LLIO: A lot of things are difficult to understand in Cwmllynfach.

MAGISTRATE: But I don't understand, what was your object?

LLIO: To wreck the ghost train.

MAGISTRATE: If this goes on, I shall be adjourning the case for medical examination.

LLIO: I have never been so clear-sighted.

MAGISTRATE: Your interests were all the other way. Your husband was one of the loyal workmen. You can't try to persuade me that you had any interest in wrecking that train. . . . Tell me, Mrs Jones, has anybody been trying to intimidate you?

LLIO: Life.

MAGISTRATE: I beg your pardon. You must speak up. What did you say?

LLIO: I'd rather not repeat it.

MAGISTRATE: Now give your evidence properly. Don't be frightened. Whatever anybody else has been saying outside this Court, you will be protected.

LLIO: I'm not one to be easily frightened.

MAGISTRATE: So much I'm gathering. Now answer my question. Did you, or did you not, have anything to do with the riot of Gaergwaun Hollow?

LLIO: Depends what you mean by having anything to do with it.

MAGISTRATE: Did you throw any stones?

LLIO: No.

MAGISTRATE: Did you push the coping-stone?

LLIO: No.

MAGISTRATE: Very well then.

LLIO: It is not very well. You've another question to ask me.

MAGISTRATE: I've asked all the questions I wish to.

LLIO: You should ask, did I incite.

MAGISTRATE: You are doing your best to get into prison, Mrs Jones.

LLIO: I have been in prison all my life. I am doing my best to get out.

MAGISTRATE: I wish you wouldn't talk so cryptically.

LLIO: Your Worship, I incited. I incited to riot, I incited to violence, I incited for all I was worth, with all my might. Is that enough?

MAGISTRATE: Quite enough, I should have thought. Stand aside then. This needs a more learned head than I have.

WILL LEWIS: Before she stands down I want to ask some questions.

MAGISTRATE: I should have thought you had expressed yourself pretty freely already.

WILL LEWIS: You cannot refuse. I am asking formally.

MAGISTRATE: Very well.

WILL LEWIS (*To Llio*): Were you put up to this by anybody?

LLIO: No.

WILL LEWIS: If you had not told the crowd and incited them,

the train would not have been stoned nor the coping-stone pushed over?

LLIO: No.

WILL LEWIS: In short, you are a provocative agent and an inciter?

LLIO: Yes – no – no.

WILL LEWIS: Yes – no – yes – no – yes –no!

GWEVRIL: Leave her alone, Will Lewis. She meant it for the best.

WILL LEWIS: Meant it for the best and got it for the worst. Listen, Mrs Llio. We have heard all about your changed heart and being in prison all your life. We are the people that prisoned you, by keeping you out. When you come in there is hell to pay. You belong to the other side and you should stay there.

(*Llio bursts into tears.*)

GWEVRIL: Leave her alone, Will Lewis. You are wrong.

MAGISTRATE: Enough of this nonsense.

WILL LEWIS: Yes, but it is your fault, you and your system. You turned her bad like cheap mutton.

MAGISTRATE: Sit down, please.

BOXER JONES (*from the audience*): Before you finish with this item I want to give evidence.

MAGISTRATE: Who are you?

BOXER: I am her husband.

MAGISTRATE: Certainly you can give evidence. Come up into the box.

(*Boxer goes into the witness-box.*)

CLERK: Take the Book in your right hand. Do you solemnly swear to tell the truth, the whole truth, and nothing but the truth, so help you God?

BOXER: Aye.

MAGISTRATE: Now, what do you want to say?

BOXER: I have come to say that I have renounced blacklegging and all organised job stealing.

MAGISTRATE: I thought you were going to give evidence.

BOXER: I came to say this publicly. I was going to put it in the paper, Miss Gwevril was going to write it: but now you have pinched her and I do not trust my spelling.

MAGISTRATE: Mr Jones, I've given you a lot of rope. If you have anything to say bearing on the case, please say it. Otherwise I must ask you to get down.

BOXER: No. I have said it. I wanted to give the statement publicity. There are hundreds of the general public (*pointing to the audience*) down there. It will do.

MAGISTRATE: Stand down, please.

BOXER: Sure—I've done my stuff.

WILL LEWIS: We've all done our stuff.

MAGISTRATE: Well, I haven't.

BOXER (*pointing to the audience*): There are a few more down there that haven't either.

MAGISTRATE: Prisoners, I want you to listen. You are committed now for your trial. That does not mean that you are guilty or innocent but simply that you will be tried before a judge and jury at the next Assizes.

BOXER (*shouting*): If you could make a dock big enough to hold all of us—

MAGISTRATE (*angry*): Go back to the public seats.

BOXER (*hesitates*): All right.

MAGISTRATE: Go back to the public seats.

BOXER: The public seats and the dock is the same in this business.

(*Boxer backs slowly towards the steps leading to the auditorium.*)

BRONWEN: Before you sentence us—

MAGISTRATE: I'm not sentencing you, Mrs Jones. I'm committing you for trial.

BRONWEN: I've got to say something.

MAGISTRATE: What is it?

BRONWEN (*to the audience*): You people of Cwmllynfach –

MAGISTRATE: No more speeches, please.

BRONWEN (*with great emphasis*): Tell the world.

MAGISTRATE: Please.

BRONWEN: Tell England and Scotland.

MAGISTRATE: I said no speeches.

BRONWEN: Tell them to join Wales.

CURTAIN

JAMES BOSWELL:

An introductory note to the work of the 1930s

James Boswell was born on 9 June 1906, at Westport, New Zealand. His father, Edward Blair Buchanan Boswell, was of Scottish descent. He earned his living as a school teacher, and was an amateur watercolourist, a designer of his own furniture, and a collector of shells and geological specimens. Boswell's mother was Ida Fair, daughter of a local draper, of Irish stock.

In 1917 the family moved to Auckland, where Boswell attended the grammar school. Seven years later, in 1924, he began studying at the Elam School of Art, Auckland, and in the following year he came with his mother and sister to London, and began to study at the Royal College of Art. Boswell has left us his own account of those years.

In 1925 I started at the Royal College of Art, at that time with William Rothenstein as Principal. I disliked him and his work but he was ill much of the time so I didn't often see him. You can have no idea how provincial and awful London was in the 1920s. Painting was dreary, academic and rubbishy. I was fascinated by modern painting but couldn't find anyone to talk about it until I met Fred Porter. I had seen a couple of his land-scapes in Auckland at a show and admired them a lot. I got a letter of introduction to him from his mother and we became great friends. Eventually I took over his studio at 8 Fitzroy Street. Porter had gone to Paris in the early 1900s and his early work was very strong Fauve painting. He worked at Julien's and stayed in Paris for years. Before the war broke out in 1914 he had come to London and as, like many artists of the period in Paris, he was a Radical Socialist, he refused to do war service. He had a rough time in London and was directed into a job as a mortuary attendant. He lived in Fitzroy Street all through these years and was a close friend of Harold Gilman and others of the Camden Town Group. He was a friend of Walter Sickert's who had a big studio at the back of No. 8. He was a marvellous little man and when in 1926 I was fired from the R.C.A. painting school he took me in and taught me to paint. I don't suppose he was a great artist but what he had to teach was *la belle peinture* and how it should be done. It was as different from painting taught in England as a good claret is from coca-cola. When I went back to the College they left me alone and I went on with my work. I took my diploma and won a scolarship to go on painting. But I was too restive to work in the place and spent most of my time in my studio and so they fired me again.

I worked away at group shows, London Group and one or two galleries – Zwemmer, Lefevre, Mrs Wertheims. I sold a few pictures, did a few commissions, tried a bit of teaching and hated it. By 1932 the Great Depression hung over us all. I joined the Communist Party, gave up painting, took to illustration and graphic design and helped found the Artists' International Association which at that time was a mixture of agit-prop body, Marxist discussion group, exhibitions organiser and anti-war, anti-fascist outfit. It did an excellent job at the time in a very wide range of activity.[1]

Boswell's involvement in party matters became of crucial importance when, together with James Fitton and James Holland, he began to contribute work to *Left Review* (1934-1938). The work of the 'Three Jameses', as they became called, was one of the review's strongest features, and helped to give the journal its punch. As Paul Hogarth points out, Boswell was the most memorable of all the artists whose work appeared within the *Review's* covers.

> The Great Depression of 1929-1936 made James Boswell the draughtsman of the history of those years and the decade afterwards. He took an active part in much of what he depicted and led the characteristically double life that such an artist invariably leads. By day, he was a successful graphic designer, and later the charismatic art director of Shell's publicity organisation. But he spent his nights and weekends exploring the streets and pubs of working-class London. Like Daumier and Grosz he had a passion for justice, and the opportunities the executive post gave him to observe City of London types – crooked stockbrokers, lawyers and bankers – enables him with a few strokes to define what he felt could be villainy and double-dealing. Yet he is a satirist, not a caricaturist. Few of his drawings actually deal with a single event or a known person, but they are *all* dealing with realities.[2]

Hogarth remarks that the influence of Boswell's work on the 'radical student generation' of the 1930s 'was enormous'. Certainly, there can be no mistaking the energy of Boswell's commitment to the cause of marxism, nor the ways in which such energy is controlled and redeemed by wit and sharp severity of line. James Friell recalls that 'The James Boswell I met in the mid-thirties was a young man of . . . gusto and vehemence and he was unmistakably in the struggle.' His work 'added a graphic pungency to the *Left Review*', and it sprang from a commitment that led him to become, among other things, 'a leader of the Artists International Association, a natural organiser . . .'.[3] Boswell also worked as a cartoonist for the *Daily Worker*. (Most of his work for the paper appeared under the pen-name of 'Buchan'.)

One inevitably thinks of Boswell in the 1930s as above all a satirist. For the satiric work *was* wonderful, it *did* have a ruthless economy and savage pointedness reminiscent of Grosz. Yet as Friell points out, Boswell was also busy in the thirties 'producing line and colour sketches of market places, public houses and shabby streets in the hinterlands of Camden Town',[4] and of Soho and London's East End. Not just line and colour sketches, either. For in those years Boswell was learning the art of lithography and much of his finest work of that decade is lithographic. (A point Montague Slater makes in his note on Boswell, first printed in *Our Time*, March 1942.)[5] Richard Cork refers to these depictions of street life as 'surprisingly mellow';[6] yet it can hardly be thought surprising that Boswell should want to capture, lovingly and uncensoriously, the lives of ordinary people at work or play, lounging in pubs, sitting in cafés, selling from street barrows, talking to friends and clients. And his drawings and lithographic work of the 1930 alike testify to his great skill in recording London life of the time.

Then came the war, and with it a whole new impulse, a new direction. We cannot follow it here, for to do so would take us beyond our chosen limits, and anyway what is needed is a full-length study of Boswell at war. But it can be said that his sketches of army life during the phoney-war period have, variously, such rancorous wit and power, such gimlet-eyed awareness of what bullshit and blanco mean, and then such chuckly acceptance of 'the eccentrics and the silent walkers,/The dumpy and the tall', that all other artists of the second world war ought to be judged by reference to Boswell's work during those years.

JL

NOTES

1 *James Boswell, 1906-1971; Drawings, Illustrations, and Paintings.*
Catalogue of an exhibition held at Nottingham University Art Gallery,
1976. pp. 8-9.
2 *Ibid.* p. 10.
3 *James Boswell: a Memoir of the thirties,* by James Friell.
4 *Ibid.*
5 Reprinted in the *Catalogue, op. cit.* p. 20.
6 *Ibid.* p. 25.

Photography by Brian Shuel

"He hath made for us a pathway
To the ends of the earth."

JAMES BOSWELL

Blackmail set-up

Path to Glory
Boswell '37

Cartoon/satiric
work for the
Left Review

Cartoon/satiric work for the *Left Review*

'Commercial Pub' 1938

'Amusement' 1938

'The Dying Street' 1938

Street scenes: 'Free Speech' 1938

'Ace Dining Rooms' 1938

Three sketches from a series of six, of the Sphinx, a celebrated Paris Brothel, which Boswell visited in 1939. Paul Hogarth remarks that the work that came out of Boswell's stay there is 'equal to Pascin in revealing the butterfly existence led by its inmates'

Three works from the phoney war period
(1) 'Candidates for Glory'
(2) 'Waterloo Station'. 1940
(3) 'Medical Inspection'. 1940

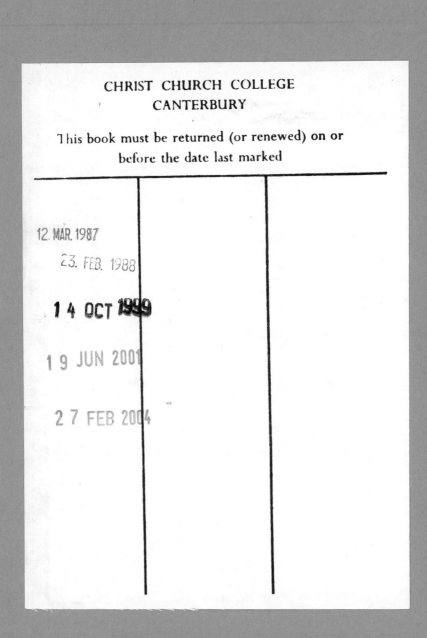

CHRIST CHURCH COLLEGE
CANTERBURY

This book must be returned (or renewed) on or
before the date last marked